First World War
and Army of Occupation
War Diary
France, Belgium and Germany

4 DIVISION
Divisional Troops
32, 37 and 127 Brigades Royal Field Artillery
3 August 1914 - 21 May 1916

WO95/1467

The Naval & Military Press Ltd
www.nmarchive.com
Published in association with The National Archives

Published by

The Naval & Military Press Ltd

Unit 10 Ridgewood Industrial Park,

Uckfield, East Sussex,

TN22 5QE England

Tel: +44 (0) 1825 749494

www.naval-military-press.com

www.nmarchive.com

This diary has been reprinted in facsimile from the original. Any imperfections are inevitably reproduced and the quality may fall short of modern type and cartographic standards.

© **Crown Copyright**
Images reproduced by permission of The National Archives, London, England, 2015.

Contents

Document type	Place/Title	Date From	Date To
Heading	4 Division. Troops. 32 Brigade R.F.A. 1914 Aug To 1919 Jan. 37 Brigade R.F.A. 1914 Aug To 1914 Dec. 127 Brigade R.F.A. 1915 Aug To 1916 May.		
Heading	4th Division War Diaries 32nd Brigade R.F.A. August To December 1914		
Heading	32nd Bde. R.F.A. War Diary For Period 10th-31st October 1914 Is Missing. 4th Div, R. A. 32nd Bde, R.F.A. War Diary. Aug-Dec 1914		
Heading	32nd Bde R.F.A. 2.11.14-31.12.14		
Heading	32nd Bde RFA War Diary For Period 10th-31st-October 1914 Is Missing		
War Diary	Woolwich	03/08/1914	18/08/1914
War Diary	Harrow	22/08/1914	22/08/1914
War Diary	Boulogne	23/08/1914	23/08/1914
War Diary	Bohain	24/08/1914	24/08/1914
War Diary	Briastre	25/08/1914	25/08/1914
War Diary	Ligny	26/08/1914	09/10/1914
War Diary	Point '63'	02/11/1914	02/11/1914
War Diary	Nieppe	03/11/1914	10/11/1914
War Diary	Petit Pont	11/11/1914	29/11/1914
War Diary	Menegate	02/12/1914	02/12/1914
War Diary	La Menegate	12/12/1914	12/12/1914
War Diary	Point '63'	13/12/1914	21/12/1914
War Diary	Petit Pont	22/12/1914	31/12/1914
Heading	4th Division War Diaries 32nd Bde R.F.A. January 1st To 31st December 1915		
Heading	32nd Bde R.F.A. Jan 1-30.04.15		
War Diary	Petit Pont	01/01/1915	05/01/1915
War Diary	l'Hallabeau	06/01/1915	19/01/1915
War Diary	Petit Pont	20/01/1915	16/04/1915
War Diary	L'Hallobeau	17/04/1915	30/04/1915
Heading	32nd Bde R.F.A. Vol III 1-31.05.15		
War Diary	L'Hallobeau	01/05/1915	13/05/1915
War Diary	Ypres	14/05/1915	31/05/1915
Heading	4th Division 32nd Bde R.F.A. Vol IV 1-30.6.15		
Miscellaneous	War Diary 32nd Bde R.F.A. June 1915. Appendix I.		
War Diary	Ypres	01/06/1915	30/06/1915
Heading	4th Division 32nd Bde R.F.A. Vol V 1-31-7-15		
War Diary	Elverdinghe	01/07/1915	09/07/1915
War Diary	Houtkerque	10/07/1915	25/07/1915
War Diary	Thievres	26/07/1915	31/07/1915
Miscellaneous	Appendix To Folio F.		
Map	Ferme 14		
Heading	32nd Bde. R.F.A. Vol VI Aug + Sept 15		
War Diary	Englebelmer	01/08/1915	31/12/1915
Miscellaneous			
Heading	32nd Bde. R.F.A. January To December 1916		
Heading	32nd Bde. R.F.A. January 1916		
War Diary	Englebelmer	01/01/1916	05/03/1916
War Diary	Halloy	05/03/1916	05/03/1916

Heading	32nd Bde. R. R. A. March 5th To August 2nd. 1916		
War Diary	Halloy	05/03/1916	05/04/1916
War Diary	Bienvillers Fonquevillers	05/04/1916	05/04/1916
War Diary	Bienvillers	05/04/1916	06/05/1916
War Diary	Outrebois	06/05/1916	21/05/1916
War Diary	Coulon Villers	21/05/1916	27/05/1916
War Diary	Outrebois	01/06/1916	09/06/1916
War Diary	Vauchelles	09/06/1916	09/06/1916
War Diary	Mailly-Maillet	15/06/1916	02/08/1916
Heading	32nd Bde R.F.A. August 1916		
War Diary		08/08/1916	04/09/1916
Heading	32nd Bde. R.F.A. September 1916		
War Diary		05/09/1916	02/10/1916
Heading	8700/1372 Files. Army. Duplicate G.S. War Diaries. G.S. First Army. 1917 (i) War Diary For Period 1st To 31st October, 1917. (ii) Files Of Messages 1st To 31st October, 1917. (iii) Weekly Summary Of Operations. 28th September To 26th October, 1917.	26/10/1917	26/10/1917
Heading	32nd Bde. R.F.A. October 1916		
War Diary		03/10/1916	28/10/1916
Heading	32nd Bde R.F.A. November 1916		
War Diary		05/11/1916	29/11/1916
Heading	32nd Bde. R.F.A. December 1916		
War Diary		01/12/1916	31/12/1916
Heading	32nd Bde. R.F.A. January 1st To 31 December 1917		
Heading	February 1917 32nd Brigade R.F.A. Vol 30		
War Diary		01/01/1917	28/02/1917
Heading	32nd Brigade R.F.A. March 1917		
War Diary		04/03/1917	31/03/1917
Heading	32nd Brigade RFA April 1917		
War Diary		14/04/1917	28/04/1917
War Diary		01/04/1917	13/04/1917
Heading	32nd Brigade RFA May 1917		
War Diary		03/05/1917	30/05/1917
Heading	War Diary 32nd Bde RFA June 17		
War Diary		01/06/1917	30/06/1917
Heading	32nd Brigade RFA July 1917		
War Diary		01/07/1917	31/07/1917
Heading	32nd Brigade RFA August 1917		
War Diary		01/08/1917	26/08/1917
Heading	32nd Brigade RFA September 17		
War Diary		02/09/1917	30/09/1917
Heading	32nd Brigade RFA October, 1917		
War Diary		01/10/1917	31/10/1917
Heading	32nd. Brigade R.F.A. November, 1917		
War Diary		01/11/1917	30/11/1917
War Diary	In The Field	01/12/1917	31/12/1917
Heading	32nd Bde R.F.A. January To December 1918		
War Diary	In the Field	01/01/1918	31/01/1918
Heading	32nd. Brigade, R.F.A. February, 1918		
War Diary	In The Field	01/02/1918	28/02/1918
Heading	Headquarters, 32nd Brigade, R.F.A. March 1918		
Heading	War Diary. 32nd. Brigade R.F.A. March, 1918		
War Diary	In The Field	01/03/1918	31/03/1918
Heading	4th Divisional Artillery. 32nd Brigade R.F.A. April 1918		

War Diary		01/04/1918	30/04/1918
War Diary	In The Field	01/05/1918	31/05/1918
War Diary	Bellerive	01/06/1918	30/06/1918
Heading	32nd. Brigade, R.F.A. July, 1918		
War Diary	Bellerive	01/07/1918	23/08/1918
War Diary	Erny St Julien	24/08/1918	24/08/1918
War Diary	Hernicourt	25/08/1918	25/08/1918
War Diary	Esterre Cauchie	26/08/1918	26/08/1918
War Diary	Anzin (Arras)	27/08/1918	27/08/1918
War Diary	Bois De Vert	28/08/1918	28/08/1918
War Diary	Bois Des Vert O. 9c 8095	28/08/1918	31/08/1918
War Diary	Hernicourt	26/08/1918	27/08/1918
War Diary	Estree Cauchie.	27/08/1918	27/08/1918
War Diary	Anzin	28/08/1918	28/08/1918
War Diary	Bois De Vert	28/08/1918	03/09/1918
War Diary	Savy	04/09/1918	19/09/1918
War Diary	Monchy	19/09/1918	09/10/1918
War Diary	Cambrai	09/10/1918	12/10/1918
War Diary	Naves	12/10/1918	12/10/1918
War Diary	Villers en Cauchie	13/10/1918	14/10/1918
War Diary	Rieux	14/10/1918	22/10/1918
War Diary	Haspres	23/10/1918	31/10/1918
War Diary		01/11/1918	30/11/1918
War Diary	Coron K (2) 1535	01/12/1918	31/12/1918
War Diary		14/12/1918	25/12/1918
Heading	4th Division War Diaries 32nd Bde R.F.A. Royal F Artillery Jan-Feb 1919		
War Diary	Boussoit	00/01/1919	00/02/1919
Heading	37th Brigade R.F.A. August, To December 1914		
Heading	37th Brigade R.F.A. 4th Division 4-30.8.14		
War Diary	Woolwich	04/08/1914	18/08/1914
War Diary	Camp (4th Divn) Harrow.	19/08/1914	20/08/1914
War Diary	Camp Harrow	21/08/1914	23/08/1914
War Diary	Camp Boulogne	24/08/1914	25/08/1914
War Diary	500 x SW Of Haucourt	26/08/1914	30/08/1914
Heading	37th Brigade R.F.A. 4th Division Volume II 31.8-30.09.14 Sept 1914		
War Diary		31/08/1914	02/09/1914
War Diary	Camp	02/09/1914	30/09/1914
Heading	37th Brigade RFA 4th Division 1-31.10.14		
War Diary		01/10/1914	31/10/1914
Miscellaneous	Copy. From O.C. 31st Battery R.F.A. To Commanding 37th Bde. R.F.A.		
Heading	37th Bde. R.F.A. Vol. IV 1-30.11.14		
War Diary		01/11/1914	30/11/1914
Heading	37th Bde R.F.A. Vol V 1-31.12.14		
War Diary		01/12/1914	31/12/1914
Heading	4th Division War Diaries 37th Bde. R.F.A. To IV. Carps 07-02-15 January + February 1915		
Heading	37th Bde R.F.A. Vol VI. 01-31.01.15		
War Diary	Nieppe	01/01/1915	05/01/1915
War Diary	Le Bizet	06/01/1915	18/01/1915
War Diary	Nieppe	19/01/1915	31/01/1915
Heading	4th Division 37th Bde R.F.A. Vol VII 1-28.2.15		
War Diary	Nieppe	01/02/1915	03/02/1915
War Diary	H Ploegsteert	04/02/1915	28/02/1915

Heading	4th Division War Diaries 127th (How) Bde. R.F.A. Formed 06-08-15 August To 31st December 1915		
Heading	127th Bde R.F.A. Vol I Aug To Oct. 15		
War Diary	Mailly-Maillet	06/08/1915	31/10/1915
Heading	127th Brigade R.F.A. Nov. 1915		
War Diary		01/11/1915	30/11/1915
Heading	127th Bde. R.F.A. Dec Vol III		
War Diary		01/12/1915	31/12/1915
Heading	4th Division War Diaries 127th Bde R.F.A. January, To 21-5-16 1916		
Heading	127th Bde. R.F.A. January 1916		
War Diary		01/01/1916	31/01/1916
Heading	127th Bde R.F.A. February 1916		
War Diary		01/02/1916	29/02/1916
Heading	127th Bde R.F.A. March 1916		
War Diary		01/03/1916	31/03/1916
Heading	127th Bde. R.F.A. April 1916		
War Diary		01/04/1916	30/04/1916
Heading	127th Bde. R.F.A. May 1916		
War Diary		01/05/1916	21/05/1916

4 DIVISION. TROOPS.

32 BRIGADE R.F.A.
1914 AUG TO 1919 JAN.

37 BRIGADE R.F.A.
1914 AUG TO 1914 DEC.

127 BRIGADE R.F.A.
1915 AUG TO 1916 MAY.

4 DIVISION. TROOPS.
32 BRIGADE R.F.A.
1914 AUG TO 1919 JAN.
37 BRIGADE R.F.A.
1914 AUG TO 1914 DEC.
127 BRIGADE R.F.A.
1915 AUG TO 1916 MAY.

4nd Division
War Diaries
32nd Brigade R.F.A.

August to December
1914

Index..........

SUBJECT.

32nd Bde. R.F.A.
War Diary for period 10th – 31st October 1914
is missing.

No.	Contents.	Date.
	4TH DIV, R.A. 32ND BDE. R.F.A. WAR DIARY, AUG-DEC, 1914	

121/4538

4th Division

82nd Bde R.F.A.

Vol I. 2.11.14 — 31.12.14

32ND BDE RFA
WAR DIARY
FOR PERIOD
10th – 31st October 1914
is MISSING

32nd Brigade R.F.A.

WAR DIARY
or
INTELLIGENCE SUMMARY.
(Erase heading not required.)

Army Form C. 2118

A 1

Hour, Date, Place	Summary of Events and Information	Remarks and references to Appendices
1914		
WOOLWICH August 3rd 5 p.m.	Orders to Mobilize Received.	
4th	First day of Mobilization.	
7th	134 & 135 Batteries sent to EDINBURGH & CROMER respectively about 11 p.m.	
15th	134 Battery returned to WOOLWICH	
18th	Brigade ordered to HARROW where Concentration of 4th Division took place. Brigade under Canvas.	
HARROW 22nd	Brigade Entrained for SOUTHAMPTON - H.Q. Embarked at 2 p.m. on S.S. THESPIS.	
BOULOGNE 23rd	Disembarked at BOULOGNE - H.Q. & 27th Entrained at 9 p.m.	
BOHAIN 24th	134 135 & Am Col Entrained at BOULOGNE 27th & HQ arrived at BOHAIN & bivouaced a mile North of Rail Term - 134 joined 12 noon later.	
BRIASTRE 25th	H.Q. 27th & 134 ordered to move at 2 A.M. due North by march route - 135th & Am Col ordered to follow on arrival at BOHAIN.	
	8 A.M. HQ. 27th & 134th arrived at BRIASTRE.	
	9 A.M. 135th arrived at BRIASTRE followed by Am. Col.	
	4 P.M. 27th went into action in support of 10th Inf Bde who were holding an entrenched Position. They did not open fire. After dark Brigade withdrew to LIGNY EN-CAMBRESIS where they bivouaced for the night.	Reference Map. FRANCE - CAMBRAI. Sheet 13 $\frac{1}{80,000}$

WAR DIARY or INTELLIGENCE SUMMARY

Army Form C 2118

Hour, Date, Place	Summary of Events and Information	Remarks and references to Appendices
LIGNY August 26th 8.30 AM	Enemy reported advancing on LIGNY from N & N.E. Bde. took up position in action as follows:- 27th Battery on ridge ½ mile west of LIGNY in the open - 134th Battery astride the road just S.W. of village under cover - 135th Battery on left rear of 27th Battery, under cover, but did not open fire from this position. 27th & 134th searched for guns behind ridge FONTAINE AU PRE - CAUDRY and later at massed infantry crowning the railway South of FONTAINE.	
9.30 A.M.	Capt. Haskard, who had been reconnoitring position N. of LIGNY for the defence of the village itself now brought the 135th Battery into action in open and sections in ridge along N. & N.E. edge of village.	
3.30 P.M.	One gun of 135 Battery moved to position near LIGNY railway station but did not open fire. Remainder of Battery fired in direction of heavy enemy infantry advancing on railway from direction of CAUDRY - BEAUVOIS. 2/Lt Hislop's section was reported to have been quite successful on Prussian guns. The Battery was under fire all day & remained in action till about 5pm when they & our infantry being ordered to LIGNY. Battery was too as was the enemy in coming on there were signs to withdraw with the horses, we were being shelled from all 27th Battery were subjected to a very heavy shrapnel fire all day & lost one killed & 7 wounded. They eventually withdrew	

WAR DIARY
or
INTELLIGENCE SUMMARY.

(Erase heading not required.)

Army Form C 2118

Hour, Date, Place	Summary of Events and Information	Remarks and references to Appendices
4.45 pm.	lost last about 200 guns & six wagons. One gun was too damaged to move. The Bde. commenced to withdraw & assemble in a position Vg Kashunga under cover 1½ miles S.W. of CLARY. The Bde. having joined up with the remainder of the Div. Artillery withdrew at dusk passing through MALINCOURT & VILLERS - OUTREAUX	
11.30 pm.	Column halted & bivouaked by roadside on road between LE CATELET & VENDHUILLE. Capt. Stevenson R.A.M.C. & Lt. B.L. Armitage (wounded) 27th Battery were missing. Batt. was left in the Dressing Station at LIGNY. All medical equipment & supplies of mobile was also lost.	
August 27th 3.30 A.M.	Retirement continued through VENDHUILLE - LEMPIRE - RONSSOY & TEMPLEUX-le-GUERARD where orders were received to harass PERONNE (at time was cancelled) - Bde in action on point 144 South of TEMPLEUX but did not open fire. Bde was withdrawn through HERVILLY & position in ridge S. of HANCOURT where guns were dug in, 27th in right facing N. 134IC & 135IC on left facing E. Supports to French artillery in this left. The maximum range of the guns was 5000 x.	
Noon.	The Enemy having got his attack in, chuck the Bde. in & withdrawn & became Rearguard to 4th Div. with	

Army Form 211

WAR DIARY
or
INTELLIGENCE SUMMARY.
(Erase heading not required.)

Instructions regarding War Diaries and Intelligence Summaries are contained in F.S. Regs., Part II. and the Staff Manual respectively. Title pages will be prepared in manuscript.

Hour, Date, Place	Summary of Events and Information	Remarks and references to Appendices
9.30 p.m.	12th Inf. Bde. under Brig. Gen. Wilson – Column marched on VOYENNES through VRAIGNES. The Bde. lost 14 pairs of horses & pack bcs. & enemy Infantry at VOYENNES. Column continued forward all night.	Reference Map. FRANCE – LAON. Sheet 22. 1/80,000
August 28th 7.30 A.M.	Arrived just N. of VOYENNES. II Army Corps. retiring through HAM. Bde. came in to action just west of SANCOURT with a view to displaying enemy advancing on HAM. Bde. did not then fire a retired at noon to a position 1½ miles 1 mile W. of ESMERY–HALLON–	
Noon		
2 p.m.	Retirement continued via LIBERMONT – FRENICHES – FRETOY to MUIRANCOURT where Bde. bivouacked for night. Orders to move by night to NOYON however cancelled just after had commenced –	
29th	Bde. moved to GENVRY escort & mounted detachment R 36 men from the Bde. Halts at GENVRY the rest. Numerous reconnaissance carried out by officers during afternoon. After parade march to NOYON & crossing the OISE & the PONT l'EVEQUE bivouacked at Kings midnight at LES CLOYES.	
30th 4 a.m.	Retirement continued through CARLEPONT – TRACY-le-MONT to BASCULE where Bde. came into a position of readiness	Reference Map. SOISSONS Sheet 33. 1/80,000
3 p.m.	At 3 p.m. a receiving their Bde. broke when it moved into bivouac at PIERREFONDS.	

WAR DIARY or **INTELLIGENCE SUMMARY.**
(Erase heading not required.)

Army Form C. 2118

Hour, Date, Place		Summary of Events and Information	Remarks and references to Appendices
August 31st	6. A.M.	Retirement continued through PIERREFONDS – ST JEAN AUX BOIS – ST SAUVEUR – Bde. bivouacked in wood S.E. of St. VAAST.	Reference BEAUVAIS. Sheet 32 1/80000
Sept. 1st	4. A.M.	Bde. ready to move off. Very foggy – Very heavy gun & M.G. fire heard from S.E. This fired out to come from NERY where L Battery RHA + 1st Cav. Bde. were surprised by hostile cavalry to bivouac. Gen. Briggs ordered Bde. into action just N.W. of bivouac to cover retirement from NERY - 5th + 9th Lancers from Bde. Groups with 19th Inf. Bde. on Rear front occupied. Successive positions to cover retirement on BARONNE via RARY + RULY. Bde. also was then fired + eventually bivouacked with 19th Bde. at FRESNOY.	Reference PARIS Sheet 48. 1/80000
"	2.–	Bde. withdrew at dawn to position of readiness under cover to own withdrawal & 19th Bde. from FRESNOY.	
	6.30 A.M.	Retirement continued through BARONNE & EVE. 13th came into action N. of EVE. again withdrew without firing.	
	2 p.m.	13th + 15th came into action E. of EVE to cover withdrawal. No attack was made. 2nd remained in reserve S.E. of EVE. During afternoon information was received that 2 German Cavalry Bdes. were trying from ERMENONVILLE towards MONTAIGNY + Rothuin were ordered to try to stall them. This was not done as the Bde. was relieved by 14th R Bde.	
	3.30 p.m.	RFA + continued its retirement to DAMMARTIN where it bivouacked.	

WAR DIARY
or
INTELLIGENCE SUMMARY.

Army Form C. 2118

Hour, Date, Place		Summary of Events and Information	Remarks and references to Appendices
September 3rd	12.45 AM	Bde. marched with 4th Bde. via CLAYE-SOUILLY and ANNET to LAGNY & westwards to LAGNY. Arrived here / mile SE of that town.	
	2 p.m.	Moved bivouac through CHANTELOUP.	
" 4th	6.15pm	Remained in bivouac till 6.15pm. When Bde. moved with 12th Inf Bde. to bivouac at FERRIERES.	Reference MELUN sheet 65- corno
" 5th	5 a.m.	Left FERRIERES marching via PONT CARRE	
	11 a.m.	Arriving bivouac at BRIE COMTE ROBERT	
	5 pm.	Bde. ordered to move at once to join Cavalry Division.	
	6.30 pm	Marched via GUIGNES to MARMONT joining Cavalry Division. Then	
		& bivouac.	
		A.C. left behind & attached to 27th Bde. RFA.) night at 12.30 a.m. (S.A.A. Section of	
" 6th	7 a.m.	Advanced with 4th Cav. Bde. to GASTINS	Reference PROVINS sheet 66 corno
	10 a.m.	Bde. went into action in observation 134 Bde. went to GASTINS. The 27th on left of 134 — 135 in reserve S.E. of GASTINS. Bde did not come into fire.	
	11.30 AM	Bde. moved forward with 4th Cavalry Bde. to position of readiness just S.W. of CHAMPMOULIN. 134 Bde. coming into action in observation just North Second L in BEAULEY.	
	6.45 PM	Advanced to JOUY le CHALET & bivouaced there at 8.30pm.	
" 7th	5.45AM	Moved off with Cavalry Division.	
	8 AM	135 Bty. came into action in observation 2 miles N of JOUY. Remainder of Bde. lillied in position of readiness under cover.	

Army Form C. 2118

WAR DIARY
or
INTELLIGENCE SUMMARY.
(Erase heading not required.)

Instructions regarding War Diaries and Intelligence Summaries are contained in F. S. Regs., Part II. and the Staff Manual respectively. Title pages will be prepared in manuscript.

(7)

Hour, Date, Place	Summary of Events and Information	Remarks and references to Appendices
September 8th	Heavy firing last to East. Bde. advanced though DAGNY + CHEVRU. 135 Bty. came into action west of CHEVRU against ridge N.W. of CHOISY but did not fire. Bde. advanced bridge N.W. of CHOISY + eventually relieved 6 Les PETITS COURBANS for the night. Marched via LEUDON joining Cavalry Division just south of LA FERTE GAUCHER then via ST LEGER to a point just S. of P in CHAMP-LA-BRIDE where Bde. found up in rear. 134 Bty was brought into action near les MIKATS against a column of the enemy near SABLONIERES. 135 Bty. Later came into action on right of 134 Bty - 27 Bty remaining in reserve. Bde. advanced, one section of 134 Bty being detailed to escort towards BOITRON but afterwards recalled. 135 Bty. was sent forward with 4th Cavalry Bde. towards BASSEVILLE & came into action against while infantry retiring. Remainder of Bde. advanced to a point S.W. of BASSEVILLE eventually the whole Bde. bivouacked at LA VOVE le PRETRE.	Reference Map. MEAUX Sheet 49 $\frac{1}{80.000}$

Army Form C 2118

(8)

WAR DIARY
or
INTELLIGENCE SUMMARY.
(Erase heading not required.)

Hour, Date, Place	Summary of Events and Information	Remarks and references to Appendices
September 9th	Joined up with 4th Cav. Bde. at a point S.W. of Bois de la HUTBORNE. 27th R.G. came into action facing west in relief of R.H.A. Remainder moved with 4th Cavalry Bde. to la BOISSON & thence via CAEZY sur MARNE, AZY, Mt. de BONNEIL to la CROISETTE where 27 Battery who had crossed the MARNE at NOGENT rejoined & came into action at LUCY-le-BOCAGE. Bde. returned to Mt. de BONNEIL for tonight.	Reference Map. SOISSOUS Sheet 33. 1/80000
10th 6.30 AM	Assembled one mile way of LE THIBLET in the Wellens & marched via TOURESCHES to MONTHIERS. Here few June of 135 Bty. was detailed & came into action firing 145 against enemy retiring. Remainder of Bde. moved on via BONNES, Bois de BONNES to Château just hutts of GRISSOLLES when 27 Bty came into action & fired a few rounds at a German Battery. Bde. bivouaced at the Château - 135 Bty. rejoined Bde. between LA CROIX & GRISSOLES.	

WAR DIARY or INTELLIGENCE SUMMARY

Army Form C. 2118

Hour, Date, Place	Summary of Events and Information	Remarks and references to Appendices
September 11th	Moved with 4th Cav. Bde. via LA CROIX - BRENY - OULCHY le CHATEAU - SERVENAY - ARCY to cross roads one mile N.N.E of ARCY. Batteries with 4th Cav. Bde. N.E. of BRANGES did not come into action. Billetted at VAUX.	
12th	Bde. H.Q. moved with H.Q 4th Cav. Bde. to LESGES and thence to CERSEUIL - 134 Battery moved with 4th Cavalry Bde - 27 & 135 Batteries via LOUPEIGNE to LESGES. Considerable opposition was met with at BRAINE L. Bde eventually advanced to fork road 1 mile N.E of MONTHUSSART farm and bivouacked at follows:- H.Q of VAUXCERÉ, 134 Battery at VAUXTIN, 27, 135 Batteries + Am. Col. near PAARS.	
13th	134 Battery covered horses from rest of Bde. & became a mobile Battery acting as Horse artillery. 134 with 4th Cav. Bde. moved to EPINE de VAUXCERE + thence to la Cour aus MOINET farm. later the Battery advanced to just South of BOURG. 27 & 125 Bty. moved via FE de PINÇON & went into billets in VILLERS at Clark - Am. Col. at FE de PINÇON. No Battery came into action.	Reference Map. RHEIMS sheet 34 $\frac{1}{80,000}$
14th. 15th	Moved from VILLERS to TOUR de PAISSY 3 Batteries came into action in a position just South of the TOUR de PAISSY Farm and assisted to drive off a vigorous counter attack near the FABRIQUE de TROYON with very excellent shooting - The Bde. billetted at PARGNAN.	

Army Form C 2118
(10)

WAR DIARY
or
INTELLIGENCE SUMMARY.
(Erase heading not required.)

Instructions regarding War Diaries and Intelligence Summaries are contained in F.S. Regs., Part II. and the Staff Manual respectively. Title pages will be prepared in manuscript.

Hour, Date, Place	Summary of Events and Information	Remarks and references to Appendices
September 16th 1914	The 27th & 134th Batteries came into action South of TOUR de PAISSY farm. The 135th Battery with N of this farm. The latter Battery was afterwards pushed forward to support the French attack on HEUTE BRISE farm. The 27th & 134th Batteries engaged guns near CERNAY.	
17th	Guns occupied same positions as yesterday & fired steadily all day. 27th & 135th Batteries towards LA CREUTE & 134th Battery towards FARROQUE & TROYAN - Bde. billeted at PARGNAN.	
18th	134th & 135th Batteries came into action S. of TOUR de PAISSY farm, HQ being at the farm. The farm was heavily shelled, several men & horses being killed. Batteries were located & enemy at 3pm were heavily shelling the 135th Battery losing 2 guns, 2 men killed & 14 wounded. The location of the Bde. was found & both ranks & skin.	
19th	The 32nd Bde. moved out of billets at 5 a.m. & remained in reserve all day.	
20th	Village of PAISSY heavily shelled. The 134th Battery came into action N. of PARGNAN & 135th Battery W. of Tour de Paissy. & German shelling which they gd. 27th were in reserve - Bde. billeted in PARGNAN.	

Army Form C 2118

(11.)

WAR DIARY
or
INTELLIGENCE SUMMARY.
(Erase heading not required.)

Hour, Date, Place	Summary of Events and Information	Remarks and references to Appendices
1914 September 21st	Bde. in action N. of PARGNAN. One Section of 135th Battery under 2nd Lieut. McKay & Rogers pushed forward to N. of PAISSY & for heavily shelled.	
" 22nd	Bde. in action lying in N. of PARGNAN, no heavy shelled. The Section 135th Bty stopped yesterday returns to billets.	
" 23rd	Bde. in action as yesterday. Aeroplane observer located 36 guns massed which Bde. shelled.	
" 24th	Orig Gleam stalling 27th & 135th Batteries altered their positions. 27th occupied position in a class just north of 2nd N. of PARGNAN, 135th Battery just North of CUSSY farm. The 27th were completely covered from aeroplane observation.	
" 25th	The 134th & 135th Batteries proceeded at 5.20 am to rendezvous at CUSSY farm. 27th remained in billets. 134th Bty. Came into action N. of PARGNAN and 135th west of CUSSY farm.	
" 26th	134th Battery came into action just N. of PARGNAN - 27th remained in reserve - 135th Bty. returns to billets.	

WAR DIARY
or
INTELLIGENCE SUMMARY.
(Erase heading not required.)

Army Form C. 2118

Instructions regarding War Diaries and Intelligence Summaries are contained in F.S. Regs., Part II. and the Staff Manual respectively. Title pages will be prepared in manuscript.

Hour, Date, Place	Summary of Events and Information	Remarks and references to Appendices
September 27th	The Bde. Hdqrs. in billets. 134th R.G. remaining as yesterday all day ready for use as between not required. Bde. resting.	
28th, 29th, 30th	First reinforcement of 2 men & horses arrived for Bde. from 4th Division.	
October 1st	Resting in billets. Message received for Bde. to hold itself in readiness to rejoin 3rd Corps.	
2nd	Message received 12.45 am ordering Battery Commanders in one after other each to report themselves at 7am at B. of BRENELLE. At 2pm. Bde. moves to BRAINE & took up position N.W. of BRENELLE at sunset. This position had previously been held by 2nd Corps. The 27th Battery employed detached sections – 135th R.G. were in Reserve.	Reference Map. Soissons sheet 33. 1/80,000.
3rd	Communication established with same officers owing to Corps O. State that wire had been left in.	
4th	Same position occupied. Useful reports sent in from forward observing officers.	

WAR DIARY
or
INTELLIGENCE SUMMARY.
(Erase heading not required.)

Army Form C 2118

Hour, Date, Place	Summary of Events and Information	Remarks and references to Appendices
1914		
October 5th	Same position occupied. Various objectives engaged with considerable effect on enemy's trenches & observing officers. Area of Supectirea H.Q. night killer.	
6th	Section of Defence Lansdowne & Lt. Col. Sandilands RFA. Bde. moved at 6 pm to CHACRISE Killer & rejoined 4th Division.	
7th	Bde. relieving the morning & moved at 7 pm. to RIZET ST ALBIN also at billetes at 5 SeSte Fachin. Extraordinary hospitality shown by ——— owner of same.	
8th.		
9th.	Bde. again moved at 7 pm. AVAUCIENNES. Arrives VAUCIENNES at 4 a.m. moves again at 6.30 a.m. to DURY.	

J. Palmer Capt Adjt
for Lt.Col. RFA.
Cmdg 32nd Bde R.F.A.

32nd Bde RFA.

WAR DIARY or INTELLIGENCE SUMMARY.

Army Form 2118.

Hour, Date, Place	Summary of Events and Information	Remarks and references to Appendices
PONT '63' 2nd Nov. 1914.	Batteries in action as follows. 27th 500 yds. N.E. of PLOEGSTEERT. 134th Batt. 600 yds. South of La PLUS DOUCE Farm. 135th Batt. near Boncenelles Farm (T18a NW) Bde. Hqrs. in the farm. All 3 Batteries & HQrs. were subjected to v.y. heavy rifle fire from direction of HESSINGS. Fixed huts were obtained in 134 & owing to heavy casualties detachments were withdrawn from the 135. Headquarters were shelled and to a farm further west. Later in the afternoon Headquarters moved again to MLLE ROSENBERG & later telephonic communication was restored with all 4 Bn. Casualties amongst officers. 2nd Lieut. Hopps (H.Q.) & Major Irving (135) 2nd Lieut. Rogers (135) 2nd Lieut. Makins (135). The 134 & 135 Batteries were withdrawn to NIEPPE during the night & HQ moves to Farm in T11c South.	Reference Map "Belgium & France" (1:13 Series) Sheet 26 S.W. Casualties to Rank & File on 2nd November 1914. 27 Batt. wounded 2. 134 " wounded 10 135 " killed 4 wounded 4 2nd Lieut Taylor was slightly wounded in the hands at LE GHEER.
NIEPPE. 3rd	HQ moved to Nieppe & were placed by HQ 37th Bde- under Lt. Col. Ballecombe. 27th Battery remained in action near PLOEGSTEERT.	
4th	HQ & 134 & 135 Batteries resting at NIEPPE.	

WAR DIARY or INTELLIGENCE SUMMARY.

Army Form 2118.

Hour, Date, Place	Summary of Events and Information	Remarks and references to Appendices
1914. NIEPPE Nov. 5th	One Section 134 Battery under Lieut Hutton went into action in V19B. This Section was withdrawn at night. Remainder of Battery remained in reserve near PETIT PONT.	
" 6th	Same as for Nov 5th. Very foggy.	
" 7th	Heavy attack on the line ST. YVON — LEGHEER — 27th Batty. heavily engaged & fired 1500 rounds. German penetrated the line East of PLOEGSTEERT Wood — The day was extremely foggy & firing consequently lost to them by the mist.	
" 8th	French attacking MESSINES. 134 & 135 in billets at NIEPPE. 27th in action at PLOEGSTEERT.	
" 9th	Same as for Nov 8th.	
" 10th	134 Battery relieved the 27th at PLOEGSTEERT. 27th to rest.	
" 11th	HQ moved to farm at PETIT PONT (T23?) & took over Artillery Command known as North Artillery Group, consisting of 4th & 6th Siege Batteries R.G.A, 31st & 35th Howitzer Siege Batteries, 125th & 134 & 135 Batteries.	
PETIT PONT " 12th	A day of shelling.	
" 13th	135th relieved 125 Bty in position T17Z. 134 & 135 Batteries fired at enemy N.E. of LE GHEER.	
" 14th	Heavy shelling on point 63. Batteries replied.	

WAR DIARY or INTELLIGENCE SUMMARY

Army Form 2118.

Place	Hour, Date	Summary of Events and Information	Remarks and references to Appendices
PETIT PONT	Nov. 15th 1914	Villa ROSENBERG burnt by German shell fire.	
"	16th	Germans attacked ST YVON. The evening attack was repulsed.	
"	18th	135th Bty. co-operated – 18th-27th into action T.17c relieving J Bty, RHA	
"	19th	134 Bty. moved back to a position South of PLOEGSTEERT –	
"	20th	ROMARIN Rd in T.30.c SE. 135 Bty. heavy shelled by H.E. one shell fell in one of their Try nts. Detachment lay flat, been withdrawn, Enemy station on point 63 leaving shelled, Neighbourhood of HQ farm shelled all night.	
"	21st	135 Bty. moved to new position 200 yds. futher South of N. of BELHEEN Farm (U.3.c) Task. 27 Bty. fires on lines N. of LA HENEGATE & was	
"	24th	134 Bty. went into rest S of LA HENEGATE & was relieved by 125 Battery	
"	25th	Shelled. Came near HQ farm + 27th A.S. horse lines. Horse lines were moved further back. 125th Battery relieved the 135th Bty.	
"	29th	27th Bty. were relieved by 127th Battery & they went into rest at NIEPPE.	
HENEGATE	December 2nd	HQ relieved by HQ 29th Bde. under Lt Col. Stockdale. + went into rest at LA HENEGATE. at 3pm - dismounted parties on shore on permilla from each Battery were inspected by H.M. The King at NIEPPE. Major Valentine was presented with the D.S.O. by H.M.	

WAR DIARY or INTELLIGENCE SUMMARY.

(Erase heading not required.)

Army Form C. 2118.

Hour, Date, Place		Summary of Events and Information	Remarks and references to Appendices
1914.			
LA MENEGATE Dec. 12th			
POINT '63'	13th	The Brigade took up action on point 63. Three Batteries in line facing North. HQ at PETIT MUNQUE Farm. Batteries registered as follows. 27th Batt. on German trenches west of MESSINES – WYTSCHAETE Ridge. 134 & 135 Batteries on the PETIT BOIS & point 74 & WYTSCHAETE WOOD.	
"	14th	3rd Division attacked the PETIT BOIS. 134 & 135 Batteries at 7 a.m. bombarded point 74 & WYTSCHAETE wood till 7.45am & then fired on long programme till 3pm. From 3.30 pm till 4-15 pm the whole Bde. shelled point 74 & WYTSCHAETE wood – the infantry captured the PETIT BOIS – General Smith-Dorrien greeted the 32nd Bde. with as small gun in the success.	
"	15th	Attack continued. Programme of firing for the 14th Bde repeated.	
"	16th	Batteries in same position by did not fire.	
"	17th	134th Battery registered HAEDELSTEDE Farm (N.24.d.)	
"	18th	27th fires on trenches opposite 5th Division. 134 & 135 on point 73 & wood. 134 turned one section on to the ground East of MESSINES. 135 Batty. after dark changed position to T18c so as to be able to fire on TILLEUL – 927 Batty. to T18b to fire on the AVENUE.	

WAR DIARY or INTELLIGENCE SUMMARY.

Army Form C. 2118.

(Erase heading not required.)

Instructions regarding War Diaries and Intelligence Summaries are contained in F.S. Regs., Part II. and the Staff Manual respectively. Title pages will be prepared in manuscript.

Hour, Date, Place		Summary of Events and Information	Remarks and references to Appendices
1914			
POINT '63' Dec 19th		General bombardment of Phoenix line opposite & Western from. Infantry attacked at 2.30 p.m. & drove German out of the 3rd CAGE East of PLOEGSTEERT Wood. They subsequently lost relief. At 7.20 a.m. a general bombardment of the enemy's trenches commenced. Continued throughout the day. 275 Battery & HQ	
" 20th		were shelled by 6 inch howitzer. In the evening 134 Batt withdrew to NIEPPE. 135 Batt. relieved the 126 Batt. HQ took over the Command of the North Artillery Group & went into the Farm at PETIT PONT. 275 Batt. relieved	
" 21st		the 127th Batty.	
PETIT PONT 22nd		During the night 21–22 all Batteries slow & normal. 135 Batt. opened fire during the night on enemy massing opposite 11th Inf. Bde.	
" 24th		Enemy shelling one man 275 Batty. & one horse 135 Batty wounded by Shrapnel fire.	
" 27th		27th Batty. fired on Observation post near the AVENUE (U9c)	
" 28th		27th Batty. fired on enemy's trenches & wth battyl on house & entrenchment South of the AVENUE. 135 Batty. on enemy's guns.	
" 29th		27th Batty. fired on AVENUE trenches. 135 Batty. on guns & H.Q. emplacements.	

Army Form C. 2118.

WAR DIARY
or
INTELLIGENCE SUMMARY.
(Erase heading not required.)

Instructions regarding War Diaries and Intelligence Summaries are contained in F. S. Regs., Part II. and the Staff Manual respectively. Title pages will be prepared in manuscript.

Hour, Date, Place	Summary of Events and Information	Remarks and references to Appendices
1914		
PETIT POUT Dec. 30th	27th Batty. sent one gun into position in front of LA HUTTE Chateau (U14 c West) to enfilade Enemy's trench west of MESSINES. 135 Batty. fired on M.G. emplacement.	
" 31st	27th detached gun fired on Enemy's trenches.	

6.

4th Division

War Diaries

32nd Bde. R.F.A.

January 1st To 31st December

1915

121/52854

4th Division

32nd Bde: O.T.A.
Jan!
Vol III   30.4.15.

WAR DIARY
INTELLIGENCE SUMMARY
(Erase heading not required.)

Army Form C. 2118

F. Bty
32nd Bde R.F.A.

Place	Date	Hour	Summary of Events and Information	Remarks and references to Appendices
	1915			
PETIT POINT	Jany. 1st		During the night 31st-1st 135 Batty. fired on enemy's trench to stop sniping.	
"	2nd to 5th		Various targets engaged to keep them hostile fire in co-operation with infantry.	
L'HALLABEAU	6th		Brigade went into rest in billets at L'HALLABEAU, near STEENWERCK.	
"	7th to 19th		At rest. Anti typhoid inoculation carried out. Instruction of young officers & Reinforcements.	
PETIT PONT	20th & 21st		Bde. relieved 29th Bde. at PETIT PONT for the next few days were employed regaining their guns. 134 Batty. in old position west of PLOEGSTEERT	
"	24th		134 Batty. in rest work & trenches East of LE GHEER. 135 Batty. in AU CHASSEUR CABARET. Trenches huntby ST YVON.	

WAR DIARY or INTELLIGENCE SUMMARY

Army Form C. 2118.

Hour, Date, Place	Summary of Events and Information	Remarks and references to Appendices
1915.		
PETIT PONT. Jan. 26th	27th fired on enemy's flanking Pts. ghicken - 135 Batty on snipers in cooperation with infantry - 126 Battery joined the North Artillery Group in anticipation of attack on Kaiser's birthday.	
" 27th	Kaiser's birthday - No attack!	
" 29th	Genl Fx to S.O. succeeded Genl Milne in the command of the No. Arty.	
Feb. 3rd	Stonewall of the North Artillery Group. Redistribution of Bries. 32nd Bde. is allotted 3 Bries. from AU CHASSEUR CART (W.16 & West) to MESSINES.	
" 4th	134 Batty took up a position just north of the H.Q. Farm. Battery zones were allotted as follows :- 27th Batty MESSINES to DOUVE RIVER. 134 Batty DOUVE RIVER to South end of AVENUE. 135 Battery South end of AVENUE to AU CHASSEUR CART. Retaliation Gun (27th Batty) enfilading trenches West of MESSINES. Retaliation scheme has been instituted by which 134 & 135 Batteries fire on trenches nearest line of hostile fire.	
" 8th	275 Batty opened fire on parts of the enemy who appeared to be having lunch S.E. of MESSINES. Scattered them.	

WAR DIARY
or
INTELLIGENCE SUMMARY.
(Erase heading not required.)

Army Form C. 2118.

Hour, Date, Place	Summary of Events and Information	Remarks and references to Appendices
PETIT PONT Feb 11th	134 Battery altered their night lines to regiment of the Infantry required them.	
" 17th	135 Battery located a hostile howitzer Battery east of BASSE VILLE but found it out of range. It was however engaged by 31st Heavy Battery & caused to retire.	
" 24th	134 Batty. located in the gun & support limber immediately stopping their fire. 135 Batty. dispersed an enemy party & fired on a breastwork which they held up.	
" 27th	134 Batty. located M.G. Emplacements. Trapped it. Later on a working party employed in rebuilding the emplacement were surprised by a well directed shell & only one man was seen to escape.	

Jeffery M. Tly
Lieut Colonel N°2

Army Form C. 2118.

WAR DIARY
or
INTELLIGENCE SUMMARY.
(Erase heading not required.)

Instructions regarding War Diaries and Intelligence Summaries are contained in F.S. Regs., Part II. and the Staff Manual respectively. Title pages will be prepared in manuscript.

Hour, Date, Place	Summary of Events and Information	Remarks and references to Appendices
1915		Reference Map – Belgium + France (B Series) Sheet 28 S.W.
PETIT PONT March 4th.	134 Battery silenced hostile Battery 1500 East of MESSINES.	
" 5th	Battery located by 135 on 17th Feb. again located behind the rest house further back & was engaged by 31st Howitzer.	
6th	135 Battery fired on trenches east of St YVES & to slip ferry & rifle pits – Thin Battery traffic almost daily with good results. Capt. Crossman (Adjt) left Bde. on appointment to 2nd Group Arty. G.H.Q.	
7th	Orders received from 3rd Corps to show increased activity Gray. Bde. took part in bombardment of enemys first line trenches from 4.15 pm till 4.45 pm. 134 located & stopped hostile Battery & stopped its fire. Bombardment of enemy's trenches repeated from 4:30 pm till 5 pm.	
8th	27th Battery gun exchanged further north so as to enclose hostile trenches W.S.W. of MESSINES.	
9th	Yesterdays programme of bombardment repeated by 134 & 135 – 134 Battery shelled machine gun emplacement in the AVENUE	
10th	Yesterdays programme repeated – Tenth infantry Brigate report on artillery fire yesterday on enemy's trench "very accurate" – 10th Inf. Bde. trench heavily shelled from our Battalion retaliated – at 7.25 pm infantry called for artillery support as they had heavy rifle fire & an attack on the 10th Bde. front appeared imminent – 27th & 134 fired fire. Enemy did not attack & rifle fire stopped.	

Army Form C. 2118.

WAR DIARY
or
INTELLIGENCE SUMMARY.
(Erase heading not required.)

Instructions regarding War Diaries and Intelligence Summaries are contained in F.S. Regs. Part II. and the Staff Manual respectively. Title pages will be prepared in manuscript.

Hour, Date, Place	Summary of Events and Information	Remarks and references to Appendices
PETIT PONT March 11th	Bombardment of Enemy's trenches from 12 noon to 12.30 p.m.	
March 12th	27th Battery acted to be prepared to support a group sent up MESSINES – WYTSCHAETE ridge in support of 2nd Corps. 27th Battery ceased firing at 12.30 p.m. & silenced hostile battery. Enemy very active shelling our trenches in the DOUVE valley. 134 Battery retaliated.	
" 13th	Our trenches on R. DOUVE shelled from 3 a.m. till 5.30 a.m. – St YVES shelled. 135 retaliated. 134 & 27th Battery retaliated – St YVES retaliates.	
" 15th	135 Battery shelled working parties near CHASSEUR CABARET. Orders received that 32nd Bde. to be relieved by 5th Div. Arty. 4th Division Extending their line to the South. 32nd Bde. to relieve 2nd Bde. RFA at HOUPLINES. 10th Inf Bde relieved 5ght. Inf. Bde.	
" 16th	Orders received at 6.30 p.m. cancelling relief.	
" 17th	134 Battery shelled avenue farm at report of Infantry.	
20th to 22nd	Very bright days – Germans use several captive balloons up – Very quiet along our front.	
" 24th	134 Battery fired at machine gun Replacements in avenue. 135 Battery scattered a working party near German second line trench west of BASSEVILLE.	
" 25th	Observing officers reports considerable amount of traffic on WARNETON – YPRES Road mostly moving north	

WAR DIARY
or
INTELLIGENCE SUMMARY.
(Erase heading not required.)

Army Form C. 2118.

Hour, Date, Place	Summary of Events and Information	Remarks and references to Appendices
PETIT PONT March 26th	Mare traffic seen on WARNETON-YPRES Road.	
27th	27th Battery shelled working party + German observing Station. 2nd Lieut VENNING (27th) was wounded in the shoulder (a bullet while observing from the infantry trenches.	
28th	135th Battery fired at working party at BASSEVILLE and scattered them.	
29th	27th Battery fired at some German transport in YPRES. WARNETON Road — 135th Battery shelled what appeared to be a (gun) house near the Sucrerie at BASSEVILLE & billets & occupants. This Battery also fired at a house close behind German trenches. After our infantry reports that several Germans were seen being carried away on stretchers.	
30th	27 Battery shelled a party of Officers near POTERIE farm – 135 Bty. scattered a working party just South of BASSEVILLE.	
31st	27th and 135th Batteries both scattered working parties.	
April 1st	Do.	
2nd	27th Battery fired at German working party.	
3rd	134 Battery shelled machine gun emplacements. 135 Battery obtained ten direct hits on occupied house – occupied billets.	
4th	27th Battery observed a gun Battery at 134 a Battalion Hqrs. machine gun hqrs in rear of German line at Hqrs.	
5th	Resistant Shelling by R Irish Fus. Bombs in Douve Valley. Battery retaliates.	

Army Form C. 2118.

WAR DIARY
or
INTELLIGENCE SUMMARY.
(Erase heading not required.)

Hour, Date, Place	Summary of Events and Information	Remarks and references to Appendices
PETIT PONT April 6th	27th Battery shelled Enemy's working party.	
" 7th	LA HUTTE Château heavily shelled. One section Seventh Siege Battery came under orders of 3rd Bde. for Tactical purposes. Considerable traffic observed behind German lines. 135 Battery fired at traffic on WARNETON - YPRES Road.	
8th	27th & 134th Batteries shelled working parties.	
9th	27th Battery shelled working party of 5 men. 9 shells they appear to kill one wounded two. One working party in Douve Trenches were heavily shelled during the night. 27th Battery retaliated -	
10th	135 Battery shelled working party near SUCRERIE with great effect.	
11th	Four 10 c.m. Shrapnel burst over 135 wagon line wounding 9 men & 13 horses. 2 of the men afterwards died of wounds.	
12th	135 Battery shifted their wagon line to near ROMARIN. Their old wagon line was being shelled shortly after they left.	
13th	134 Battery shelled working party.	
14th	135 Battery shelled working party near SUCRERIE & afterwards saw two wounded men being carried away -	

Army Form C. 2118.

WAR DIARY
or
INTELLIGENCE SUMMARY.
(Erase heading not required.)

Instructions regarding War Diaries and Intelligence Summaries are contained in F.S. Regs., Part II. and the Staff Manual respectively. Title pages will be prepared in manuscript.

Hour, Date, Place	Summary of Events and Information	Remarks and references to Appendices
PETIT PONT April 16th	27th & 130 Batteries shelled working parties. During the night 16/17 134th & 27th Batteries were relieved by Batteries of 2nd South Midland Bde, & went into rest billets at HENEGATE.	
L'HALLOBEAU. 17th	32nd Bde. H.Q. relieved by 2nd South Midland Bde (T) & went into rest billet at L'HALLOBEAU.	
18th	135 Battery relieved by Battery of 3rd South Midland Bde (T) 135 Battery went into action near LE BIZET. Came under orders of 14th F.A. Bde. for tactical purposes.	
19th to 30th	27th & 134th Batteries resting at L'HALLOBEAU & were joined there on 28th by 135 Battery	

J. Murray Hay
Lieut-Colonel R.F.A.
Comdg. 32nd Bde., R.F.A.

121/5354

4th Division

32nd Bde R.F.A.

Vol III 1 — 31.5.15

Nil

Army Form C. 2118.

WAR DIARY
or
INTELLIGENCE SUMMARY.
(Erase heading not required.)

D-

Instructions regarding War Diaries and Intelligence Summaries are contained in F.S. Regs., Part II. and the Staff Manual respectively. Title pages will be prepared in manuscript.

Hour, Date, Place	Summary of Events and Information	Remarks and references to Appendices
L'HALLOBEAU May 1st to 3rd	Whole Bde. Resting.	
4th	27th Battery moved into action ½ mile S. of NEUVE EGLISE in Support of South Midland Div. & came under order of S.M. Div. Arty.	
5th	Brigade less 27th Battery marched at 2pm via BAILLEUL & LOCRE to POPERINGHE + bivouacked 1 mile east of that town.	Reference Map. BELGIUM (B series) Sheet 28 N.W. 1/20,000
6th	Brigade remained in bivouack while positions were reconnoitred North of YPRES.	
8th	In the evening Batteries came into action in support of 11th Infantry Bde. - 134 Battery 1 mc C.8.8. - 135 Battery 1 mc B.2.6. Head Quarters just west of 134 Battery.	
9th	Batteries registered their zones (farm in C.15a to farm C.23 c4) 135 Bty. on the right of 6th Battery covering SHELL TRAP FARM (C22%) Enemy attacked about 6 SHELL TRAP. Our Batteries retaliated.	
10th	Heavy shelling of our trenches. Batteries retaliated.	
11th	Our trenches heavily shelled at 8pm. but no attack.	
12th	Quiet day	
13th	Enemy bombarded our trenches heavily from 4.15a.m. B.K. Batteries retaliated. Later enemy reported massing in rear of their lines. Fire was directed against them & effect reported good by our infantry - Enemy	

79 / 3298

(9 26 6). W 257—976 100,000 4/12 H W V

Army Form C. 2118.

(2)

WAR DIARY
or
INTELLIGENCE SUMMARY.
(Erase heading not required.)

Instructions regarding War Diaries and Intelligence Summaries are contained in F.S. Regs., Part II. and the Staff Manual respectively. Title pages will be prepared in manuscript.

Hour, Date, Place	Summary of Events and Information	Remarks and references to Appendices
YPRES. 14th	Ham attacked but successful counter attack was delivered at night of the 4th Division line was restored by 11 am. – Two Batteries engaged fired 2800 rounds. Fourth Division received the congratulations of General Joffre.	
15th	Enemy were reported to be massing in front of the Royal Irish Regt. – Batteries maintained a slow fire but no attack developed. Enemy shelled our first line trench, in fifth Division of SHELLTRAP FARM & also Second line trench. Both Batteries retaliated.	
16th	French 45th Division attacked 13m & 135 Batteries Cooperating by bombarding German trench opposite our front. – Our fire was to increase to 6pm at advance on heavy bursts between 5.15 & 6.25pm. Enemy retaliated by shelling our trench with H.E.	
18th	134 Battery fired at Shrapnel 135 shelled enemy's trench near SHELLTRAP FARM.	

WAR DIARY
or
INTELLIGENCE SUMMARY.
(Erase heading not required.)

Army Form C. 2118.

(3)

Hour, Date, Place	Summary of Events and Information	Remarks and references to Appendices
19th	134 Battery registered on Shrapnel Trench & two direct hits. 135 Battery Shelled Infantry trench off ST JULIEN ROAD.	
20th	27th Battery rejoined the Bde. & came into action 200 yards west of 134 B.g. 5th Indian How. Battery also came under 32nd Bde. for tactical purposes.	
21st	Batteries retaliated	
22nd	27th & How. Repulses	
23rd	Quiet day	
24th	2.30 am Enemy starts gassing on french South of SHELL TRAP FARM. All Batteries immediately opened fire on Enemy's trenches. 4 am 2 Observers came in to Canal bank in our A.G. They were repairing 5 am 2 Observers report. Owing to Fog - heavy shelling SHELL TRAP FARM & trench to South were evacuated. A counter attack was launched at 8 am against SHELL TRAP FARM but was unsuccessful. Our first line trench South of WIELTJE road held out all day. Battery	

76 / 3298

WAR DIARY
or
INTELLIGENCE SUMMARY.
(Erase heading not required.)

Army Form C. 2118.

Hour, Date, Place	Summary of Events and Information	Remarks and references to Appendices

Trenches were heavily shelled with shell which affected the eyes & 134 Regt had to leave their guns for 15 mins.

11. a.m. Enemy started dropping in S.W. of SHELLTRAP. Batteries covered this line to stop the enemy. Our infantry then held the support line S.W. of SHELLTRAP. German attack was not pushed any further.

2.45 p.m. French Battery unlimbered SHELLTRAP with fire effect. Shelling gradually died away about 6 p.m. During the night division retired to the line WIELTJE M (exclu.) — WIELTJE — ST. JULIEN ROAD — C 21 D 2 — Role zone was shifted to VERLORENHOEK & were from night 6 Sept 27 — 134 — 135. Role & position 10 & 14 How. Lying in followg Battn dumps in m m m

Major Grey, Lieut Hunter & Lieut. Barclay were wounded. Batteries registered on new zones.

26th | Quiet day.

27th | Batteries dispersed enemy's working party.

28th & 30th | Quiet in our front. Batteries obtained hostile working parties & retaliated to shelling from trenches.

Army Form C. 2118.

(5)

WAR DIARY
or
INTELLIGENCE SUMMARY.

(Erase heading not required.)

Hour, Date, Place	Summary of Events and Information	Remarks and references to Appendices
31.8	134 Battery got several direct hits on enemy's parapets – 135 Bg: shelled enemy's trenches East of WIELTJE – 134 Battery were heavily shelled in the morning & Capt Bennett Stewart & 2Lt Atkinson Bartlett were wounded, the latter seriously.	

Walker Capt & Adjt.
for Lieut. Colonel.
Cmg. 32nd Bde. RFA.

137/5845

4th Division

32nd Bde R.F.A.

Vol IV 1 — 30.6.15

War Diary 32nd Bde R.F.A. (E)
June 1915.   Appendix I.

The following awards have been made for gallant conduct in the field during June

Major H. Ward (134)   D.S.O.
Lieut. T. J. Hutton (134)   M.C.

B.Q.M.S. Mitchell (135)   D.C.M.
Cpl. Kempster (135)   D.C.M.
Bmdr. Cooper (135)   D.C.M.

Mentioned in Despatches.
  Major Ward (134)
  Major Hawkesley (135)
  Lieut. Hutton (134)

30/6/15.

[signature]
32nd Bde R.F.A.

Army Form C. 2118.

WAR DIARY
or
INTELLIGENCE SUMMARY.
(Erase heading not required.)

(E) (1)

Hour, Date, Place	Summary of Events and Information	Remarks and references to Appendices

YPRES. June 1915

1st — 27th Battery fired at Ration Party & silenced a french mortar.

2nd — The town of YPRES was very heavily shelled 5 guns of large calibres.

3rd — Germans very busy constructing their position. 134th Bde. Airplanes a working party. 134 + 135 Battery shells working parties the latter Bde with considerable effect.

4th — Observed on at BELLEVUE Farm Battery withdrew to Afd. park one section per Battery withdrew to wagon line.

5th — Working parties again. Shells of all Batteries. Afd. park remaining guns of Batteries withdrew to wagon lines. Section from each Battery went into action in positions alongside French Battery which the Bde. has been relieving. The Bde. was relieved on its O.P. by the VI Division.

6th — Bde. H.Q. withdrew to Bde. Am. Col. bivouac near VLAMERTINGHE. Section from each Battery stood registration from new position which was a shell hollow. 27th Bde. B22 d 6.5. 134th Bde. in a barn

Army Form C. 2118.

WAR DIARY
or
INTELLIGENCE SUMMARY.
(Erase heading not required.)

Instructions regarding War Diaries and Intelligence Summaries are contained in F.S. Regs., Part II. and the Staff Manual respectively. Title pages will be prepared in manuscript.

(2)

Hour, Date, Place	Summary of Events and Information	Remarks and references to Appendices
		Reference Map. (B Series) 28 N.W. 1/20,000
7th	B 22 d 3.9. – 135 Battery B16 Centre – The new Bde. Zone extended from C 8 c. 0.0 to Hill 14 C 7 a c (inclusive) – During the night 12th Inf. Bde. took over right half of new 4th Div! front from 45th French Div. Batteries went into action during night 7/8 relieving "Sensibles Groupe" of French Artillery. Bde. HQ. at farm B 15 d 4.7 S.E. Elverdinghe. Tenth Infantry Bde. took over left half of new 4th Div! front. G in G French. 32nd Bde. was then covering Bde. of 10th Bde. front & part of left Battalion of Right Bde. 4th Div. The Batteries divided almost Bde. Zone taking a third back in following order from right to left 27 – 134 – 135. One section of 86th 4.5 How. Battery joined the Bde. & took into action at B 22 d 10.5 purpose of came into action to cover the whole Bde. Zone –
8th	Batteries registered their new Zones.	

Army Form C. 2118.

WAR DIARY
or
INTELLIGENCE SUMMARY.
(Erase heading not required.)

Instructions regarding War Diaries and Intelligence Summaries are contained in F.S. Regs., Part II. and the Staff Manual respectively. Title pages will be prepared in manuscript.

Hour, Date, Place	Summary of Events and Information	Remarks and references to Appendices
9th	Registration continued. 27 Bty. Snipped trench mortar	
10th	at C.B.C. 2.4. Enemy's trench mortars fairly active. 27 F.Bty. Shelled form Joss'n believed to be an observing station & obtained 3 direct hits - 27 Shells. Trench mortar near farm at C.7.d. 6.6. Germans exploded a mine under Rt. Half Fusilier trench at 9.15 am but did not do much material damage.	
11th & 14th	Batteries chiefly occupied in retaliating to enemy's trench mortars which were very active firing on our front line - On night 11th these (our?) trench mortars Bde. was relieved in the front line by Eleventh Bde. (8th Pruss.)	
15th	On nights 15/16, 16/17 Enk Infantry Bde. took over part of the line from Eleventh & Twelfth Bde. 32nd Bde. slightly adjusted the right of its line so as to cover only the front held by Eleventh Infantry Bde. Three trench mortars were fired Infantry from Snipers of Am.Uchin (66.R.Bde) & 135.R.Bde. 135.R.Bde. also engaged enemy's observing station. Shelled	

WAR DIARY or INTELLIGENCE SUMMARY

Army Form C. 2118.

Hour, Date, Place	Summary of Events and Information	Remarks and references to Appendices
16th	About 2.20 am - heavy mist & rifle fire was down on front line. 135 Battery opened rate of section fire on enemy's front trenches. No attack developed. 86th Hvy. Section obtained 3 direct hits on supposed enemy's dressing station. 135th Battery was shelled. 4.2 How & Shrapnel. Wounded. 27th Battery shelled mostly running N.T.S C and C. 8.1 shrapnel, in afternoon heavy enemy aeroplane fire. 135th we gain shelled. Shrapnel Fitter Staff Sergt. wounded.	
17th	All Batteries retaliated daily to shelling of enemy's trench mortars. Obtained a direct hit on 7.5 HG's enemy's trench mortar. One Observing station hit & two enemy heavily shelled. Three other front trench were heavily shelled. One man of heavy Battery & trench mortars 6 brought in with rifle fire wounds.	
18th & 25th	Aeroplane one fell near Souchez. Th's Occupants were wounded.	

WAR DIARY or INTELLIGENCE SUMMARY

Army Form C. 2118.

(5)

(Erase heading not required.)

Hour, Date, Place	Summary of Events and Information	Remarks and references to Appendices
21st	134 & 135 Batteries retaliated to shelling of our trenches.	
22nd to 24th	Batteries retaliated to hostile machine & shelling of Canal Bank. Otherwise very quiet.	
25th	On night of 25/26 one Section 128th How. Battery joined 86th How. Battery Section to form new Bde (86th Battery) known as "Knuttor" under Captain Knutton. Bde.	
26th	Battery - Knutton Bde. Came under 32nd Bde. for tactical purposes. 4th Siege Bde. also came under Bde. for tactical purposes. At 10 p.m. two great explosions occurred in enemy's trench - large heaps of debris blown to westerly.	
27th	Bde. did not fire.	
28th	134th Battery moved one gun to new position at B.15.B.8.7	
29th/30th	A good deal of hostile shelling in rear of front trenches. 134 Gun started registering from new position. Otherwise quiet day.	

R.R. Weer Capt & Adjt
32nd Bde R.F.A.

4th Division

121/6308

32nd Bde R.F.A.
Vol V
1-31-4-15

WAR DIARY
or
INTELLIGENCE SUMMARY.
(Erase heading not required.)

Army Form C. 2118.

F O

Hour, Date, Place	Summary of Events and Information	Remarks and references to Appendices
ELVERDINGHE July 1st 1915	German guns very active. Fired markers did considerable damage to our trenches. 134 Battery retaliated with "International trench". 135 Bty shelled Enemy's observing station at about 8pm on Sappers Combermere + blew up a German mine in front of the S.L.I trenches. Germans at once opened rifle fire with 4.2 + 5.7 Howrs. All Batteries 9.02 RB retaliated on Enemy's trenches.	Reference Map Belgium (5 Series) Sheet 28 N.W 1/20000
2nd	Farm used as observing station by 134 + 135 Batteries was shelled.	
3rd	135 Battery fired a successful salvoes at a party who were apparently starving. All Batteries retaliated to the shelling from trenches + Canal Bank. Between 7-8pm there was a heavy bombardment from trenches with short shells. An attack appeared	134 Battery clamped v/s position after trench 2 section firing into action at B156 b64 Likely but did not materialise on section of B11 C 6.6

WAR DIARY
or
INTELLIGENCE SUMMARY.
(*Erase heading not required.*)

Army Form C. 2118.

F(2)

Hour, Date, Place		Summary of Events and Information	Remarks and references to Appendices
July 4th		A Corps meeting quiet day. There were some Hvy heavy bursts of rifle firing thro' night to which 135 Bty. retaliated. 134 Battery replied from its new position on the Yzenstein ridge. Engaged enemy prepared attack.	
	5th	134 Bty. shelled hostile B.S.L.P. Company. 135 Bty. searched for searchlight sited in enemy's working trenches. One gun of 135 Battery under Lieut. R'Quin was taken into action after dark in replacement in our front trench for tomorrow's attack.	
	6th	The task for this gun was to destroy the enemy S(Capt G) with H.E. then switch on enemy's wire to assist S sap with Lime Sprayers. At 3am 32nd Bde. H.Q. moved to support just S of BOESINGHE on the YPRES Road - Lieut. Statetalon (Capt Pyres) joined H.Q. Rifle Bde. an liaison with attacking Battalion.	Reference Larger Map attached –

Army Form C. 2118.

F(3)

WAR DIARY
or
INTELLIGENCE SUMMARY.
(Erase heading not required.)

Hour, Date, Place	Summary of Events and Information	Remarks and references to Appendices
	Telephone Communication was passed from Bde. H.Q. August to 115th Bde. + H.Q. R.B. The bombardment of Enemy's position commenced at 5 a.m. in accordance with attack programme. Owing to mist the Enemy's trenches could be seen from the observing stations till about 5.40 a.m. but infantry reported that wire had been successfully cut & 2nd Rifleman's Gun + Section 13th Bde. Rifle Bde. occupied in ten columns at 6 a.m. + has no difficulty in	
8 a.m.	occupying the Enemy's first line trenches. Batteries continued a slow rate of fire till 7 a.m. to cover the construction of the position gained. Heavy xxxx xxxxxxx N.E. of xxx. heavy thin xxxx Batteries searched the area. from Pr. 10 stick their first counter attack from Pr. 14 stick was easily dealt with & 134 Bg. 134 + 135 still communication trench. A + B.	
3 p.m.	Another Counter attack from same direction Similarly dealt with.	

Army Form C. 2118.

F

WAR DIARY
or
INTELLIGENCE SUMMARY.
(Erase heading not required.)

Hour, Date, Place	Summary of Events and Information	Remarks and references to Appendices
10 a.m.	Major Hulim saw Enemy debouching from farm C8a.5.2 opposite from the hill in close formation. 27 Bty fired with excellent effect but almost 750 men appeared to reach the trench at the bottom of the hill. They were large seen again almost 20 mins later running across gap in ridge at C7 c 9.8. 27 Bty again opened fire & did great execution piling up a number of bodies in the gap. No counter attack developed from this quarter.	
2.30 p.m.	Another hostile, probably reinforcement, line 2 Bn occurs of troops attempted to cross the gap & 27 Bty meanwhile 13th Bty shelled reinforcements coming from a village with 1st Bty, formed curtain in front & was turning back. The night was comparatively quiet & the French gun 2135 Bty. was successfully withdrawn after dark. The Gun captured Fr Coy. the Sap had during the bombardment firing 184 rounds in 9 mins. One of the detachment was slightly wounded after the assault on Bean ridge.	

Army Form C. 2118.

WAR DIARY
or
INTELLIGENCE SUMMARY.
(Erase heading not required.)

Hour, Date, Place	Summary of Events and Information	Remarks and references to Appendices
July 7th	From daybreak Batteries were busy with day firing at German Jäger parties. These proved to be unique targets & great execution was done. All our trench especially the Copses were very heavily bombarded all day, our infantry suffering heavy casualties. From 1pm till 2.15pm there was a heavy bombardment with shell shells during which enemy were seen massing men from 14. All Batteries fired & the counter attack died following up very effectively. I. The Left Hants counter attack said we pressed [?] a heavy bombardment on trenches, were easily disposed of. Annon [?] the afternoon. At 7 pm. a few German succeeded in reaching SP running along left of S and D trench C. They were however eventually driven out by our bombers under a covering fire from 13th Bttn.	

WAR DIARY or INTELLIGENCE SUMMARY

Army Form C. 2118.

F 6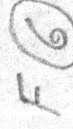

Hour, Date, Place	Summary of Events and Information	Remarks and references to Appendices
July 8th	Bde. HQ. returned to their billet at about 10 a.m. Enemy shelled our section per Battery with Gas & incendiary during the night (7/8). There was a C.B. Shelley returning during the night (7/8). The bombardment of our trenches was recommenced at 6.30 a.m. & continued with intense barrage fire. The Enemy made 3 more Counter attacks at 10.15 a.m. 11.30 a.m. & 2.10 p.m. all repulsed. The Enemy's trench area very heavily damaged & no shrapnel fire. The Enemy's trench area very heavily shelled. All 3 Reinforcements lines & Sap & shelters were all shelled. Communication trenches. All 3 Battery shelled German working parties apparently digging new trenches. One section per Battery & ½ Am. Col. withdrew after dark on relief § 49th Div. A/F & withdrew to Keltkellen at HOUTKERQUE (sheet 27) Lt. Col. M°Carthy C.M.G. left the 32nd Bde. on appointment to Brig. Genl. Comdg. 515th Div. Art. Major Tilney posts to command the Bde. from 'B' 135. RHA.	

WAR DIARY or INTELLIGENCE SUMMARY

Army Form C. 2118.

F (7)

Hour, Date, Place	Summary of Events and Information	Remarks and references to Appendices
July 9th	Fourth Div. landed and its Section of the Frd of 49th Div. & went into reserve with H.Q. at WATOU. 32nd Bde. H.Q. after handing over to 33rd heavy Battery withdrew to its billets near HOUTKERQUE. One Section per Battery of Bde to C.C. was left behind in support of number the orders of 49th Div. A.G. These Sections were eventually withdrawn to HOUTKERQUE on the night 14/15.	Reference Map. AMIENS Sheet/12. 1/80,000
HOUTKERQUE 10th till 23rd	Bde. Resting.	
12th	Bde. inspected by Gen.l Plumer Cmd.g 2nd Army.	
19th	Siege Artillery Inspects 9″ mountings of F.M. Sir John French C-in-C.	
23rd-24th	32nd Bde. entrained at CASSEL & proceeded by rail to MONDICOURT & went into rest billets at THIEVRES preparing to 4th Div. taking over the Sector of position of 5, 218th French division.	
25th	2/Lt. Robinson (135) awarded the M.C. for his good work when in Charge of Retaches gun in the trenches on 6th July.	

Army Form C. 2118.

F 

WAR DIARY
or
INTELLIGENCE SUMMARY.
(Erase heading not required.)

Hour, Date, Place	Summary of Events and Information	Remarks and references to Appendices
THIEVRES July 26th to 28th	Bde. in rest billets – Battery Commanders reconnoitring next positions –	Reference Map. AMIENS Sheet 12. 1/80,000
29th	27th & 135th Batteries (less one section each) moved up into action – 135 Bty. on east edge of village of VITERMONT 135 about ½ mile S.E. of ENGLEBELMER. Bde. H.Q. at ENGLEBELMER. An O.P. at ACHEUX. 134 Bty. remained at its wagon line in wood 1½ miles W. of ENGLEBELMER as replacements. Gun positions were taken over from French Battys. The Bde. was in Support of Sleventh Infantry Bde. & covered the front from a point 700 yds. S. of BEAUMONT-HAMEL to the River ANCRE near St PIERRE DIVISION.	
30 & 31st	27th & 135th Batteries Registered – 134th Battery preparing emplacements on the immediate left of 27th Battery.	

Rolleston Capt & Adjt
32nd Bde RFA

32nd Bde, RFA

Appendix to Folio F.

Allotment of Objectives for attack on 6th July 1915

PHASE	1	2	3	4
27 {2 Section / 1 Section}	TL / WE	} TL	JTL	line BTL
135 {less 1 gun / one gun}	A / G South	AB / wire	AB / —	AB / —
134 {2 section / 1 Section}	C / D north	C lifting / Pause	C / F North	C lifting / K (east)

Target refer to target map attached.

Programme of Bombardment.

Phase I 5 am till 5.37 am. { wire cutting & destruction of defences.

— II 5.37 am till 5.47 am Observation Period.

— III 5.47 till 6. am. Destruction of Defences.

— IV 6 am. Assault – Barrage.

4th Division

32nd Bde. R.F.A.
Vol VI
Aug & Sept. 15

32nd Bde. R.F.A.

WAR DIARY
INTELLIGENCE SUMMARY

Army Form C. 2118

G (1)

Hour, Date, Place	Summary of Events and Information	Remarks and references to Appendices
ENGLEBELMER Aug. 1st 1915	All Batteries Registered.	Reference Map. French Plan Directeur 2 + 2bis. 1/20000
2nd	6th. Remainder of French Battery came out of action.	
7th	3rd Section of 135 Bty. came into action. Battery wagon lines except 4-horse gun teams moved back to SARTON on account of difficulties in watering horses at present position.	
8th	After dark 27th Battery fired at transport on BEAUCOURT - MIRAUMONT Road after which transport was heard moving off at a gallop. 135 Bty. fired at a working party in German front trenches. Firing was followed by squeals from the working party.	
14th	HESNIL was heavily shelled by field guns. All Batteries retaliated with salvos on BEAUCOURT.	
18th	27th + 134th Batteries fired salvos on transport in conjunction with an infantry also signallers O.P. with lamp when enemy transport had reached registered point. Transport heard at a gallop. 2/15 R.G. have detected section of Auchonvillers to Hamel shelling on the days of the month chiefly consists in retaliation to enemy's fire with occasional shells at working parties + transport. The enemy are very quiet on the front. There is very little sniping on gun fire. The enemy only appear to have a few field guns + a few Batteries of field How. Guns near HAMEL	

WAR DIARY
or
INTELLIGENCE SUMMARY.
(Erase heading not required.)

Army Form C. 2118

G (2)

Hour, Date, Place	Summary of Events and Information	Remarks and references to Appendices
ENGLEBELMER Sept 1st & 2nd	Our trenches near HAMEL. Some 5.9 heavy shells & trench mortars to which 275th Battery retaliated in German lines + St. PIERRE DIVION.	Reference Map French Plan Directeur Sheet 2 v 2 bis. 1/10,000
4th	134th Battery successfully shelled working parties near the RAVIN R. Y.	
5th	Spare Section of 134th Battery came into action N 18. MESNIL shelled GRANDCOURT to which its retaliated by violent shelling of AUTHUILE. This section is normally kept in reserve of the weapon line but can into action whenever it may be required.	
6th	135th Battery fraction was repeatedly fired guns. Observation balloon appeared to be observing its fire. No damage was done. MESNIL + MAILLY MAILLET were heavy shelled. 5 field guns. All Batteries retaliated on BEAUCOURT.	
10th	9.25 pm. working party was seen at F.23.b.6.0. 134th Battery fired + shouts & firers were subsequently heard from infantry.	
11th	135th Battery fired 28 rounds to time Enemy's line after dark on relief was believed to be in progress. A dummy Battery unbuilt the Bde. H.Q. in conjunction with the firing of 135th Battery succeeded in drawing enemy's fire	

WAR DIARY or INTELLIGENCE SUMMARY.

Army Form C. 2118

G (3)

Hour, Date, Place	Summary of Events and Information	Remarks and references to Appendices
ENGLEBELMER. Sept 14th	AUCHONVILLERS, MESNIL, HAMEL & positions of 275 & 134th Batteries were shelled. Field Guns, Headquarters & A & C Batteries of 99th Bgd. R.F.A. joined the Bde for attachment. A & C Batteries came into action in alternative positions of 275 & 135th Batteries respectively.	
16th	Attached Batteries positions were supervision of our Battery Commanders. Attached Batteries left after dark.	
18th	135th Battery registered a point on BEAUMONT – BEAUCOURT Road with aeroplane observation. Communication satisfactory.	
20th	ENGLEBELMER was shelled. 275 Battery fires 5 rounds on a machine gun emplacement. Others a direct hit on a machine gun emplacement.	
23rd	Coincident with the Allied Offensive 134th & 135th Batteries bombard enemy front trench from the RAVIN S.Y. Bombardment repeated at 10 am to 10.20 am & 4.30 pm to 4.50 pm. Ammunition allowance for the 2 Batteries 150 Shrapnel & 100 H.E.	
24th	Bombardment continued 10.35 am till 10.55 am, 2.20 pm to 2.40 pm & 3 pm to 3.10 pm. Ammunition allowance 215 Shrapnel + 150 H.E. During these bombardments Amiezville barrage was such the enemy's trench. Retaliation was very slight & ineffective.	
26th	Some repairing damage was successfully dealt by 134 R.S.	

WAR DIARY
or
INTELLIGENCE SUMMARY.

Army Form C. 2118

G 4

Hour, Date, Place	Summary of Events and Information	Remarks and references to Appendices
ENGLEBELMER Sept. 27th to 30th	Very quiet indeed & practically no hostile fire.	

J. Arthur Cap. & Adjt.
for Lt. Col. RFA
Cmdg. 32nd Bde RFA.

WAR DIARY or INTELLIGENCE SUMMARY.

Army Form C. 2118.

Hour, Date, Place	Summary of Events and Information	Remarks and references to Appendices
ENGLEBELMER Oct. 1915		Reference Map 57DSE 1/20,000
1st to 9th	Very quiet with occasional thick mist. On 7th a few trench mortar bombs fell in our trenches.	
10th-9/11/15	Regt. HANCOCK joined the regt. HAMEL to which 27th & 135th Batteries retaliated. Considerable mortar shelling of our trenches. Especially by	
12th	Heavy trench mortars to which our Batteries retaliated. Shelling of our trenches continued — 27th Battery fired at a German trench in neighbourhood of ST PIERRE DIVION with good results. They attained a direct hit on supposed dressing station. Timber + what lit on appeared like a man's body were thrown into the air. A hostile Battery South of GRANDCOURT at Rqd 4.0 immediately stopped firing.	
13th/16/20th (18th)	Very quiet — Misty. The personnel of a Section from each Battery was exchanged with personnel of 124th Bde. 37th Division for a fortnight, attached for instruction.	
21st	Our trenches were shelled especially on our right. All Batteries retaliated.	
2nd 23rd	Major Bray # D.S.O (134th Battery) left the Rgt. on promotion & was posted to 22nd Division. (SG)	
22	2nd Lt J W WOODROFFE joined the regt and was posted to 134th Battery	

Army Form C. 2118

WAR DIARY
or
INTELLIGENCE SUMMARY.   H (2)

(Erase heading not required.)

Instructions regarding War Diaries and Intelligence Summaries are contained in F.S. Regs., Part II. and the Staff Manual respectively. Title pages will be prepared in manuscript.

Hour, Date, Place	Summary of Events and Information	Remarks and references to Appendices
ENGLEBELMER Oct. 24th to 31st 1915	Very quiet. Occasional slight shelling from front line trenches with feed guns to which our Batteries retaliated. The whole week it was wet & misty + very little could be seen from the observing stations. Monday 25th a party of 50 men from the Bde. Ammunition Column paraded at ACHEUX for the visit of the Major.	

JRArthur Capt & Adjt.
32 Bde R.F.A.

Army Form C. 2118.

WAR DIARY
or
INTELLIGENCE SUMMARY

(Erase heading not required.)

32 Bde R.F.A.

Instructions regarding War Diaries and Intelligence Summaries are contained in F. S. Regs., Part II. and the Staff Manual respectively. Title Pages will be prepared in manuscript.

Place	Date	Hour	Summary of Events and Information	Remarks and references to Appendices
ENGLEBELMER	Nov	1-7	Very little hostile fire. Germans fairly busy on their trenches. Strongpoints destroyed. working parties.	Reference Map 57 D S.E. 1/20,000
		8	ENGLEBELMER shelled. One man slightly wounded and two horses. Bridges retaliated on GRANDCOURT, BEAUCOURT, BEAUMONT along with 157 Bde.	
		9-14	Batteries engaged in retaliation on enemy trenches and shelling machine gun emplacements and working parties. Heavies daily between ACHIET and BAPAUME. Constant movement on ACHIET-BIHUCOURT Road and BEAUCOURT-MIRAUMONT Road	
		15	Very heavy hostile shelling. They seemed to be searching up the valley of the ANCRE and also JACOB'S LADDER. O.P. attempt to be at Q.5.D.98 as a single tree in the area was observed. 27th Battery registered target 1 (Road Junction R.13.c.4.4) by aeroplane.	
		6	2 Lt H.T. VACHELL (Temp) joined Brigade and posted to 134 Battery	
		6	2 Lt H.V. SQUIRES (Temp) 135 Battery	
			2 Lt S.G. SIMPSON (Temp) 27 Battery	
			2 Lt G. Keogh from the 27th Battery, 2 Lt PARSON & 134 Battery and Lt MOTION 135 Battery left the Brigade and were posted to 124th Bde. 37 Division	
			The personnel of a section from each battery were exchanged with the personnel of 124th Bde 37 Div.	

Army Form C. 2118.

WAR DIARY
or
INTELLIGENCE SUMMARY

32 Bde R.F.A.
T (2)

(Erase heading not required.)

Place	Date	Hour	Summary of Events and Information	Remarks and references to Appendices
ENGLEBELMER	Nov 16-18		Misty. Battery fired at odd intervals so as to catch Germans working in the open.	
		19	27th Battery bombarded German trenches in Q.2.4 and R.19 in conjunction with 51st Division.	
		20	2/Lt. C.T. COBBOLD joined Bde and was posted to 27 Bty. 2/Lt. J.E. NICHOLS — 134 Bty 2/Lt. D WILLIAMS — Divm. Col.	
		22.	Capt Lord CRANWORTH joined Bde and took over command of the Column.	
		24.	Major SWANN joined Bde and took over command of 134 Battery.	
		23.	At 1 pm in conjunction with the Boers and the Yorkshires 134 and 135 Batteries bombarded RAVIN en Y. 134 searching the trench Q.10.D.6.7. to Q.10.B.8.1. and 135 searching the Southern arm of the RAVIN from above G.11.C.6.3. Several bombs derived very successful	
		25.	Enemy hard at work during night. Wire. First line trench in Q7A and Q2B considerably strengthened. New wire in second line trench between Q.11.B.1.9 and Q.11.C.8.3	
		26.	HAMEL shelled. Direct hits on Battalion HQ 27th Bty retaliated	
		30.	HAMEL shelled. Strong retaliation by 27th Battery on Q.1.B.c.6.7 and 127 Bde.	

O.S. Baines Lt. Adjt
32 Bde R.F.A

Army Form C. 2118.

WAR DIARY
or
INTELLIGENCE SUMMARY

32 Brigade R.F.A.

(Erase heading not required.)

Place	Date	Hour	Summary of Events and Information	Remarks and references to Appendices
ENGLEBELMER	1915 Dec 1		27th Battery at 6.45 p.m. shelled near Bridge in Q.18.B.6.3. and also BEAUCOURT Station Road and at 10 p.m. road in BEAUCOURT.	Reference Map 57.D.S.E. 1/20,000.
		2	134 Battery took a gun into action at Q.22.A.4.1. and shelled trenches in Q.6.A and Q.6.c.	
			155 Battery retaliated on Beckport Trenches in Q.17.A and B.	
		2	German Trench Mortar busy at WHITE MOUND opposite LANCASHIRE POST at Q.3.C.5.3. It was killed by 27th Battery.	

Army Form C. 2118.

32 bde. R.F.A
J.B.

WAR DIARY or INTELLIGENCE SUMMARY.
(Erase heading not required.)

Hour, Date, Place	Summary of Events and Information	Remarks and references to Appendices
ENGLEBELMER 1915 DEC. 2	This French Mortar is rather troublesome. It is tucked under a hill on the East of it, so that it is difficult to reach. The Brigade on our right can reach it and the Howrs on our left can get to it so lest it can be effectively dealt with. Our part of the line is very interesting as the Battery of the ANCRE interrupts the trenches on both sides. We drill in the them land is visited by patrols on both sides. The 27th Battery shell it when occupied by German.	
3.	134th Battery fired detached gun from Q22.A.4.1 on trenches Q5.A. Heavy German Battery of our trenches in Q10.D and Q16.B. 135th Battery retaliated with good effect, some 5 direct hits being got on dug-outs with H.E. Machine Gun emplacements were also hit. German Trench Mortars in R16.C and D were again very active the signal box in our line being destroyed. 27th Battery and 16th Heavy (Whitehall) 27th Battery supported bombardment by the 51st Division to BEAUCOURT. Battery fired on weapons from MIRAUMONT to BEAUCOURT.	
4.	Captain C.P. HUGHES-GIBB R.G.A. 135th Battery proceeded to England to report to the War Office to take up a new appointment. No 5 gun of 135th Battery fired out of action owing to premature. Muzzle was blown off. Only one man slightly injured.	Q17 A.8.9, Q11.c.8.2 Q11.c.2.5
5.	135th Battery heavily shelled 134th Battery destroyed working parties	

WAR DIARY or INTELLIGENCE SUMMARY

Army Form C. 2118.

35 Bde R.F.A.

(Erase heading not required.)

Instructions regarding War Diaries and Intelligence Summaries are contained in F.S. Regs., Part II. and the Staff Manual respectively. Title pages will be prepared in manuscript.

Place	Hour, Date, Place	Summary of Events and Information	Remarks and references to Appendices
ENGLEBELMER	1915 Dec 6	27th Battery Attached X at AUCHONVILLERS supported 57th Brigade bombardment shelling Q.7.d.B.5.1. Q.20.B.4.30.05 and R.19.c.5.5.	
	7.	German forces single rounds at 10 minutes intervals. Pre-arranged bombardment carried out by the detached section fired with good results. 130th Battery Attached Guns at Q.22.c.0.6 cut wire successfully in front of Y Q.17.B.2.0.13. 135th Battery fired on the front dots intervals during night to prevent the being repaired.	
	8.	D. Battery (ue2t Bde) in position at Q.19.13.4.6 attached to this Brigade for one week.	
	10.	27th Battery fired on S PIERRE DIVION observing down hit with H.E. and direct hit also with H.E. on Observation Station at O.5.D.9.5. 135 Battery fired on working party in Q.17.B.2.4 at 6.20 am	
	13.	D 145 Battery registered BEAUCOURT CHATEAU and bombarded French trenches running NE from sunken road in Q.12.c.1.3. and Q.12.A.3.4 and Q.12.B.6.2.	
	14.	27th Battery shelled trenches in R.19.c.4.7 in conjunction with 57th Brigade. Heavy mist AUCHONVILLERS shelled by Germans. All batteries fired at intervals on roads. D 145 Battery left.	
	17.		

Army Form C. 2118

WAR DIARY
or
INTELLIGENCE SUMMARY
(Erase heading not required.)

32nd Brigade R.F.A.

Place	Date	Hour	Summary of Events and Information	Remarks and references to Appendices
ENGLEBELMER	1915 Dec.	18	D/150 Battery in position at 135 altogether. Position	
		22	Lieut Col CRANWORTH left to join staff of General SMITH DORRIEN	
		23	D/150 Battery registered BEAUCOURT CHATEAU, dug outs in R.7.A.D.2.%0 in Q.11.B.65	
		24	D/150 Battery registered huts Q5, D, Y, 5 and trench dug outs R.7.A.0.2	
		18–25	A quiet week. Usual shelling of working parties and retaliation	
		25	Christmas passed very quietly. Particular precautions were taken to prevent any surprise	
		26	11.45 HAMEL and Yr (Q.2.2.B) heavily shelled in reply to bombardment of S. PIERRE DIVION by 51st Division. 27th Battery at once retaliated on Q.24.B and Yr Q.16.C Hours also shelled Yr Q.16.C	
		28	135 Battery (detached from Brigade) Q.22.A.2.0 sent Germans were at Q.14 B.20.13. Considerable damage but not certain whether clear lane was cut. At night 135 Battery shelled Q.17.B.20.13 at irregular intervals to prevent wire being repaired	
		30	D/150 Battery taken out of action – 105 mm and 150 mm. At 1.30 pm the Hours and 27th B Battery recover German guns at june. S. PIERRE DIVION retaliated strongly on S. PIERRE DIVION	
		31.	PROSPECT POINT and CHARLES AVENUE (Q.23 D) very accurately registered by Germans. Germans took in the New Year with rifle fire and flares and 27th Battery fired a salvo.	
		23.	0.21 C.R. Sanfoir 27th Battery left the Brigade to go to the Second Army School	

A. C. Loaumo Lt. Col
32 B.G. R.F.A.

4th Division
War Diary
32nd Bde. R.F.A.

January to December
1916

4th DIVISION.

32nd BDE. R. F. A.

JANUARY 1916.

WAR DIARY
INTELLIGENCE SUMMARY

32nd Brigade R.F.A.

Place	Date	Hour	Summary of Events and Information	Remarks and references to Appendices
ENGLEBELMER	19/6 1/7		The following were mentioned in despatches. Major Saunders R.F.A. Comdg. 135' Battery and awarded D.S.O. today, & Lt. W.G. COMERVILLE R.A.M.C. att. 4/Shropt. 32 V Brigade and awarded Military Cross. No.59078 Sergt. J. DEAN, 134 Bty. and awarded Distinguished Conduct Medal. No. 59097 Corpl. E. JAMES 125 Bty. and awarded a Distinguished Conduct Medal. VIII B/131 Bdr. J. IRVIN 134 Bty. "	
	4/7		To-day the Germans made an attempt to 'eat out' on this front. They heavily bombarded HAMEL all day and all along our trenches. Communication with battalion HQ at HAMEL was broken off and 27th Battery O.P. was shelled. At 4:30 p.m. the bombardment ceased for a few minutes then it was started again very severely all along the line. The fire was lifted at HAMEL and a barrage laid behind it. At the same time there was heavy rifle fire. Lt. Patterson of 96th Brigade got down to section fire on their barrage lines and the Boers joined in and by Zero hour everything was quiet again. It was undoubtedly a serious attempt to feel out on perhaps even more just to test the opposition had it did not succeed. Considering the flattening of trenches the casualties were quite insignificant.	
	5/7		27, 134 and 135 batteries took part in the bombardment at 10 am in retaliation to the German attack of the day before.	

Army Form C. 2118.

WAR DIARY
or
INTELLIGENCE SUMMARY
(Erase heading not required.)

32nd Brigade R.F.A.
K (2)

Place	Date	Hour	Summary of Events and Information	Remarks and references to Appendices
ENGLEBEL- MER	Feby Jany 1916	6-10.	The usual trench warfare. In the most thought was had about the aeroplane targets R.13.c.6 and Q.15.B.4. 27th Battery opened fire over the transport appeared to be in great confusion. The Germans replied their fire at about 2 rounds very rapidly into HAMEL reflecting about our own Line.	
		10.	A patrol party of the 2nd Royal Irish with Col Sloggett controlling the whole operation were to enter the German trenches in Q.10.D.6.,134 and 135 Batteries were ready along with the Heavy to open fire in support at 1 a.m. (11-1-16) but at 5.30 a.m. the patrol returned as they were unable to get the wire cut.	
		13	2 Lt P.G. HOLMS joined Brigade and was attached to 135th Bty	
		18	On trenches in Q.10 c & Q.10 D were heavily shelled between 9.30 and 10.30 a.m. and Germans without reply. 27th Battery retaliated on BEAUCOURT-MIRAUMONT Road, B & Battery shelled Q.11.C.1.8 and 135 Battery fired H.E. on Q.10.D.8.4	
		20.	Several small parties of Germans in light blue uniforms seen known cross of Hers were on Statio Road in Q.11.D.3.6 at 10.15 a.m. they were shelled and one was seen to fall	
		27.	GAS started by 48th Division nothing happened. F. 2/Lt RUTHERFORD	
		29	2/Lt RUTHERFORD 134 Battery were wounded. A party of infantry had been 2/Lt F. CASSIDY formed hole cut was posted to the command of 3 Ammunition Column	

2449 Wt. W14957/M90 750,000 1/16 J.B.C. & A. Forms/C.2118/12.

WAR DIARY
or
INTELLIGENCE SUMMARY

32nd Bde R.F.A. K (3)

Army Form C. 2118.

Place	Date	Hour	Summary of Events and Information	Remarks and references to Appendices
ENGLEBELMER	1916 Jany 29		The roof lifted and a German machine gun was turned on. One of the party was wounded and 2 Lt RUTHERFURD was hit and at once got over the back of the trench to 75.3 his rescue. 2 Lieut RUTHERFURD was wounded in four places	
		3.0	A German Patrol was on the Hill and it was arranged to send a Patrol to explore the. It was very thoroughly done however, and is head 27th battery at 6 p.m. were noted & still [illegible]	

O.C. [illegible] Bty RFA
32 Bde R.F.A.

Army Form C. 2118.

WAR DIARY
or
INTELLIGENCE SUMMARY
(Erase heading not required.)

32 Bde RFA Vol (1)

Place	Date	Hour	Summary of Events and Information	Remarks and references to Appendices
ENGLEBELMER	Dec 27th		4th Division (less Divl Arty) relieved by 36 Division in that portion of the line held by 4th Division south of MAILLY-MAILLET — SERRE Road.	
	5/1/17		11th Infantry Brigade relieved by 108th Inf Bde — Whites Rifles were supporting the latter. The 91 Royal Irish Fusiliers, 13th Royal Irish Rifles, and 11 Royal Irish Rifles were occupying the trenches.	
		13th	134 Battery placed tactically under 14th Brigade RFA as 14th A/P Brigade were taking over from the right Brigade the line of the front supported by the 134 Battery	
		12.	Major C.J.H. SWANN 134 Bty was attached to Army Cavalry Div and in much of the strength. He was present by us on 3rd January 1916.	
		10.	Hostile artillery rather more active. Trenches Q16B Q16D and AUCHONVILLERS been heavily shelled by the Germans. 27th Bty OP and 135 Bty OP were shelled.	
		11.	Between 4 and 4.30 pm HAMEL Q16A and centre by Q17A73 were heavily shelly. The Brigade retaliated with about 90 rounds on BEAUCOURT vicinity A.E. The trenches (127th Bde) also shelled BEAUCOURT.	
		12.	About 50 rounds 105 mm burst on ME SNIL. Between 27th and 135 Batteries retaliated strongly along with the 8 guns on BEAUCOURT. The Germans reply was a fairly heavy bombt west of AUCHONVILLERS from 5 to 5.15 pm. 134 & other recd Scan on THIEPVAL normal respected 2 points in Q10D and Q11C.	

Army Form C. 2118.

WAR DIARY
or INTELLIGENCE SUMMARY

32 Bde R.F.A. L (2)

(Erase heading not required.)

Place	Date	Hour	Summary of Events and Information	Remarks and references to Appendices
ENGLEBELMER	Feb	14	The Germans shewed great deliberate shelling, round at 9.30 minutes. There were more casualties than usual. 27th and 13th Batteries retaliated with single rounds at intervals of 10 min. 30 minutes on Q.18.A.5.6. the German Batteries H.Q.	
	15	at 7.20 p.m.	27th Battery fired on junction of roads and dumps in R.7.B. and then switched on to the Battery position at R.J.B.3.8. Battery to retaliate the German Battery retaliated on 27 Battery for fire at [illegible] [crossed out text]	
	17	2 Lt	H.J. IVENS joined the Brigade and was posted to 13th Battery.	
	15-29		Hostile Artillery inactive.	
	26		Major J.P.V. HAWKSLEY D.S.O. L.23.135 R.F. May left to take up the command of 110th Brigade R.F.A.	
	29		Two bombs were dropped from aeroplanes on ENGLEBELMER close to 135 Battery Mess. All the windows were shattered and about 12 foot hole was made but no one was hurt.	

A.E. Loring Lt Col
32 Bde R.F.A.

Army Form C. 2118.

WAR DIARY
or
INTELLIGENCE SUMMARY

32nd Brigade R.F.A.

M.D.

(Erase heading not required.)

Instructions regarding War Diaries and Intelligence Summaries are contained in F. S. Regs., Part II. and the Staff Manual respectively. Title Pages will be prepared in manuscript.

Place	Date	Hour	Summary of Events and Information	Remarks and references to Appendices
ENGUELBELMER	March 1	2	Between 2 and 2.30 am 20 105m/m shells fell on 37th Battery position. One man slightly wounded. 27th Battery retaliated on battery at R.20.c.37.85	
	2/5		Brigade relieved by sections of 143 Brigade of the 36th Division	
HALLOY		5	9 am Brigade marched over to 143 Brigade. Brigade went into rest at HALLOY	LENS 1/100,000 F.5
BIENVILLERS			Brigade returned into action relieving the 35th Brigade and our section of 37 Battery of the 37th Division. Itself near wounded near by section	57 D.N.E. 1/—

A. E. Cairns
Lt & Adjt
32 Brigade R.F.A.

4th DIVISION

32nd BDE. R. F. A.

MARCH 5th to AUGUST 2nd.
1916.

Army Form C. 2118

WAR DIARY
or
INTELLIGENCE SUMMARY
(Erase heading not required.)

32nd Brigade RFA No. 1

Place	Date	Hour	Summary of Events and Information	Remarks and references to Appendices
HALLOY	Mar to April	5	Brigade in rest at HALLOY	1/10,000 57D NE sheets 14z (Parts) FONQUEVILLERS
	April	5	2/Lt J.W. CORBISHLEY joined Bde and posted to 135 Battery	
		2		
		3/4 4/4	Batteries moved up in sections relieving sections of 37th Div Arty at BIENVILLERS and FONQUEVILLERS.	
BIENVILLERS & FONQUEVILLERS		5	At 10 a.m. 32nd Brigade took over from 125th Brigade. The Ammunition columns moved SOUASTRE and the Waggon lines at HENU. 32nd Brigade R.F.A. supported II Infantry Brigade on the left, from E.28 A 85.85 to 5.5 C 85.85. The 29th Brigade R.F.A. and the 2nd South Midland Brigade R.F.A. were on the left and right respectively of this Brigade. Batteries rebuilt wire making metallic circuits and also made ammunition pits for dumping. Battery positions were as follows:- 27th Battery E.20 D 5.1. 134 Battery E.14 D.I.P. 135 E. & D.I.9 each about section E.1 R 6.590 (POMMIER) Telephone O.P. scheme made at E.16 C. 2.9. The usual trench warfare was carried out. The German trenches at E.23 C (the "Z") being shelled for the most part. The Germans made a new trench across the Z from E.23 C 6.5 to E.23 C 6.4. They also did a great deal of new work, M.G. emplacements &c at & E.23 D.1.4 and back area from the front at Z E.23 C 6070 to the Settler at E.23 C.2.9 and 6 E.23 D.5.6 27 and 134 batteries distributed ammunition pits	

WAR DIARY or INTELLIGENCE SUMMARY

Army Form C. 2118

37 Bde R.F.A.

Place	Date	Hour	Summary of Events and Information	Remarks and references to Appendices
BIENVILLERS	April 19		Traffic altering ESSARTS in E.3.4.B, trenches in E.5.D and E.11.B, machine guns in COMMEROUT Wood and also a trench there were shelled.	1/19000 57 D.NE (sheet 19 a) map of our trenches
			The German Batteries provided much firing. Among the heaviest guns and 12ca and 27 Battery positions were shelled. One shell fell in amongst a detachment of 13ca Battery. 1 134 Battery horses and wagons. 1. 134 Battery was hit by a shell near houses at E.5.B.5.3. A Minewerfer gun (27th Battery area) at E.5.B.5.3 was destroyed but the detachment had left when the gun was not damaged. The gun was recovered and the emplacement was again heavily shelled.	
		15.	Bombardment along with 29th Brigade and 137 How., 155 Battery bombarded hostile trenches E.5.D.05.36 to E.5.D.4.3.20 and hostile wire and trench at E5Duc30. When they lifted on to E.5.D.57.04 to E.M.A.5.6 our trench trajectory E.5.D.60.45 and troops in the trench signalled the relief.	
		25.	Bombardment by 1st and 4th Division at German trenches from E.5.C. 37.73 to E.5.9.B.2.2. — 27 Batteries tasks being trenches E.23 & 37.23, A.E.25 & B.C.c.a	
	May	6.	2/Lt R.W. FORAGUE 2/5cm Thomas Commando Red R.F.A. attached for fortnight instruction to 135 and then to 136 Battery.	
		30. 3/4 ? 3	2/Lt P.G. HOLMS Orderly Officer U/A to be A.D.C. to R.G.F.A. 4th Division 27 Battery placed temporarily under 35 Bde R.F.A. Group on MONCHY Salient. Relieved by batteries of 12 & 125 Bdes. 37 Bde relief completed by batteries of H.Q. Batteries & H.Q. moved to OUTERS E.BOIS.	

Army Form C. 2118

WAR DIARY or INTELLIGENCE SUMMARY

323rd Bde R.F.A. O.O.

(Erase heading not required.)

Place	Date	Hour	Summary of Events and Information	Remarks and references to Appendices
OUTREBOIS	1916 MAY	6	Batteries in training.	1/109,000 LENS
		15	2/Lt. J.H.C. SIMPSON joined Brigade as orderly officer. Major P.H. WILSON commanding 27th Battery, left Brigade on his appointment to Brigade Major of Ammunition.	
		16.	2/Lt. H.V. COCKLE posted to 31st Battery from Brig. Ammn. Col.	
		16.	33rd Brigade ammunition column transferred to 4th Division Ammunition column, leaving the 3rd Section. Lieut CASSIDY and 2/Lt WILLIAMS of the Ammn. Col. transferred to 4th Div. Ammn. Col.	
		16.	2/Lt. E.C. RAYNER joined the Brigade and posted to 27th Battery	
		19.	2/Lt. H.V. MATTHEWS joined the Brigade and was posted to 135 Battery	
		21st	2/Lt. J.D.H. DICK joined the Brigade and was posted to D/82 Battery (D/32)	
		21st	On the re-arrangement of 127 (How) Brigade a 4 Gun Battery came under the command of the O.C. 33rd Brigade	
		21.	Capt W.B. MACKIE, Lt E.G. WALLER, Lt. G.R.S. PRANCE and 2/Lt H.G.B. THOMAS of D/82 Battery, joined the Brigade	
COULON VILLERS	21		Brigade moved to COULON VILLERS for training as 1st Brigade reserve division	
	23 24 25 26		Batteries carried out rehearses as by Brigade execution order.	

Army Form C. 2118

WAR DIARY
or
INTELLIGENCE SUMMARY
(Erase heading not required.)

32nd Bde R.F.A. D(?)

Place	Date	Hour	Summary of Events and Information	Remarks and references to Appendices
COULON VILLERS	1916 MAY	26-29	Brigadier Lawrie & Staff HQ 32nd Bde went to T.M. School Journey N4 T.M. Battery ran 3rd Bde Bombardment Artillery scheme. Rehearsal of attack N. of BEAUMONT HAMEL	Map 57D LENS
		30.	4th Divisional Artillery relieved	
		31.	Returned to OUTREBOIS.	
		26	Lt. H. CORMAC WALSHE posted to 134 Battery.	
		27	2/Lt. J.E. NICHOLS 134 Bty appointed Orderly Officer	

WAR DIARY
or
INTELLIGENCE SUMMARY

Army Form C. 2118.

(Erase heading not required.)

32nd Brigade R.F.A. P.1

Place	Date	Hour	Summary of Events and Information	Remarks and references to Appendices
OUTREBOIS	8 Dec. 1915 13-14		Brigade at OUTREBOIS.	1/10,000 LENS
VAUCHELLES	15		Lt. T.H. HAWKE joined B/32 and posted to D/B/32 Battery.	1/40,000
			Brigade marched to VAUCHELLES.	
MAILLY-MAILLET	15/16		C.64, 135th, 26th (How.) met D/32 (How.) which act here as Howitzer Bde. 12 guns 13 pdr, 12 guns × 18 pdr, 6/4·5" How. Battery.	MAILLY-MAILLET 1/40,000 S.E.
	16/7		2 7-pdrs 13-pdrs 18-pdrs relieved 2 guns × 18 pdr Battery.	
	16	6 p.m.	Lieut. Lathro 6th 135th 26th (How.) D/B/7 How. and 12th Grenadiers. Lt. Col. 35·41st Bde. (Lt-Col. TILNEY, R.F.A.) met Liaison of 32nd Group. The Artillery O.C. 32 Group taken command of 29th Div. taking over 35th Bde Fd. Artillery which left the Tenth Brigade front line but on night of 15/16 was relieved by 104 Infantry Brigade infantry from H.Q. D.2.9. R. 6. 35. 8 × 9. 135 Battery occupies the right Battalion, 130 Battery the left Battalion. 69th 26th (How.) and D/B (How.) all cover front of Brigade. During frequency of these Batteries. D/B are duty liaison out from the Capt ELLIS 135 Battery. He is in consequence of the Brigade taken a temporary duties according to the B.M. one hour attached Headquarters.	
	27 Dec 16		H.Q. Lt. Col. TILNEY R.F.A. commdg 32 Brigade R.F.A. mentioned in despatches. Capt R.B. STONEY R.F.A. commdg 134 Battery mentioned in despatches.	

WAR DIARY
or
INTELLIGENCE SUMMARY

Army Form C. 2118.

33rd Bde R.F.A. P(2)

(Erase heading not required.)

Place	Date	Hour	Summary of Events and Information	Remarks and references to Appendices
June rept 22/23 27			27th Battery in action at Q.15.B.20.15. Communications tested.	1/23,000 S73. NE sheet 35. 1/10,000 French Maps HEBUTERNE and BEAUMONT
	24	5 am	U day. 68th and 86 (Hows) Batteries ordered to be grouped with 33rd Brigade and occupy waiting positions R.96.'a Rd. O.C. 33rd Bde Battle Section H.Q at TENDERLOIN. 33rd Brigade frontage Q's A.33 (4 pieces) to K.35 c 5 y (inclusive) Permanent barrage lines allotted to all batteries In all special bombardments Batteries to fire on own lines. See also before S.O.S. lines (OAD4 '8'1/147 Jan 7)	4th Divisional Artillery Orders 19/2/147 CRA 19.2.16
			Action prior to assault Prior to U to Y days, 33rd Brigade tasks were as follows:— (1) By day D/33 Battery bombarded TEN TREE ALLEY after East of BEAUCOURT-STATION (2) By night (a) Harassing with their 18th and 29th [?] Brigades each evening notified 3 areas selected and portion of wire cut during day. Bk 32 HRH observed batteries in the last yds left fire over less wire. O.G. 32 Bde alloted tasks each night (to harassing fire on enemy front line PUISIEUX-SERRE near Pt 3, 9, 20, 25, 30 c5 c6 and 55 after each c8 of hour, between 9 p.m. and 5 a.m. (Annex 4) (b) Night bombardment 6.15 an hour counting Wire [?] on their points in the area East of MUNICH TRENCH from K.30. A. 75.75 (Serre Road) to not including 61.10 c uo Rough Junction in irregular intervals. 8 Cables Rendezvous or communications roughly junctions u—ave area	

Army Form C. 2118.

WAR DIARY
or
INTELLIGENCE SUMMARY
(Erase heading not required.)

32nd Bde R.F.A.   P(3)

Instructions regarding War Diaries and Intelligence Summaries are contained in F.S. Regs., Part II. and the Staff Manual respectively. Title Pages will be prepared in manuscript.

Place	Date	Hour	Summary of Events and Information	Remarks and references to Appendices
	June 1916			1/20,000 57.D NE & SE
	24	10 p.m. to 10.10 p.m. 10.10 to 12.30 a.m.	T.Day DRESDEN Gas released. Batteries shared fire on enemy front line trenches for 10 minutes & Mine 8. Intense enemy bombardment. Ours in answer as in our front trenches.	Wagon Lines Acheux Hedauville BEAUMONT
	25.	4-5.30 p.m.	U.day Special Bombardment. June 6. 16 hrs. with H.E. on selected trenches opposite our own front. N/85 and N/186 each expended 160 rounds. Battery fire 40 rounds.	4th Div Op O No. 95 Order 1814/a/7 51/14-5-15
	26	2.30 a.m. 9 a.m. to 10.20 a.m. 11.30 p.m. to 12.10 a.m.	W.day Night firing - keeping wide view and cross roads N of Thiepval as ordered. DRESDEN Gas released. Heavy in front of trenches held by we to 3 Somerset from where it being all morning. Front of batteries was cover front for check. Special Bombardment. Smoke discharged (10.15 a.m.) Night firing - firing was then at at concentration 27th and 134 Batteries bombarded trenches as ordered (4th DA 1817/a/6) in Sheet of 10th Divisions Target raid on enemy trenches at K 31.C 21.35.	
	27	4.30 - 5.50 a.m.	X.day Special bombardment. Smoke discharged 5.45 a.m. Wire cutting by 27th Battery on trench Q5 A 8.1 to Q5 A 4.0.35. Night firing as ordered.	
	28	12.40 a.m. to 2.2 a.m. 11.45 to 2.30 a.m.	Y.day Subaltern's rifles and machine gun but and flares constantly lit. Enemy put a heavy barrage on our line. Red rockets were sent up. 134 and D/52 joined in counter-bombardment as ordered. Other batteries carrying out several tasks of keeping wire cut and under fire most of time. Point 5.5 - Point of June Log L.	

Army Form C. 2118.

WAR DIARY
or
INTELLIGENCE SUMMARY
(Erase heading not required.)

32nd Bde R.F.A. P(4)

Place	Date	Hour	Summary of Events and Information	Remarks and references to Appendices
	June 1916			
	28	4 day	During the night wire cutting and preparation was carried on	1/29, 30 S7D 1/5 and S2
		6 am to 7.30 am	Steady bombardment assisted by Trench Mortars shelling the WHITE CITY. Smoke discharged 7.15 & 7.25 am	Yapes Bombay HEBUTERNE BEAUMONT
		10.52	Some of 96th Siege bomb. advanced and 27th battery came to near OSA 81 and OPA near 44 Div HQ	
		2.30 pm	Junction of A.8.6 trench and A TENDERLOIN heavily shelled with 150 r.g.m. ideas AUCHONVILLERS	18/2/147
			Lero hour pont hour 48 hours	2/19 = 2-7-15
		9.44 pm	Heavy two worst from VAUCHELLES to BEETEAUCOURT	
		3 pm	BEAUSSART to the position of moderate	
			Heavy fire returns to VAUCHELLES	
	29	41 day	Left firing as orders. Enemy doubled hostile artillery active during the night and during forenoon and afternoon 8:9th WHITE CITY shelled by 4.32 and 5.9s	
			Our two batteries seem to have fire are allotted when their just a barrage	
			Reconnaissance of wire carried out	
	28	10 pm to	Raids on enemy's trenches	
	29	4 am		
		1.30 am	Enemy put heavy barrage on our front trenches in OSA. Many flares and red lights sent up	
		2-2.15 am	Special attention directed to prevention of hostile movement both by day and night and exhibition of livine ceiling	
		4 to 5.20 am	Special Bombardment as ordered	

Army Form C. 2118.

WAR DIARY
or
INTELLIGENCE SUMMARY

(Erase heading not required.)

32nd Bde R.F.A. P.(3)

Instructions regarding War Diaries and Intelligence Summaries are contained in F. S. Regs., Part II and the Staff Manual respectively. Title Pages will be prepared in manuscript.

Place	Date	Hour	Summary of Events and Information	Remarks and references to Appendices
	June 1916 30		Y/2 day	1/20,000 57 D N.E and S.E
		12.30am	Infantry raid K35C.2.2 and K35C.0.4. No Artillery fire level at line K35C.9.7 - K35C.20.00. Infantry reconnaissance 10.30 pm to 11.50 pm (31st)	1/10,000 Trench Maps HEBUTERNE and BEAUMONT
		8.9.70 am	Programme as for Y day. Special bombardment ordered	
		6 pm	New frontage Q5 A 53 (exclusive) to K 35 C 2.0 (inclusive) Night firing guns of 126th Army Bty 127th Battery in place of 134 and 135 Batteries	4th Div Orders order 1812/147 dated 19-6-16
		10 pm	134 and 135 Batteries pull out and take up position of new divisions at BEAUSSART ready to march under orders of BG RA at too late to No Mans Land. Wagon lines move up to BERTRANCOURT and 134 and 135 to BEAUSSART. Night firing as usual	
	July 1st	2 day Zero time 7.30 am	All guns cut wire on their own and 27th Kitchy artillery attacking 3rd and 11th Brigades frontages (33) to hour (6.2) moved for gun fire 13th Brussille. D/32 1st two guns fired rounds from K35C.B4.15 to K35C.B.45	4 Div Orders 1812/197 Q/2.6.16 based on the written order 638 d (N.G.N)
		6.25 am to 6.50 am	All guns on front trench in their several area. Incurred the positive received H.E	
		7.20 am	Rate of fire 3 rounds per gun per circuit (H.E.) D/32 2nd rounds be gun for secondly 11-4-35	
		7.30 am	Zero time all guns lift by step. No advance at the rate of 100 yds in every two minutes firing their rounds of gunfire at each lift. Attack commenced 11th Infantry Brigade to advance over "No Mans Land" Hohenzollern Redoubt seen to blown up.	

Army Form C. 2118.

WAR DIARY
or
INTELLIGENCE SUMMARY
(Erase heading not required.)

32nd Bde R.F.A. P 6

Place	Date	Hour	Summary of Events and Information	Remarks and references to Appendices
	JULY 1916			1/28,000 57D
	1	Zero 7.30	German barrage very futile. No particular barrage. Volunteers gun barrage	N.E. corner S.E.
		8/10	German barrage in No Man's Land weaker	Map of HEBUTERNE
		8.25		Map and BEAUMONT
		8.45	3 very lights from Pt(15) (Bocuvet Trench) Men crossing No-mans land	1/10,000 57D Pts 14/15
		8.30		bombing d
		9.12	3 red – no shots from about (30) but not below (91)	26-6-16 somewhat in 7/5
		9.25	Heavy German barrage from Redan welcome to the North	New position Dates to 2.9
		9.40	Sappers beeldens [?] bridge over front trenches have excavator access, invaders people	27 (10-6-16)
		10.16a	Hostile barrage beyond 17th Bde objective is E of MUNICH TRENCH	
		10.30am	Received orders from to Adv Arty to hold green on BLUE BARRAGE (Kara 15)	
		10.55am	36 Devonion doing well. 2 B Division have not taken BEAUMONT redoubt	
		11 am	Return serretts wanted by order	
		11.45	ESSEX held up over MUNICH TRENCH by German snipers 2d/31 consented all Guns on Pt(31)	
		12.15pm	Position now is Essex Rifle Brigade and Somersets not about of MUNICH TRENCH some Germans still in the Redan and BEAUMONT still held out	

WAR DIARY or INTELLIGENCE SUMMARY

Army Form C. 2118.

37th A.Bde R.F.A. P(y)

Place	Date	Hour	Summary of Events and Information	Remarks and references to Appendices
	July 1916			1/20,000 57D NE and SE
	1.		SEAFORTHS sent to receivers used with heavy machine gun fire	
	2.		134 and 135 batteries return to their original gun positions. Limbers & firing batteries move to PAVEIELLES. first line wagon at BERTRANCOURT	1/10,000 Trench Map HEBUTERNE
	3.		66, 32 & Ade Rebecco 96, 14th Bde, with the letter W.R. at POMMIER HEDGE Batteries w. Grenfeld. 32 ca Group - with bat TIDNEY - Remained at 6854 265 27 134 135 and D/32 Batteries	
	4.		27th Battery, w/ Adam, 88th Battery come under command of A.6. 32 Group 27th Battery moves to BERTRANCOURT then to AMPLIER firing batteries wagons and gun limbers move to AMPLIER 88th Battery moves G Q7, C 63, 18	
	5.		first Lt wagons moves from BECTRANCOURT to LOUVENCOURT 134 Battery change wagon section with 32 group in group zone Q5a 23.75 to R15 9.18 Batteries carried out harassing and a direct	
	7.	7-45am		
	7-16		By day were cutting and firing on individuals and enemy parties in MINSUT WOOD PUISUEX trenches, firing at irregular intervals on all communication trench in ANCRE VALLEY bombardments is ordered. By night batteries were open German batteries harbors roads & Junction and	
	9. 16		enemy billet areas. 32 Ade HQ FLAWMETIN was shelled to 135 his Bde HQ relieved by 147 Bde HQ 32 Ade HQ proceeded KAMPUER	
	22	6pm	Batteries relieved by batteries of 12th X Division	

WAR DIARY or INTELLIGENCE SUMMARY

Army Form C. 2118.

32nd Brigade R.F.A.

Place	Date	Hour	Summary of Events and Information	Remarks and references to Appendices
	July 1918		Brigade marched with 4th Div Arty from AMPLIER - BONNEVY-SUR-CANCHE.	HAZEBROUCK 52. 1/40,000
	23.		" " " " " VERCHIN.	
	24.		" " " " DELETTE	
	25.		" " " " OUDEZEELE	
	26.		During the period 15th - 27th July, the guns of the Brigade were exchanged for	
	27.		guns of the 3rd, 4th, 48th, & 6th Divisional Artillery.	
	28.		The Brigade moved into action by half-batteries relieving the GUARDS DIV ARTY.	BELGIUM 28 N.W. 1/20,000
	29.		Distribution of batteries as follows:—	
			Right Group (Lt. Col. J.H.G. Lloyd D.S.O.)	
			27th Bty. 5 guns J.7.a.8.9 } OP C.28.a.3½.1 Zone C.22.a.6.5 - C.15.d.8.5	
			1 " C.26.d.5.4 } " C.35.d.8½.3 - C.15.a.7.2	
			135th Bty. 6 " B.28.c.4.5½ OP C.21.c.7.7½ " C.22.d.9.½ - C.16.b.2.½.½	
			D/32 Bty. 2 " B.30.c.2.3 OP C.19.d.2.8	
			Left Group. (Lt. Col W.S. Tristram)	
			114.2 Bty. 4 guns B.15.b.9.7 } OP B.27.b.8.1½ " C.7.d.2.8 - C.7.a.0.2	
			2 " B.14.b.9.7 }	
			D/32 Bty. 2 " I.2.b.2.0 OP C.21.c.7.6 " C.16.b.5.3 - C.7.a.0.2	

Army Form C. 2118.

WAR DIARY
or
INTELLIGENCE SUMMARY

(Erase heading not required.)   32nd Brigade R.F.A.   P.

Place	Date	Hour	Summary of Events and Information	Remarks and references to Appendices
	July 31.		32nd Brigade Hqrs in rest at PROVEN. Lt.C. A.F. Drummond 135th Bty. wounded by shrapnel near his battery O.P. and evacuated to CASUALTY CLEARING STATION	
	August 2.		Lt. R.W. Talbot in appointed Adjutant, vice Lt. A.G. Lewis, evacuated to CASUALTY CLEARING STATION sick	

W.J. Dun Lt Col
C.9.32nd Bde R.F.A.

4th DIVISION.

32nd bde R. F. A.

AUGUST 1916.

Army Form C. 2118.

WAR DIARY
or
INTELLIGENCE SUMMARY
(Erase heading not required.)

32nd Brigade R.F.A.

Instructions regarding War Diaries and Intelligence Summaries are contained in F. S. Regs., Part II. and the Staff Manual respectively. Title Pages will be prepared in manuscript.

Place	Date	Hour	Summary of Events and Information	Remarks and references to Appendices
	8/8/16		During the evening a German gas cloud was released, but no attack delivered about 300 yds. per battery were fired on enemy lines.	
	9–20/8/16		Normal trench warfare. 27th Battery had one gun wrecked by shell fire on the 10th our man was killed.	
	20/8/16		Brigade was relieved by 38th Div. Arty. and went into rest at Wagon lines.	
	21/8/16			
	24/25/8/16		Brigade went into action relieving 3rd Canadian Div. Arty. and forming equal group under Lt Col N.E. Young. 45th + 46th Bty. 4th Australian Div. were included in the group. Battery positions as follows:—	Ref. ZILLEBEKE No wo Tr. MAP.
			Position	
			Group H.Q. I.21.c.5.5	
			27 Bty (4 guns) I.27.b.5.2	Zone
			N (4 guns) I.16.b.4.7½ I.35.a.8.8 – I.30.b.8½.4½	
			134 I.15.b.5.4 I.29.d.3.5 – I.30.d.5.8	
			135 I.10.c.5.8 I.30.c.0.8 – I.30.b.1.6.1	
			D/32 I.29.d.2½.1½ I.30.b.1½.1 – I.19.c.0.3	
			group supported the 10th Yk. Inf. Bde. I.35.a.6.8 – I.30.b.9½.9½	
	26/8/16		During heavy bombardment of our trenches 2/Lt. N. Matthews 135th Battery was killed by shell fire	

Army Form C. 2118.

WAR DIARY
or
INTELLIGENCE SUMMARY

32nd Brigade R.F.A.

(Erase heading not required.)

Place	Date	Hour	Summary of Events and Information	Remarks and references to Appendices
	25/8/16 –2/9/16		Normal Trench Warfare.	
	3/9/16		Brigade was relieved by 1st Bde A.F.A. 1st Australian Division, guns being handed over, moved back to WATOU, & CO & BC's reconnoitring new positions.	
	4/9/16		"	

W.E.Warhurst Lt for Lt-Col
comdg 32nd Bde R.F.A.

4th DIVISION.

32nd BDE. R. F. A.

SEPTEMBER 1916.

WAR DIARY or INTELLIGENCE SUMMARY

32nd Brigade R.F.A.

Army Form C. 2118

Place	Date	Hour	Summary of Events and Information	Remarks and references to Appendices
	6/9/16		32nd Bde. moved into action relieving 91st Bde. 20th Div. Arty. H.Q. at Menin Gate Ypres, batteries in action to the left of the town.	
	6/9/16–18/9/16		Normal trench warfare. 29th Div. Arty carried out a successful raid, supported by 77th Bde. on Vermuly night of 11/12th	
	19/9/16		Bde. relieved by 15th Bde. R.H.A. 29th Div. Arty. went into rest at WATOU.	
	20/9/16		Bde entrained at PROVEN and reached ST SAUVEUR 21/9/16. near AMIENS.	Ref FRANCE ALBERT positions Sheet 1/20000
	24/9/16		Bde marched to BOIS DET AILLES (K18b+d)	
	25/9/16		32nd Bde. took over from 106th & 109th Bdes R.F.A. 24th Div. Arty in action round T25b & T26a. 134th D/n battery moved forward to T14c. 4th A.F.A. Reserve 135th & 84th R.F.A. & brigade wounded.	
	29/9/16–30/9/16		Captain R.B. Storey, 134th Bty R.F.A. wounded in head neck and hand, evacuated to hospital.	
	1/10/16		Bde took part in bombardment on T35.	
	2/10/16		Captain Brown took command of 134th Battery.	

W Walkerton Lt. for Lt. Col
Comdg 32 Bde R.F.A.

Boxes (1) (2)

8700/1372

Files.

ARMY.

Duplicate G.S. War Diaries.

G.S. First Army.

1917

(i) War Diary for period   1st to 31st October, 1917.
(ii) Files of Messages   1st to 31st October, 1917.
(iii) Weekly Summary of Operations. 28th September to 26th October, 1917.

4th DIVISION.

32nd BDE. R. F. A.

OCTOBER 1916.

WAR DIARY or INTELLIGENCE SUMMARY

Army Form C. 2118.

Vol 1 32nd Brigade R.F.A.

(Va)

Place	Date	Hour	Summary of Events and Information	Remarks and references to Appendices
FRANCE	3/10/16		2/Lt. [?] Offord R.F.A. 2nd D Bty killed in action.	
ST OS WFA	4/10/16		2/Lt [?] Robinson R.F.A. 131st D Bty. wounded in leg. admitted to hospital.	
	7/10/16		Attack one line (Brown) at 1.45 p.m. N 29 c 5-5 - N5.5 d S.W. covered by Regtl group (32nd Bde & 2 Btys) with creeping and standing Barrages. Attack unsuccessful.	2000
	8/10/16		Fire straightened up after heavens days bombard.	R.E.X. HOR
	9/10/16		25 minutes bombardment at 7.15 p.m.	X A 2
	12/10/16		Attack on Brown line resumed at 2.5 p.m. (by 4th Division 32nd Bde + 284 (Right group) Bde) Attack on Duke of Wellingtons Regmnt (D Batt) The whole attack unsuccessful on several of the objectives.	
			1 long range machine gun fire from LE TRANSLOY.	
	15/10/16		Bayonet attack on DEWDROP unsuccessful.	
	18/10/16		Right group, consisting of 32nd Bde, 15th Bde, 112 + 125 Bty under Lt-Col NETHAMAY supported part of attack by 4 DIV on SPECTRUM, DEWDROP, RAINY, FROSTHAMAY but was unsuccessful.	
	25/10/16		Tr.s Attack commenced at 3.40 a.m. (34/10) Attack as above repeated at 6.0 a.m by 4th Divn, but again unsuccessful owing chiefly to very bad weather.	
	28/10/16		RAINY + DEWDROP taken at 6.0 a.m. by 98th Inf Bde 33rd Divn supported by Right group.	Withdrawal of 32 Bde R.F.A.

4th DIVISION.

32nd BDE R. F. A.

NOVEMBER 1916.

Army Form 'C. 2118.

WAR DIARY
or
INTELLIGENCE SUMMARY
(Erase heading not required.)

32nd Brigade R.F.A.

Instructions regarding War Diaries and Intelligence Summaries are contained in F. S. Regs., Part II. and the Staff Manual respectively. Title Pages will be prepared in manuscript.

Place	Date	Hour	Summary of Events and Information	Remarks and references to Appendices
	5/11/16		General attack by III & IV British & VI French Armies. 32nd Bde (Right group) covered attack on trenches BORITSKA, MIRAGE & HAZY in M.34.c. which was gained by 33rd Div. Infantry. In the night of 3rd–4th, 27th & 135th Batteries had moved to forward positions in T.q. central under very trying weather.	FRANCE 5/8 SW 1/20000
	7/11/16			
	10/11/16		27th & 135th Batteries moved back to their old positions in Trone Wood night 7/8 inst. Right group came under command of 8th Div. Arty.	
	19/11/16		NORMAL TRENCH WARFARE. Captain E.R.G. Griffith-Williams took over command of 134th Bty, vice Captain W.C. Count to 63rd Bde R.F.A.	
	22/23 25/24/11/16		Right group relieved by 20th Div Arty.	
	26/11/16		32nd Bde marched to DAOURS.	
	27/11/16		" " " ST SAUVEUR	
	28/11/16		" " " HORNOY, Major L.J. W. Robinson took over Bde whilst Col Tilney went on leave	
	29/11/16		" " " rest billets at SENARPONT	

W.W. Newton Major H. Col
Comdg 32nd Bde R.F.A.

4th DIVISION.

32nd BDE. R. F. A.

DECEMBER 1918.

Army Form C. 2118.

WAR DIARY
or
INTELLIGENCE SUMMARY
(Erase heading not required.)

 32nd Brigade R.F.A.

Instructions regarding War Diaries and Intelligence Summaries are contained in F. S. Regs., Part II. and the Staff Manual respectively. Title Pages will be prepared in manuscript.

Place	Date	Hour	Summary of Events and Information	Remarks and references to Appendices
	1/12/15 -4/12/15		Brigade rested at SENARPONT.	Ref:- ALBERT 1/40,000 continued
	5/12/15		135th Battery marched to CAMP 14, 2 miles S.W. of BOIS DE TAILLES, stopping a night en route at HORNOY.	
	7/12/15		ST SAUVEUR, SAILLY-LE-SEC, arriving 7th.	
	8/12/15		H.Q. + 134 Battery marched as above, arriving Camp 14 the 10th	
	9/12-10/12		27th Battery " " " " 11th	
			D/32 " " " " 12th	
			Batteries relieved 39me Regiment d'Artillerie (FRENCH) on nights, 13th, 11th/12th at B12272	
				13th/14th " B12274
			134, 12th/13th " " B5225
			27, 27pr. } 13th/14th " " B11456
			H.Q, } 20th/15th " " B5408
			D/32,	
	13/12/15 -28/12/15		Normal trench fighting.	
	29/12/15			
	3.12.15 to		Normal trench fighting.	
	30.12.15		Men in Batteries relieved by H.Q. 32d R.F.A. 28.3. relieved D/32 batteries 3"- O.P B12.0.P
	31.12.15			584 " 134 " 22.47.4
				599 " 135 " 52.27.4
			Relieved half batteries marched to their wagon lines at 44.21.central	

2449 Wt. W14957/M90 750,000 1/16 J.B.C. & A. Forms/C.2118/12.

4th Division
War Diaries
32nd Bde. R.F.A.

January 1st to 31st December
1917

War Diary
February 1917
32nd. Brigade RGA

WAR DIARY
or
INTELLIGENCE SUMMARY

(V) 32nd Bde. R.F.A.   Vol 22

Army Form C. 2118.

Place	Date	Hour	Summary of Events and Information	Remarks and references to Appendices
	2.1.17		Brigade marched by half batteries into rest at Y Z E OX, via VAUX-SUR-SOMME, ARGOEUVES.	Ref. AMIENS
	5.1.17			
	14.1.17		D/32 Bty broken up on reorganisation of Divnl Artyr. 36th (How) Bty joined 32 Bde.	
	15.1.17		Brigade marched to LAMPRÉ-AMIENS. Nr R.T. refitted (to be continued if in the field)	
	16.1.17		Brigade marched to Camp 14.	
	18.1.17		Brigade marched into action by sections relieving 31st Regiment of Artillery (French) B23.b.50.50	Ref. BRONFAY 62c.N.W
	19.1.17		positions as follows:— HQ 32nd Bde (Right Group) B23.b.50.50	
			2) F 134	
			135	
			36	
			B25.c.0.1	
			B23.b.50.50	
			BRONFAY	
20-31/1/17			Relieved French Bde.	

W.T.Hunter Major F.C.R.F.A
commdg 32nd Bde R.F.A.

Army Form C. 2118.

WAR DIARY
or
INTELLIGENCE SUMMARY (V8) 32ⁿᵈ Bde R.H.A.
(Erase heading not required.)

Place	Date	Hour	Summary of Events and Information	Remarks and references to Appendices
	15.2.17		32ⁿᵈ Brigade assisted in Heavy bombardment of enemy trench system on XV Corps front	Ref BOUCHAVESNES 2. EDITION 4A. 1/10,000.
	16.2.17		32ⁿᵈ " " " " " " " " " " in C.16 and C.15d	
	17.2.17		134ᵗʰ + 135ᵗʰ Batteries cut wire about in front of German front line in C.21.	
			32ⁿᵈ Brigade assisted in bombardment of trench system in L.2.	
	20/21/2/17		H.Q & 134ᵗʰ & 135ᵗʰ Batteries moved up by X.5 to positions as under:-	
	21/22/2/17		27ᵗʰ Bat. B.19.a.70.70 134ᵗʰ at B.13.c.30.50 135ᵗʰ at B.13.c.90.20	
	22/23/2/17		H.Q. at B.24.b.70.20	
	23/2/17		B Group consisting of 32ⁿᵈ Bde + D/181 (How) Bty, took over defensive zone C.16.6545 -- C.16.1535	
	28/2/17		134 + 86ᵗʰ assisted a raid to left of Group front by putting down a feint barrage from 1.02 am -- 1.20 am.	

AW Ballentine Lt for Lt-Col
Comdg 32ⁿᵈ Brigade R.H.A.

Vol 26.

War Diary
32nd. Brigade RFA
March 1917.

Army Form C. 2118.

WAR DIARY
or
INTELLIGENCE SUMMARY

(Erase heading not required.)

V9 32nd Brigade R.F.A.

Place	Date	Hour	Summary of Events and Information	Remarks and references to Appendices
	4.3.17	5.15 a.m.	25th & 23rd Bdes. 8th Division, successfully attacked FRITZ TR. 32nd Brigade + O/181 (How) Bty (B Group) covering 25th Bde on front N. boundary - L.18.d.0.50 - C.15.b.0.30 S. " - C.16.a.5.5 - C.13.d.0.0.77. Heavy firing was continued throughout the day. B Group firing approx. 6000 rds. 18 pdr and 3100 rds. 4.5 How. from 5 p.m. 3/3/17 - 6.0 p.m. 4/3/17.	Ref. BOUZINCOURT ETAPE 1/10,000
	6/7.3.17 7/8.3.17 8/9.3.17		32nd Bde. marched to :- H.Q. } SAILLY-LAURETTE 27 } 134 }	Ref. AMIENS 1/100,000
	10.3.17		" " ST. GRATIEN.	
	11.3.17		" " TALMAS.	
	12.3.17		" " OUTREBOIS.	Ref. LENS 1/100,000
	14.3.17		" " CANCHY-SUR-CANCHE	
			Rested at CANCHY-SUR-CANCHE.	
	20.3.17		32nd Bde. marched to ST-MICHEL.	
	21.3.17		" " " MARDEUIL.	
	22.3.17		" " " into action in positions as follows :- H.Q. G.15.b.60.55 27. G.16.a.20.80 135 G.10.c.70.70 134 G.10.c.20.90 86 G.16.a.70.00	Ref. Tr. Map ARRAS & NWs 1/10,000
	23.3.17 -31.3.17		Bde. in positions as above, but not registered for the line.	

Chas Sullenton Major Lt. Col.
Commdg. 32nd Brigade R.F.A.

4 Div.

War Diary
32nd. Brigade R.F.A.
April 1917.

Army Form C. 2118.

WAR DIARY
or
INTELLIGENCE SUMMARY
(Erase heading not required.)

Instructions regarding War Diaries and Intelligence Summaries are contained in F. S. Regs., Part II. and the Staff Manual respectively. Title Pages will be prepared in manuscript.

Place	Date	Hour	Summary of Events and Information	Remarks and references to Appendices
	16/4/17 – 21/4/17		Normal holding the line. Enemy kept up an intermittent bombardment of HIS lines by day & night.	FRANCE 51 N.W. 1/20,000
	21/4/17 22/4/17		Enemy shelled H.15 with gas shell from 11.10 p.m. – 5.0 a.m. Estimated no. of rds 1500. 2/Lt MURPHY 2/7 Bn. ? wounded & evacuated.	
	23/4/17		37th Div. Left; attacked GREENLAND HILL (J3) at 4.45 a.m. but only succeeded in holding the Bn. Hq. and T.c.W. – I.7a & c. – I.3.a. Another attempt made for GREENLAND HILL at 6.0 p.m. unsuccessful. 32nd Bde supported Nos two attacks on front I.12 & J.9.b. – I.12 & J.9 to E. 37th Div. Attacked GREENLAND HILL at 4.25 a.m. 32nd Bde supported ?just running E. from T.9d.60.50 – T.9b.60.32. Attack was successful, but 34 Division failed to advance on Rt. of 37 Div. so by evening 37 Div the was brought back to original line. During the day the enemy made several attempts to counter attack, but each time was driven back by the barrage. 32nd Bde received a congratulatory message from 4.0.C. 37 Div. for successful shooting. Bde ammunition expenditure 8.0 p.m. 27.4.17 – 8.0 p.m. 28.4.17 – 8804 rounds.	

W.S. Wallerton Lt. for Lt. Col
Comdg 32 B.B. R.F.A.

WAR DIARY or INTELLIGENCE SUMMARY

Army Form C. 2118.

32nd Brigade R.F.A. Vol.

Place	Date	Hour	Summary of Events and Information	Remarks and references to Appendices
	1–8/4/17		Normal Trench Warfare.	Ref. To map 51.B N.W. 1/20000 EDITION 6A
	9/4/17		Volery. Preliminary bombardment started.	
	9/4/17		9th Div. attacked on a front extending from ST-LAURENT-BLANGY – G.12.a.35 and leading to junction with II Corps, remainder of XVIII Corps and Canadian Corps.	
		5.30 a.m.	— in conjunction with II Corps, remainder of XVII Corps and Canadian Corps.	
			By 8.30 a.m. BROWN LINE (POINT DU JOUR – ATHIES) had been captured.	
			By 1.30 p.m. 32nd Bde. continued to move forward by batteries to positions about H.13. and H.7.2.0 p.m. 32nd Bde. had passed through 9th Div. by 5.3 p.m. had established on line Hermorille & 4th Div. Preliminary reports were received for 32nd Bde to FAMPOUX – HYDERABAD WORK. At 3.45 p.m. orders were received for 32nd Bde to move further forward. Positions taken up were as follows:—	
			H.Q. & 135th Bty. Hisd 2020 23rd Bty. Hisd 2060 135th Bty. Hisd 2030 26th Bty Hisd 2060	
	10/4/17		Consolidated positions	
	11/4/17		4th Div. endeavoured to advance at 12.0 noon, but were unsuccessful. Cavalry could not get through owing to hostile machine guns.	
	12/4/17		5.0 p.m.	
			Capt. R.B. Stoney posted to command 23rd Bty. vice Major F.W. Risley to 3 Bde. R.F.A.	
	13/4/17		Quiet day. Enemy bombarded H.13 & H.13 from 1.30 p.m. 13/4/17 till 3 a.m. 14/4, with gas shell Hosier killed Drs ... suffering from gas poisoning & wounded, 3 other ranks wounded.	

War Diary
32nd Brigade R.F.A.
May 1917.

WAR DIARY
or
INTELLIGENCE SUMMARY

(Erase heading not required.)

Army Form C. 2118.

(VII) 32nd Bde R.F.A.

Place	Date	Hour	Summary of Events and Information	Remarks and references to Appendices
	3.5.17		General attack made at 3.45 a.m. 32nd Bde supported part of 4th Div, whose objective was Roeux & S. of Mill. Attack unsuccessful.	
	4/5.5.17		To capture a line 400x E of GREENLAND HILL. 32nd Bde withdrew to Wagon Lines in G.S.H. for rest.	
	11.5.17 14.5.17 16./12.5.17		Batteries returned to positions as before. H.Q. shifted to H.17.a.10.10. 4th & 17th Divisions made two attacks at 3.30 p.m. and 5.30 a.m. and captured their I.7.b.80.80 – I.14.a.40.40 – I.19.b.50.00 (approx) 32nd Bde supported by E & W fires through I.22.20.40 – I.22.c.40.40	
	16.5.17		About 3.30 a.m. enemy delivered a heavy counter attack and succeeded in penetrating our lines to I.13.b. By 12.0 midday we had regained all lost ground with exception of G.W.P.10 French in I.4.a. 32nd Bde covered same front as on the 11/12.5.17. 32nd Bde, retaining in same position, passed to command of 51st Div Arty. Zone allotted to Bde as follows: – I.20.b.00.85 – I.14.c.85.80.	
	17.5.17		29th Div. attached S. of River SCARPE. 134, 135 + 81st Bdes cooperated with harassing fire from 9.0 p.m. – 10.30 p.m.	
	19.5.17		Normal trench warfare.	
	28.5.17 – 29/30.5.17		29th Div. attached S. of River SCARPE. 134, 135 + 81st Bdes cooperated by firing H.F. barrages in I.32 from 11.30 p.m. – 12.30 a.m.	

MacCulloch Major Lt. Col
Comdg 32nd Bde R.F.A.

War Diary
32nd Bde R.F.A.
June, '17.

Army Form C. 2118.

32ⁿᵈ Bde R.F.A.

WAR DIARY
or
INTELLIGENCE SUMMARY

(Erase heading not required.)

(V12)

Place	Date	Hour	Summary of Events and Information	Remarks and references to Appendices
	1/6/17 -2/6/17		Normal trench warfare.	By Sheet 51 B NW. 1/20
	3/6/17		CUPID and trenches in I 8 c, I.14 a + c successfully attacked at 8.0 p.m. 32ⁿᵈ B⁰ put down creeping barrage during the attack, starting from I.20 a.
	7/8.6.17 9/6.17		) Each night, counter-attack driven off.
	10.6.17		At 10.0 a.m. 32ⁿᵈ B⁰ put things to I 20 d 00 75 — I 20 c 80 00 — I 25 a 00 50. Assisted 3ʳᵈ Div. in attack on INFANTRY HILL in I 22 c at 7.20 a.m. attack successful.
	14.6.17		Normal trench warfare
	15.6.17		
	16.6.17 27.6.17 28.6.17 30.6.17		Normal trench warfare. 32ⁿᵈ Bde. gone changed to South of River SCARPE – I 31 d 90.60 – I 25–3 35-30 from 2 p.m. 32ⁿᵈ Bde. taken over more of its line from the 152ⁿᵈ & 159ᵗʰ R.F.A. Zone extended from I 25–3 35-30 to I 31 c 25–35.

Ashwell L/Col.
OC 32ⁿᵈ Bde R.F.A.

2449 Wt. W14957/M90 750,000 1/16 J.B.C. & A. Forms/C.2118/12.

War Diary
32nd Brigade R.G.A.
July 1917.

Army Form C. 2118.

WAR DIARY
or
INTELLIGENCE SUMMARY

(Erase heading not required.)

32nd Bde R.F.A.

Place	Date	Hour	Summary of Events and Information	Remarks and references to Appendices
	1/7/17 to 13/7/17		Normal trench warfare.	Ref. Sheet 57A France
	14/7/17		Normal trench warfare with harassing fire.	
	14/7/17		As above.	
	14/7/17 to 23/7/17			
	24/7/17		Carried out "dummy raid" on DEVILS Tr. (I.32.d.20.80 to I.32.a.60.40) Normal trench warfare.	
	25/7/17		Supported the 1st/6th Hampshire Regt. in a raid on DEVILS Tr. (I.32.c.20.80 to I.32.a.00.40) at 10.45 p.m. Raid successful.	
	26/7/17		Normal harassing fire.	
	27/7/17		Bee Battery (135.?) assist the 17th Division in counter successful raid	
	28/7/17			
	28/7/17 to 31/7/17		Normal trench warfare with harassing fire.	

Shields(?) Lt.
1st Gen(?) 32 Bde
Officer Comdg 32 Bde
R.F.A.

War Diary
32nd Brigade RGA
August 1917.

Army Form C. 2118.

WAR DIARY
or
INTELLIGENCE SUMMARY
(Erase heading not required.)

August 1917 —
32nd Bde, R.F.A.
Page 1.

Instructions regarding War Diaries and Intelligence Summaries are contained in F.S. Regs., Part II. and the Staff Manual respectively. Title Pages will be prepared in manuscript.

Place	Date	Hour	Summary of Events and Information	Remarks and references to Appendices
	1.8.17 –8.8.17		Normal trench warfare.	Ref ½ 01 57, 8 N.W. Edition 5.A.
	9.8.17		Continuous bombardment throughout the day. At 7.45 p.m. 150 men of the ESSEX and DUKES attempted to raid DEVIL Tr (I31c2080–I31c6020). Enemy put down a heavy barrage at 7.45 p.m. Attempt to raid was unsuccessful. Fire ceased at 9.0 p.m. 32nd Bde. assisted with a form, putting down a creeping barrage at zero (7.45 p.m.) over N. half of front advanced on.	
	15.8.17 (about)		A heavy T.H. assisted by 81 & 84 R.F.A. carried out a bombardment of ARCHIE Tr (I31c1080 – I31c5075) with highly successful result. 27th By. stood by to engage any Germans who might attempt to escape, and killed 4, wounded 2.	
	17.8.17		23rd Bde. R.F.A. went out of action, leaving Regt Group (Lt. Col. Tilney). 135th By. changed position to H27d4070. C/48 By. (H34c5090) came under Regt. Group.	
	18.8.17		IV Division side-slipped, 1 Battn front Southward. 32nd Brigade yours on consolidation of changes were as follows:— 27th By. I31.b85g5 – I32a1510. 135th ,, – I32a1510 – I31c5025 C/95 ,, – I32e5025 – D2b2070 (under Regt Group, Lt. Tilney.) 86 ,, – I31h85g5 – D2b2070. 134 By in rest.	

Army Form C. 2118.

WAR DIARY
or
INTELLIGENCE SUMMARY

(V14)

(Erase heading not required.)

Page 2.

Instructions regarding War Diaries and Intelligence Summaries are contained in F.S. Regs., Part II. and the Staff Manual respectively. Title Pages will be prepared in manuscript.

Place	Date	Hour	Summary of Events and Information	Remarks and references to Appendices
	25.8.17		134th Bty relieved 113th Bty who retired to Wagon lines for rest.	Ref. 1/40 000 51 b N.W. Edition 5A
	26.8.17		During the month normal harassing fire was carried out day and night, occasional small bombardments of enemy trench system and T.H.s were fired under group arrangements.	

M.J. Walker— Capt. for Lt. Col.
comdg 32nd Bde R.H.A.

4.9.17

War Diary
32nd Bde R.F.A
September 17.

WAR DIARY
or
INTELLIGENCE SUMMARY

(Erase heading not required.)

Army Form C. 2118.

September 1917

(VIS) 32nd Brigade R.F.A

Place	Date	Hour	Summary of Events and Information	Remarks and references to Appendices
	2.9.17		134th Bty shelled with about 100-150 rounds in position at H27 d 4.0.10, no casualties to personnel, but one gun damaged by shell fire and removed to workshops.	Ref. Map 57.c N.W. Edition 5.A.
	3-8.9.17		Normal harrassing fire.	
	8.9.17		1 section each of 27th, 134th, and 36th withdrew to wagon lines near STE CATHARINE, being relieved by sections of batteries of 71st Bde R.F.A 15th Division.	
	9.9.17		Remainder of B'de relieved by 71st & B'des and withdrew to Wagon Lines.	
	10.9.17		Rested at Wagon Lines.	
	13.9.17		B'de entrained at ARRAS STN. detrained at HOPOUTRE, and marched to camp just outside PROVEN.	BELGIUM in front of FRANCE.
	13/14.9.17		Batteries marched to new wagon lines near HAMMOEK in F15c + F14 a. N.W.	
	15.9.17		Batteries marched into action to positions as under:-	
	16/17/9/17		H.Q. C 19 a 20.80 27 C 8 a 15.90 134 C 8 a 30.80 135 C 26 6.00 (working party only, being in gun-shed) 86 C 8 a 80.60 The B'de being under Rgt group. Rgt. Div. Arty. XIV corps.	"A Sheet 27 and 28

Army Form C. 2118.

Page 2

WAR DIARY
or
INTELLIGENCE SUMMARY
(Erase heading not required.)

Sept. 1917
32nd Bde R.F.A.

Place	Date	Hour	Summary of Events and Information	Remarks and references to Appendices
				BELGIUM & part of FRANCE
	17.9.17		27, 134, & 81 Btys completed registration of zero zone.	
			135 Bty came into action.	
	17/18.9.17		Preliminary bombardment commenced at 5.0 a.m. by all batteries. 32nd Bde firing in Regt. Group.	
	19.9.17		Y Day. Boundaries were N. U23 b 6000 - U18 d 0000	
			S. U24 a 4010 - U19 a 0000	
	20.9.17		Z day. V Army attacked at 5.40 a.m. 32nd Bde assisted in covering 60th & 58th Bdes 20th Divn. The first attack by 60th Bde was unsuccessful, but at 6.30 p.m. a second attempt was made, which succeeded in capturing line U24 c 8090 - U24 a 1035 - U23 b 5050 (approx). On night 10/21 58th Bty had two hour [?] of action by shell fire, and lost 1 OR killed and 1 OR wounded	
	21.9.17		Enemy counterattacked in early morning but was repulsed by barrage fire	
	22.9.17		81st Bty changed position to C30/7/9 at 3.0 a.m.	
	23/24/9/17		During the night enemy fired a heavy gas shell concentration on battery positions - 5 gas casualties	
			in 33rd Bde of which 1 was evacuated.	
	24-25/9/17		Normal harassing fire, work on forward positions commenced on 25th. Therefore [?] were for new positions by other batteries, and were allotted for construction as follows:-	
			27 U28 a 00.77	
			134 U28 a 35.10	
			135 U28 55.35	

WAR DIARY
or
INTELLIGENCE SUMMARY
(Erase heading not required.)

Army Form C. 2118.

Page 3

Sept. 1917
32nd Bde. R.F.A.

Place	Date	Hour	Summary of Events and Information	Remarks and references to Appendices
	26.9.17		V Army less XIV Corps attacked at 5.40 a.m. Artillery of XIV Corps including 32nd Bde bombarded from 5.40 - 7.40 a.m. Normal Harassing fire etc.	Ref BELGIUM & part of FRANCE 1/40 Sheet 28
	27.9.17		" " "	
	28/29/9/17		During the nig. lt. enemy gas shelled Bty-positions. Casualties. 2 D.R. died of gas poisoning, B.O.R's evacuated with wounded with gas poisoning	
	30.9.17		Normal Harassing fire etc.	

M Wallacker Capt. for Lt. Col
Comdg 32nd Brigade R.F.A.

1.10.17

War Diary.
32nd. Brigade R.G.a
October, 1917.

WAR DIARY
INTELLIGENCE SUMMARY

Army Form C. 2118.

Place	Date	Hour	Summary of Events and Information	Remarks and references to Appendices
	1st to 31st action		During the whole of this month the billowing of the 32nd Brigade lived under very severe conditions. The guns were in open pits with camouflage spread over them. The ammunition was kept in small shelters and shell holes, and the men lived chiefly in such weather proof shelters as the nature of the ground and proximity to our forward gun positions. Rain was continuous throughout the month, the whole of the month and towards the latter end of the month the weather was stormy & cold. Ammunition to our positions was either brought up by pack or decauville wagon tow up and rung to the truck to batteries being constantly shelling and traversed supposedly for anything but pack horses. Lt. Brigade Commander Col. W.E. TILNEY D.S.O. was wounded at the STEEN BEEKE on the 14th October Major W.B. MACKIE succeeded Col. NETTLENEY D.S.O. and commanded the Brigade, but the rest of the month whilst Major MACKIE was in command of the Brigade Capt. GODLEY commanded the 86th battery. Major G. STRAKER D.S.O. (very slightly on the 19th October and Capt. C.T. HUTCHISON took command) (gassed) of 134 battery. Major C.J. MACKAY went to hospital suffering from gas poisoning, his battery was temporarily commanded by Capt J.F. MICHEL V.C. Casualties other than those mentioned above are:- Asst M.J. TYERS, Lieut STACPOOLE M.C. 2 Lieut C.J. SINCLAIR 2 Lieut W.B.ORPIN, Capt. LYON-SMITH (gassed) Lieut CLAISBY (killed) Capt. W.E. GOUDIE (R.H.V. attached) wounded and about 100 other ranks were casualties. The enemy fire such as he brought to bear was very frequently of heavy calibre. Gas shell was used very considerably... his chief seeing...	BELGIUM  part of France 40.00 Blocks 2/9 28

Army Form C. 2118.

WAR DIARY
or
INTELLIGENCE SUMMARY

(Erase heading not required.)

Page 1   October 1917   V16
32 B'de R.F.A.

Place	Date	Hour	Summary of Events and Information	Remarks and references to Appendices
				part of FRANCE BELGIUM
	1-3/10/17		Harassing fire, establishment of ammunition at guns increased to 700 rds per 18 pdr per gun.	1/50,000 Sheets 27-28
	4.10.17	4.45 hour	4th Div" attacked at 6.0 a.m. and captured the line U13d 0095 - U8d 3033 - Viscoso - Visco000 - Vinq 2160 - Vinqbq070 (approx) 32 B'de assisted to support 11th Infty B'de. Counter attacks by the enemy were broken up at 2.0 p.m. and 5.0 p.m. A/RHA Regrs 23rd Bty casualties. 1/Lt AVS Cockle was B'dr wounded. B'dr 7.00 and nut each much wounded killed, seven O.R's wounded. 1/Lt AVS Cockle was B'dr 7.00 and nut each much wounded information, maintaining communication by visual. During the night work was commenced on new positions as under.	
			27 U8a 0080
			134 U23c 0040
			135 U25c 3050
			21 U29 (9905)
	5.10.17		Work & dumping of ammunition at new positions was continued, sections of 27 & battery positions to new positions during the night.	
	6.10.17		HQ moved to Vicosqs, batteries completed their move to forward positions during the night	
	7/8.10.17		Registering completed, dumping of ammunition continued.	
	9.10.17		12th Infty B'de attacked 12th Infty B'de attacked on 4th Div" frontier XIV Corps. 32 B'de formed part of the barrage covering 12th B'de. Zero hour 5.20 a.m. Final objective was not reached, and	

WAR DIARY
or
INTELLIGENCE SUMMARY

Army Form C. 2118.

October 1917

Place	Date	Hour	Summary of Events and Information	Remarks and references to Appendices
	11.10.17		at end of the day line was on 4th Our front was - V7e 8000 - V13 central - V13 d 3020 (approx) BELGIUM with R.H. Charge 56th Battery under 112th F.A.B. B.G.R.A. 4th Our Bty. Attached message attached from Brigadier Boy of same date.	Sheet 2718
	12.10.17		at 5.25 a.m. 32" B" assisting in the artillery support of the 12th Infty Brigade. Attack did not quite reach final objective, our line at end of the day running V30 9000 - V36 9040 - V14 a 3000 (approx). A German counter attack at 6.15 p.m. was broken off by S.O.S. barrage. During the night enemy bus: of approach were left under fire.	
	13.10.17		Attached message B rec'd. 86th and 133rd Batteries withdrew from old wagon lines for 96 hours rest.	
	14.10.17		It let the S Thing D.S.O. & early 32" B" wounded in action. Also left 25 G. goods B.N.R. also	
			32" B" normal harassing fire carried out. Attached message (D+E rec'd)	
	16.10.17		normal harassing fire	
	17.10.17		Regrouping of Rgt. artillery XIII Corps came into force at 8.00 a.m. 32" B" Arcane under left Sub group (39th B?) of Rgt Group, Rgt. Arty. S.O.S. lines of B". V8 c 7540 - V14 a 6573	
	18/19.10.17		Normal harassing fire. Bursts at guns increased to 1000 rds per 15 hr - 300 7 2/per 24 hour	
	20.10.17		Lt OFLV BAUNER 31st Bty R.H.A. killed in action.	
	21.10.17		Lt S. WOODS, 133rd Bty R.H.A. wounded in action.	

Army Form C. 2118.

WAR DIARY
or
INTELLIGENCE SUMMARY

(Erase heading not required.)

Page 3   October 1917

Place	Date	Hour	Summary of Events and Information	Remarks and references to Appendices
	2.10.17		XIV Corps resumed the attack, but no adequate was attempted on front of 32nd Div. 32nd B. found a barrage in accordance with Corps scheme. Major H.G. Steeler, 2nd Bty, was wounded in action.	BELGIUM + part of FRANCE 1/40,000 Sheets 27 & 28
	14.10.17		Capts. (T. Mitchum and Gridly, 27 & 28th Bty, wounded in action, still at duty.	
	25.10.17 26.10.17		Westhoek. Preparatory bombardment commenced. Infantry working parties taken to the Bde. 32 gun supported attack of 35th Divn. at 5.40 a.m. Attack was unsuccessful owing to bad weather, a final advance of about 300 yards being made. Work on forward positions stopped [unclear] gas.	
	27/28/29.10.17		Normal harassing fire etc	
	30.10.17		32 B. assisted in the artillery support of an attack by XVIII Corps on XIV Corps right. Attack was launched at 5.50 a.m and was unsuccessful.	
	31.10.17		Heavy gas concentration on 27 and 134. Casualties approximately 6 officers (1 killed) and 19 other ranks.	

NOTE. Attachments referred to their [unclear] sent to R.A. 2nd Division [signature] Capt. to Major with duplicate Copy commanding 32nd Brigade R.F.A.

1.11.17

WAR DIARY.

32nd. BRIGADE R.F.A.

NOVEMBER, 1917.

Army Form C. 2118.

WAR DIARY
or
INTELLIGENCE SUMMARY
(Erase heading not required.)

Page 1.   November 1917
                                           J2 → Brigade RFA

Place	Date	Hour	Summary of Events and Information	Remarks and references to Appendices
	1.11.17		27 and 134 Batteries withdrew from action, relieved by B and A/295 respectively	BELGIUM
	2.11.17		135th Brigade was subjected to a heavy gas shelling. No casualties.	FRANCE
	3.11.17		Lt. Colonel PATERSON D.S.O. RFA commanding the 119th A.F.A Bde. with his battery commanders inspected all battery positions and H.Q. with a view to occupying them. 32nd Bde. completed concentration to their wagon lines at POESELHOEK, being relieved at positions by the 119th Bde. RFA	HAZEBROUCK 5th
	4.11.17		At 9am the 13th marched from its wagon lines to the EECKE area. It was billeted in farms. All men and officers except the gun battery who were under canvas. Other horses and drivers in fieldsmonitored cover.	BELGIUM 1 100,000
	5.11.17		At 8.40am the Bde. marched to the MERVILLE area where it was billeted for the night under similar conditions as the day before. (N.B) Major C.E.S. BOWER D.S.O. R.F.A took over command of the 13th from Major W.B. MACKIE on the 3rd inst. Captain C.M. VALLENTIN R.F.A (late Adjutant of the 13th) took on command of the 27th battery from Captain C.T. HUTCHISON R.F.A. Lieut J.F. NICHOLS appointed Adjutant vice Capt C.M. VALLENTIN.	
	6.11.17		The march was continued to the MAZRLES Aux MINES aux, starting at 10.40am.	
	7.11.17		The Bde. marched to the VILLERS CHATEL area, and was billeted in VILLERS BRULÉ-V.	
	8.11.17		March was resumed, destination was the area of TILLOY WOOD (FRANCE Sheet 51B Edition 3) M,A + B and M.B.B. Routes of march via ARRAS-ST POL road. Men and officers were in Nissen huts and the horses in the open with no cover or standings. HQrs were in ARRAS.	
	9.11.17		Col. Adjutant + digged officer with 13C, 63rd Bdes, 12 chauffr's vc proceeded to positions of the 63rd Bde. 12 chauffrs with a view to taking over. 63rd Bde was commanded by Lt Col. Gate and had occupied their positions since Bde. attacked at ARRAS (April 9th)	

Army Form C. 2118.

WAR DIARY
or
INTELLIGENCE SUMMARY
(Erase heading not required.)

Place	Date	Hour	Summary of Events and Information	Remarks and references to Appendices
	9.11.17	cont.	In the evening 1 section per Battery of 63rd Brigade relieved 1 section per Battery of the 63rd Brigade as follows:- 275 Battery from A/63 at N11 B 82 95 134 " B/63 " H34a114.49 135 " C/63 " N4 d 35.55? 86 " D/63 " N4 d 40 70 with H.Q. with H.Q. at N6 d 11.34	FRANCE Sheet 51 B Folder 2
	10.11.17		Signal Officer remain at 63rd/13th. Remaining Sections of Battery relieved and H.Q. Staff was completed by 8pm. Position of Wgn. N5a 70.40. A/ Battery 30 & B2nd cover sector of 32nd/13th.	
	11.11.17		The wagon lines of 63" /13 were taken over by 32nd/13th & occupied in the early morning. (M63). Batteries throughout the day completed their registration & calibration of the guns. O.P.'s chiefly used were HUSSAR LANE (N23.9.9) NOVELTY (O1 C 9.7) IVANCOURT (N24 d 9.4). Good views could be obtained from all O.P.s. Summary of positions of gun, huts, wagon lines etc. Gun positions on the whole were good. The emplacements were substantial, splinter-proof, fairly strong against shell of such calibre. Dugout were sunk very deep and comfortable. Supply of ammunition was by Decauville (when available) or by pack mean. ARRAS-CAMBRAI lin...	
	13.11.17		which was have in most parts. O.P.'s were fairly good by reason good suspicions in aeroplane photographs. The approaches were by duck boards was taken? had good standings and cover for the horses. Hut huts rendered excellent... Men had wooden huts covered, and were close to the horse lines. Gun batteries... were in the main TILLOY - BEAURAIN road. It remarkable about B/... ill it with Lung yards as approach. The wagon supply lines a long tough sand of...	

Army Form C. 2118.

WAR DIARY
or
INTELLIGENCE SUMMARY
(Erase heading not required.)

Instructions regarding War Diaries and Intelligence Summaries are contained in F. S. Regs., Part II. and the Staff Manual respectively. Title Pages will be prepared in manuscript.

Place	Date	Hour	Summary of Events and Information	Remarks and references to Appendices
	11-11-17 (cont)		Officers, Breakers, stores, harness from R. were fairly good. Informants were seriously scarce, such as scavenging horse standing, was to about in reserve.	
	12.11.17.		Calibration continued. Models recently practically nil.	
	13.11.17.		2/Lt HOLLAND from 29th Battery & 2/Lt BUCK joined 13th Battery. B.O's lines were from 088 80.90 to 028 40.35. Harassing fire was carried out on enemy tracks & trench throughout the day & night. Hostile shell fire was active during the morning but was slowed by our retaliation.	
	14.11.17.		Normal trench warfare.	
	15.11.17.		2/Lt McEATLEY joined 86 Battery, 2/Lt TURNER - 13th Battery (from D.A.C) 2/Lt JEFFERIES & 2/Lt N. supporting in raid of 2nd Laws Fm. carried out together with Hannay Fm.	
	16.11.17.		At 5am 32nd Bde. supported a raid of the 12th Infantry Bde. by firing a B.O.N barrage around Porton raided at 028 05.00 to 028 4.5. The raid lasted 40 minutes. Artillery support was very round by Bde. Commander. Between 13-14 Division Rly. 49th Bde. assisted. It was not very successful but our casualties were slight.	
	17.11.17		Harassing enemy tracks in Bois Zeni and retaliated off on hostile trench areas for activity. At 6.30pm in taken assisted the artillery support of a raid by 112 A & S Highlanders. 13 Division (they 2nd Dormonts & 12 K.O.Y.L.I from the 13th supplied a raid by 12 Infantry Bde. (1st King's Sin Bg.) firing another B.O.N barrage around our rectifies 02d 55.90 - 02d 50.00. The same artillery carried out a H.E. Raid was very successful several Germans were killed & no other prisoners & identifications brought as	

Army Form C. 2118.

WAR DIARY
or
INTELLIGENCE SUMMARY

(Erase heading not required.)

Instructions regarding War Diaries and Intelligence Summaries are contained in F. S. Regs., Part II. and the Staff Manual respectively. Title Pages will be prepared in manuscript.

Place	Date	Hour	Summary of Events and Information	Remarks and references to Appendices
	18.11.17		Lieut. BROWN joined 134 Battery. At 3pm Smoke was discharged from 12" Infantry Bde front and the C.B.s Allely took part in a bombardment of the enemies defences. The effect was good especially causing great thinning to the Enemy who put down a fairly considerable barrage on our trenches and switched at from place to place as though expecting an attack. At 6pm the Batteries assisted the Artillery support of a raid by the 13th & Royal Scots (15th Division). 2/Lt DE BERSIGNEY joined 135 Battery. (NB) Up to the present 45" Groups v Flashless neutralisation have fired 16 134, 1907 of these successful and bombardments at Gunnery. 62 dinner v neutr joined the Bngatt.	
	19.11.17 20.11.17		Carried out normal harassing fire on enemies defences and tracks. Assisted the Artillery Support in a Raid carried out by the 10th Infantry Brigade. Raid a great success. Artillery fire reported excellent. 2/Lt A. BERSIGNEY joined 134 Positions for the Brigade were reconnoitered on O.7 and O.7 d and O.7 c and d (French Map). (FRAME 2 Sheet 3.7.B S.W.(20000)).	
	21.11.17		Normal trench warfare. At 6am the 15 Division carried out a raid lasting 20 mins. just North of our 13th Bde Zone. 134, 135 and 86 Batteries assisted.	
	Night 19/20		Gas was projected on divisional front North of Brigade Zone.	
	22.11.17		Normal Trench warfare.	
	23.11.17		Harassing fire and registration. Hostile trench Mortars very active but were neutralized by our fire. Many M.Gs fire opposed to our from BOYS & V.E.D.Y.	

WAR DIARY
or
INTELLIGENCE SUMMARY

Army Form C. 2118.

Place	Date	Hour	Summary of Events and Information	Remarks and references to Appendices
(N52.Y0 30)	24-11-17		32nd Bde HQ subjected to a rapid burst of H.V., 77mm. and gas shells were sund. Two casualties occurred. 27Bdy in N.13.90.80 shelled with 150 unn during the morning. There were no casualties.	
	25.11.17		Normal bursts of H.V. on targets T.M's. & trenches.	
	26.11.17		Normal Trench Warfare.	
	27.11.17		Hostile shelling very active on our front, support and reserve trenches. Back areas around N5 & N.Y searched and swept. MONCHY severely shelled between 4.30m & 4.30pm. Lt Col C.F.S.BOWER.D.S.O. took over command of 4th Div Arty while Brig Gen C.S.Sykes D.S.O was on leave. Major C.P.McKay commanded 32nd Bde during Lt Col C.F.S Bowers absence.	
	28.11.17		134 Battery in H.34.d.20.30 was very severely shelled throughout the day. About 400 shells were fired, shelling was very intense about 2.30pm. Two guns damaged. No casualties to personnel. Counter endeavoured to silence the hostile battery. Been battery refused to reach T.M's fire.	
	29.11.17		Normal trench warfare with harassing fire.	
	30.11.17		No firs. or orders from H.Q.Dn. Arty.	

			(During this month the Brigade was awarded the following honrs:-
			Capt. N.J.Ivens - M.C.
			2/Bomb CROUCHIN - D.C.M) Green DANKS - M.M 135.Bdy
			  , FISHER - D.C.M) 134 Bdy / Bomb GUILMARTIN - M.M 86 Bdy
			Sgt GIBBENS - Bar to M.M)
			  , MADIN - M.M
			134 & 31 Battries heavily shelled wund 3.qr. 134 Battery had two guns damaged.	

Army Form C. 2118.

WAR DIARY
or
INTELLIGENCE SUMMARY

(Erase heading not required.)

Place	Date	Hour	Summary of Events and Information	Remarks and references to Appendices
			96 Recruits joined the Brigade thus completing it to limits. Several reinforcements joined, causing the Brigade apt to re-establishment less Y.O.Rs. All batteries now average 6 officers each. Elwell Capt. Adjutant 322 Bde RFA 30/4/17 The only casualties in the Brigade during the month were Lieutenant Robinson RFA injured. Lieutenant "Gunner" Wilson 97th Battery RFA attached L.H.Q. He was run over slightly grazed with number of 2+5. Battery Commanders A/272 F.R.R. Cross DSO RFA Major O.N. Valentine RFA Major W Mackes MPA Major C.J. McKay MPA Major C.T. McKay RFA Major E.J. Griffith Williams RFA Major W Mackes Elwell Capt A/A.C. 322 Bde RFA	

2449. Wt. W14957/M90 750,000 1/16 J.B.C. & A. Forms/C.2118/12.

WAR DIARY or INTELLIGENCE SUMMARY

Army Form C. 2118.

32nd Brigade R.F.A.   VM 33

Place	Date	Hour	Summary of Events and Information	Remarks and references to Appendices
In the field	1-12-17		No firing was carried out in order to mystify the enemy. Orders issued from XVII Corps. Throughout the day and night hostile artillery was very active. The batteries were shelled, 134 Battery receiving most attention, about 300 130mm gas shells fired at it. Two guns were damaged by the shell fire and three dugouts demolished. During the night areas around battery were subjected to gas shelling. No casualties. At 9pm the balance of the day was taken, the Brigade put down a barrage on suspected enemy lines in O.3.c., 6.8 and I.32.a. v 3.	Ref FRANCE Sheet 57B June 1917 V.W.v SP.I. Casualties 1 20,000
	2-12-17		B/yr. Battery R.F.A. came under command of 32nd Bde R.F.A. & belonged to 31st (Oct. 1770) 15th D/A and was commanded by Major ROWDEN R.F.A. and 13th account to A/yr. R.F. Group of the Right Artillery. was commanded by Big Gen. MACHADO & LIEUT COL. DSO — OBE, 15. S.W/A. Bde S.O.S. Zones were: O.2.d.80.30 — J.32.c.15.99. Battery S.O.S. Zones: 29th O.2.d.80.30 — O.2.d.45.75 — 134th O.2.d.75.75 — O.2.d.45.90 — O.2.d.65.10. 135th O.2.d.65.10 — O.2.d.40.30 (39 guns) J.32.c.22.42 — J.32.c.15.99 (remaining guns) B/yr J.32.c.22.42 — J.32.d.05.00. 86th O.2.d.60.34 v O.2.d.45.26 v O.2.d.82.95 v O.2.d.95.60 v O.2.d.95.60.65 v O.3.c.02.04.	
	3-12-17		Sergt DEFEER 135th Battery awarded the D.C.M. Both Artilleries active all batteries shelled throughout the day. No material damage or casualties. Enemies trenches frenchies. Tracks & strong point harassed during the day v night.	
	4-12-17		Normal trench warfare. Enemy aircraft active in the early morning. Harassing fire carried out during the night areas of H.35 B.30.40. H.36 B.30.40. H.35.c.9d N. H.35.c.9d N'. & a.d N. H.35.c.15 ENEMY guns at CERPIGNY (gassed and counter battery). It was being registered trenches in H.36. B.30.40. 2nd Lt X th CERPIGNY (gassed and counter battery). It was being drawn duty with Left Battery N'y 134 a General Light Infantry. Point M-D LINDSAY 86th Battery awarded the M.C.	
	5-12-17		2/Lt Col BOWIE-BOSO returned from U.K. and resumed command of the Brigade. Major G. McRay returned to 134 Battery R.F.A. Normal trench warfare. Award M.M. received and P.d 5 over 2nd by H. 32nd Div. at 9.30 pm.	

WAR DIARY
or
INTELLIGENCE SUMMARY

Army Form C. 2118.

(Erase heading not required.)

Place	Date	Hour	Summary of Events and Information	Remarks and references to Appendices
In M/Julel	6.12.14		Normal trench warfare & harassing fire on Notch Trs and defences over around Minchy subjected to very heavy heavy barrages	
	7.12.14		London day to allow	
	8.12.14		Enemy put down a very heavy HE & Gas barrage on HAPPY VALLEY and trenches on left of Bde Zone. Usual continuous harassing fire on trenches and tracks	
	9.12.14		Enemy heavy barrage the Bde front at 12 noon and 4.30pm Duration of barrages about half an hour. Destructive fire on various new work & trench carried out by day and night. At 11pm the order was received for Battns to stand to from 6.30am to 8.30am every morning from the 10th instant. Wagon lines ordered to stand to, also Gns. In barrage gun teams were to man or have to clear the lines for exercise before gun	
	10.12.14		Brigade stood to as ordered from 6.30am to 8.30am. Enemy heavy shelled trenches & tracks in 13th Zone during the relief of the 185th US Infantry Brigade causing several casualties.
Lt.Col. C.E.S.BOWER DSO O/I 33rd Batt. to command with Batty pending return from leave of Brig Gen. SYKES CBO & Major CC McKAY joined 32nd B.J.HQ to command 33rd Bty was DCI C.E.S. Bowley	
	11.12.14			
	12.12.14		Normal trench warfare. Batteries and Bde being commanded by L BDVD Nashay DSO
AFA Brigade were ordered to present the attack posters of the 131st north & coast to occupy the lines thereof to-night	

2449 Wt. W14957/M90 750,000 1/16 J.B.C. & A. Forms/C.2118/12

WAR DIARY or INTELLIGENCE SUMMARY

Army Form C. 2118.

Place	Date	Hour	Summary of Events and Information	Remarks and references to Appendices
	12.12.17		During the night A/315 Battery pushed out a section in H34 a.no 50 (4 guns) in H34 c.50.90 (6 guns) H34 B.05.55 (4 guns) N2 a.50.90 — left sec: 4 guns B/315 D/315 315 MO Throughout a sub-group of the Staff Group (32nd Bde. RFA) A/315 Battery at I.32 c.50.40 to 02.81.0.95 B/315 " I.32 c.30.40 to I.32 a.12.10 D/315 " 1 How. I.32 c.28.96 — 1 How. I.32 c.20.30 1 How. I.32 c.60.78 — 1 How. I.32 c.55.28 Hostile T.M.s very active during the night and there was a loud enemy M.Gunness. Lym Bdy RFA fired a rapid burst of fire on hostile tracks in 08.b.70.80 to 02.9.86.10 in the 71th to Cirkach alluded from a working party of the Assaulted Battalion (10th K/134) which was taking place further North. Zero was 4 a.m and duration 15 minutes. Harassing fire between known enemy tracks and defences throughout the night. Registration carried out & completed by A/B + D/315 Bts. Hostile shelled very quiet except for the enemy gunnery and PREUX Over 134 Ineladed Hostile T.M.s. Enemy F.O. active throughout the day and harassed tracks and sunkels in O.3 ate during the night. Harassing fire on enemy defences Lym (battery had a burst of lit on gun pit damaging the gun but not observed fire prevented. L.O.Y. C.B.S. Brown Les replied the fire from the sec. Anti M.G. C.B.Shey, targets 134.B4, from 13th Enemy Shelling between Moreny & Preux served only slightly pitting around Moreny & Preux	R/FRANCE Sheet 58.3.NW + S.W. 25000
	13.12.17			
	14.12.17			

WAR DIARY
or
INTELLIGENCE SUMMARY

Army Form C. 2118.

Place	Date	Hour	Summary of Events and Information	Remarks and references to Appendices
	15/12/17		Harassing fire kept up during the morning. Our own Bde forward area at 8 a.m. from the trenches in a very light raid. Raid by 2nd Essex (South) point of entry & exit at 078 42 82). 135 + 134 By fired a short & sharp programme in support. Bois de SARTY Bois du M.O.T. operation etc. 15/minuten Bolif. Zukahlen very savage. During the afternoon Stati. 7 MS actes all along our front, firing the night harassing fire on our enemy tracks + trenches. Ordinary harassing fire carried out by 86th By R.F.A. + 27th By R.F.A. on enemy dumps in area 0.9.d.	
	16/12/17		Harassing fire by 27 By, 135 By + 86 By R.F.A. on tracks in 0.9.D. & POODLE & TREE trench in 0.3.a.	
	17/12/17		Harassing fire by 86 By + 134 By R.F.A. on BOW + BEETLE trenches. 27th By printed was heavily shelled by a 150 mm How. About 200 rds being fired at it from + direct hits being seen on the land running behind the battery at the gun on top of the run. At this was clean 20 ft no damage was done. No gun was hit. This lasted from 4.30 pm to 5 pm. The 135 By printed was also shelled by 150 mm dev during the afternoon from 2 pm to 6 pm, about 220 rounds were fired at him but no damage was caused to guns. One gun pit was slightly damaged.	
	19/12/17		Usual harassing fire carried out by 135 By on forward and rear. Hostile T.M.s were rather more active than usual.	

Army Form C. 2118.

WAR DIARY
or
INTELLIGENCE SUMMARY
(Erase heading not required.)

Place	Date	Hour	Summary of Events and Information	Remarks and references to Appendices
	20.12.17		Usual harassing fire carried out by 27th Bty & B/86 Bty during the early morning. The Hostile T.M's were very active. Our retaliation from ours was effective in stopping hostile activity.	
	21.12.17		Enemy Hostile T.M.s again active. Especially on CANISTER AVENUE which were known in several places. A concentrated bombardment was carried out at 4 pm by B/86 & Heavy artillery on CARR RIDGE trench system. T.M. emplacements were caught in that moment. Our B/15 RFA opened fire from a very heavy barrage all along our divisional front & attempts made on S.O.S. in 0.20. Fired He was unsuccessful. Our own guns & Infy + left on our own front were silently caught in our Barrage. Nerves lasts about men killed in no mans land but they also have sent similar signals for them. Ref: J.31.34.c by 27th Bty RFA. Enemy similar. Half an hour. All Battery firing slight in Aveluka in J.34.c. Enemy T.M.s again Harassing fire carried out by B/86 Bty.	
	22.12.17		Bombardment of POODLES TRENCH by 27th Bty, 135th Bty & B/86 Bty during afternoon. Enemy T.M.s again Active repeats in trench Y side in J.31.13. He was at intervals this day was nicked by our artillery was not a heavy barrage also which Hostile fire. This have been successful. This have worked a party for the 'S enemy at 6.20 pm. Stasis units + whole Strategy have him off. She have all battery fire. Co he raided the hostile front & which several canfts about 3/4 have.	
	23.12.17		hungly. lecapture 5+6 of our men. This raiders cleared + fingers was had. RA Enemy S.O.S. Snow fire has fallen + frequency was had. RA coming what in short S.O.S. Snow fire has fallen during the morning which have silence.	
	24.12.17		Our own guns harassing enemy front, After T.M.s. By our battn. Than settled in. RA	
	25.12.17		Xmas quiet Xmas day. Programmes usual harassing fire carried out by 27 Bty R.F.A. & 134 Bty R.F.A. Had 4 pm for divine which was kept by the M.O. in evening. RA	
	26.12.17		Snow fell again during the night, weather feet than two days ago. Bombardment of FRITZUN Stand by B/86 Bty RFA + How Bty + 315 Bde attached. Enemy seemed to appear in battle.	

WAR DIARY
or
INTELLIGENCE SUMMARY

Army Form C. 2118.

Place	Date	Hour	Summary of Events and Information	Remarks and references to Appendices
TREE	(Cont.) 26.12.17		Enemy were put at intervals fired shots by 86 R.G. & also fired on F. 27.H at F.13.4.08.6.	
	27.12.17		Usual harassing fire carried out by 86 Bty & 27 Bty R.F.A.	
	28.12.17		Usual harassing fire. Enemy active in the air. An enemy aeroplane came down at about 11.30 am in front of 86 B/y position. Its occupants were both Italian prisoners being taken by the flying away from it to our aerodrome. They were unhurt and the more [?] Germans attacked them & were taken away by 13th Squadron R.F.C. Guns & claims [?] Aeroplane was intact & was taken away in sections.	
	29.12.17		Nothing of importance happened. Hostile artillery fire in a while, not shown. Nothing of	
	30.12.17		Ammunition expended on Hannern [?]	
	31.12.17		importance happened. Hannern fire ceased for 3/4 hour. Enemy may in addition all batteries are preparing positions for alternative [?] from where ordinary firing sharpen positions. Guns may have been in action in front of S.O.S. + [?] operation. 275 B/y will bring into action at N.S.D. A O.S.O. 86 Bly in S.E.[?] at approximately H.24.0.30.20, 13.4.B.5 at H.34.D. A.D.3.O. at H.2.6, D.90.40. The 15th Division on our left carries practice of being relieved by The South Germans [?]	

Lt. Col. Commander
32nd Bde R.F.A.

4th Division

War Diaries

32nd Bde. R.F.A.

January to December
1915

WAR DIARY
or
INTELLIGENCE SUMMARY

Army Form C. 2118.

32 Bde ??
VM 34

Place	Date	Hour	Summary of Events and Information	Remarks and references to Appendices
JMK/JMB	1.1.18		Annual trench warfare. Enemy's attacks shelling intermittently throughout the day by way and night. Hostile artillery activity below normal.	ANNEXAIM in PAGES 1 2000
	2.1.18		As 1.1.18.	
	3.1.18		Enemy attempted a raid abt 10.40 pm. Point of assembly appeared to be L.7.0.370.70. Had own preceded by a heavy trench barrage on front line and support line in that area. The Brigade open fire on its SOS lines. Raiding party repulsed in "No Mans Land". Remaining period of the night quiet.	
	4.1.18		Hostile artillery very normal. Harassing fire and shelling eyes in fashion carried out by the Brigade.	
	5.1.18		During the day arrangements were made to pair 18 pdr batteries and exchange a number of guns with the 315" Army Fd Arty Bde who were ordered to pull out of action. During the night the following changes took place 29" Battery substituted a section to a broken N5 of 40.50. 134" Battery substituted a section to H34 d 40.80, 86 "35" Battery a section to H34 305.35: 4 guns to H34 e 85.70, 86 "Battery 4 guns to H34 305.35: 4 guns to H34 d 65.55. Hostile artillery activity very little. Registration was active Hostile shell fire was low being done a bunch of tracks burst little over lens.	
	6.1.18		Above normal. During the day you reconnoitred by me You N3 Capt P.T. Nicholson 21 Bde and Lieut G. Watson D" Batt'y arrived at N.C. General situation normal. Two enemy aeroplanes flew over our batteries during the early morning apparently on reconnaissance. D'n Battery moved a section into H.22 d 80.80. Pair guns at the 15-16f/f in position at H.23.b.95.40. Last moth's touch touch shall they attack worth them to complete.	

Army Form C. 2118.

WAR DIARY
or
INTELLIGENCE SUMMARY
(Erase heading not required.)

Instructions regarding War Diaries and Intelligence Summaries are contained in F.S. Regs., Part II. and the Staff Manual respectively. Title Pages will be prepared in manuscript.

Place	Date	Hour	Summary of Events and Information	Remarks and references to Appendices
Sully Jub	5-1-18		Normal trench warfare. Aerial activity below normal in the early morning.	
	9-1-18		As for the 8th inst.	
	10-1-18		A great deal of enemy movement observed and fired on. Several hits observed. Enemy harassed back areas around N6 and H36. with shells of all calibres.	
	11-1-18		Normal harassing of the enemies defenses. enemy hostile shelling below normal.	
	13-1-18		Hostile shelling above normal. Particularly on front and support trenches. .O2 a.c and I 31 d. during the day. This was replied to by our batteries. At 5am enemy attempted a raid, fairly about 50 strong, on SAP 12. This was repulsed by 2/Lts and artillery fire. The raid was preceded by a very heavy T.M. bombardment.	
	14-1-18		Normal trench warfare.	
	15-1-18		Green Fatal shoots on FOAL, FOX & POODLE Tr carried out at 3pm & 3.15pm. At 5.30pm neutralised hostile T.M's in I32a. Enemy artillery & nt. hostl. Quiet.	
	16-1-18		At 8am & 8.10am concentrated shots on BUCKLE Tr and area about 7pm. very active during the day and had to be neutralised several times. T.M's fire I.22 particularly active. Rain and trees rendered Trench in places impassable.	
	17-1-18		Just before morning our aeroplanes were very active. A few enemy observing place seen. One was shot down out of control behind FRESAW WOOD about 9am. Enemy carried out gas shoots around MONCHY and HAPPY VALLEY. An of present German relief was seen in progress in vicinity of KITTrench. This was fired on and casualties inflicted. Visibility good. A few gas shells were fired into HAPPY VALLEY during 15 minutes	

WAR DIARY or INTELLIGENCE SUMMARY

Army Form C. 2118.

Place	Date	Hour	Summary of Events and Information	Remarks and references to Appendices
In the field	19-1-18 20-1-18		Nothing to report. Much aircraft activity from 7.30 am to 11.30 am. Our enemy aeroplane crashed in combat in I.29.c. Our aeroplanes very active. Great deal of movement was observed chiefly enemy Germans walking about of his troops along the top of their trenches – presumably their trenches were in a bad state. Enemy shelled MONEHY, cherry tree and MUFF 135 Bys. moved this morning to a new position H34 a 80.95.	
	21-1-18		Enemy carried out an aerial short round MONEHY this Hq in N.5a 70.40 and this lane trench in N.5a during the afternoon. 24"Bys active positn N.5.d.50.50 heavily shelled left sign 894 cat the afternoon. 2 Gunpits were destroyed and one gun demolished, but owing to active (enemy) aerial recce observn, enemy battery positns in PARK WOOD etc were disposed by our fire. Special reconce hour was to tab. Normal direct air par.	
	22-1-18 23-1-18		Enemy very active with TMs on our front and support lines East of Bugachs Zons. 24"Bys broken again shelled during the afternoon.	
	24-1-18		Enemy artillery burst his artillery suffered a great deal of movement observed. Gunners walking out of their trenches. REEUX OPs on CHANCE HILL communicated.	
	25-1-18		During the day our artillery suffed hostile movement and bombarded FOX & BOOTH Trenches also PUG and TREE Trenches. At 10.30pm the enemy heavily shelled PEUVRY. H22 a1 and H34 3 pts of light minenwerfer trench mortar gas shells. Bombardment lasted until ...	

Army Form C. 2118.

WAR DIARY
or
INTELLIGENCE SUMMARY
(Erase heading not required.)

Instructions regarding War Diaries and Intelligence Summaries are contained in F.S. Regs., Part II. and the Staff Manual respectively. Title Pages will be prepared in manuscript.

Place	Date	Hour	Summary of Events and Information	Remarks and references to Appendices
‑	26-1-18		Hostile artillery quiet during the day and night. Our artillery engaged enemy work and calibrated. Aerial activity normal.	
	27-1-18		Our artillery commenced registration in a prepared raid on O8 5.d. exchanged hate. TMs in and around Steep Wood and Keiberg Copse. 86 Bty section in H22.d Sheba with 4 guns. Shelby during the night.	
	28-1-18		Registration continued. Enemy very heavy bombarded the 175th and Support lines of this Bde. The SOS was fired by our infantry. Action followed.	
	29-1-18		Registration for raid completed. 91 new from O6.13.g. action in H9.20 were evacuated gassed. Order to 92k various issues from 38 Bty holes. Also to the guns. Enemy active throughout the night. Very heavy bombardment way put down on the division front Trip of our (Guards) Div. was flying high as said which was early reported. At 10.7m Enemy barraged our trenches Nett Hostile artillery normal.	
	30-1-18		Vth SCHAPPE.	
	31-1-18		Hostile artillery quiet. Visibility very bad owing to mist orders received. Enemy own relief by a Brigade of the 75 Div.	

31-1-18

Blackb Capt
for OC 322 Bde RFA

War Diary / Intelligence Summary

Army Form C. 2118.

General Summary for the Month of January 1918.

All map points referred to are reference MAP HAMBLAIN les PRES 20000.

1. All were very comfortable accommodated in their different billets. Dugouts were mined & very high. Several dugouts were proof. The personnel of the wagon lines that we knew that all billeted and very comfortable, and all horses were under cover with securing round the sheds and rack standings.

2. The two reinforcements received were of a rougher class, physical & mentally. Several of our newly horses which had to be of the line type, and set back to be shown & other.

3. Sept. Arrangements were made for the defence of the Moyenne sector batteries had two 6 gun positions each. In one position the battery had 4 gun & in the other. A section he again positions remain silent except the S.O.S. and the section covered of all the shooting. Rear O.Ps on ORANGE HILL were constructed and Gun positions in N.23. were established top staked in N.G. 14 a Brigade position. Re: round to expand even the town of a hotel break through by an enforcing body.

6. Col. Bowes D.S.O. proceeded on leave. Officer Cmdg in England and leave a K19 was Major H. B. Mackie assumed command of the Bde.

23rd Jan. Capt B. to land R7A (mu) Lt C.E. Maggs R7A (mu) B34.

24. " " Lt C.E. Maggs R7A (mu) B34. —
The following decorations were received: Capt M C.P. HUTCHINSON R.F.A (M.C.) Lieut C. HOLMES R.F.A (M.C.)
Sergt BOX A & Sergt Edwards P (munitions) Sergt MARTIN J & Capt BURNETT A (D.C.M.)

W.C.1 C.P.S. Barr DSO RFA (munitions)

Blundell Capt
for D.C. 32, 15st. Bde

31-1-18

WAR DIARY.

32nd. BRIGADE, R. F. A.

FEBRUARY, 1918.

WAR DIARY or INTELLIGENCE SUMMARY

Army Form C. 2118.

32nd Brigade R.F.A.

Place	Date	Hour	Summary of Events and Information	Remarks and references to Appendices
Authuille	1-2-18		During the day hostile arty was active on Morchy and resumed normal and support lines. Our arty harassed enemy defences during the day. At 10.45 pm the front and support lines between MORCHY and the SCARPE were bombarded heavily with shells & TMs all calibre. At 11pm the bombardment died down and reports from MORCHY to the CAMBRAI Rd. Our arty stood on SOS lines. No infantry action taken. At 2.30am our arty stopped. A raid of the 2/13 Batt of Inf. R.F. Germans assisted 6.0.8 and was raided. By Patrol when the Batt of Batty of this Brigade assisted in the creeping barrage and two balloons proved a protection for barrage. Lieut F Park & No patrol of arty. The Royal 75 gunners fired on the enemy TM emplacements. The OSP Lewis was located. At 4.30am hostile shelling normal. Visibility fair.	CX/17/1869/1
	2-2-18		Our arty very active on 0.93 + 0.94 from 5pm to 3am in bursts. The first piece duty. Heavy hostile retaliation on front & support. wooden shelters. Visibility fair.	
	3-2-18		Very hot air report. HAPPY VALLEY was artfully & heavily hit from the direction of TUSKIN WOOD. Our arty gunfire Hostile only back by the MG. Visibility good. No abnormal seen.	
	4-2-18		About 3am enemy opened a very heavy TM barrage on the front and support lines of the Right Bge. Our arty stood firm & at 6.05 bursts sent as to infantry action followed the hostile bombardment. It lifted to Reserve TM emplacements at 6.20. Got the inf. reply after it had lifted. The rest of the day was quite. Visibility fair. Aircraft active normal.	
	5-2-18		Brigades battery practice. In the evening one section from Bty C was relieved by Germans caught a out landed over. Relief completed, and relieved by 6pm.	
	6-2-18		Hostile shelling normal. HOSTILE aircraft & HAPPY VALLEY were shelled but lonely shot in the afternoon. The sections of Y10 & Z10 Bty RFA checked & duputeered and relieved by Y14 & Y6 134 RFA. Relief was completed by 6pm as follows. B/24 Bakery RFA	
			134 " "	
			135 " "	
			56 " "	
			32/134 Bakery RFA / 32 Bat HQ /	
			The 32.134 RFA on relief took over position & batteries of operations from the Y14 134 RFA as follows.	

Army Form C. 2118.

WAR DIARY
or
INTELLIGENCE SUMMARY.
(Erase heading not required.)

Place	Date	Hour	Summary of Events and Information	Remarks and references to Appendices
Suk [Nuk?]	9.2.18 (cont)		27th Battery work from 9.9.9 Battery	Map Name Shat-i-SIB
		13.4.	" " " " B/7/.	Shat-i-SIB
		13.5	" " " " C/7/.	NW - SW
		16	" " " " D/7/.	
			The Position of Observation covers in 14.25.d the four rock posts on Q 635-224	
			were at O.9.a 30.75 (N) H.36.d 75-25 (N) H.1a 20.40 (N) H.1c 70.70	
			The Bengali old Fort Over Reception position from the Guards as under	
			27th Battery - N.3.c 20.40	
			13.4 " - H.34 c 84.55	
			13.5 " - H.34 c 54.90	
			16 " - H.34 a 55.23	
			The reinforcing positions were duly filled up & guard of 1 NCO & 4 gunners who were	
			despatched to the mountain. They were told-off to act Officer	
			The portion of the men were manned with 1 NCO & 4 men Gun & 1 Officer	
			for taking the position were good, the men practice were about 330 yards	
			clear out of the positions for Nicolas Rifle. The remaining formed from body	
			lived at the wagon lines in M.C.B.	
	10.2.18		General cleaning up by all ranks.	
	11.2.18			
	12.2.18		Wagon lines inspected by the acting CRA Lieut Col. THOMPSON DSO P+O with training	
			and all the horses in the 73rd inspected by the DDVS 3rd Army in the afternoon.	
	13.2.18			
	15.2.18		Battery carried out training on second ans'th & Programme of training	
			issued by 1st Div Arty.	
	16.2.18		Gen C.SYKES.CO 778 inspected employer positions	

WAR DIARY or INTELLIGENCE SUMMARY

Army Form C. 2118.

(Erase heading not required.)

Instructions regarding War Diaries and Intelligence Summaries are contained in F. S. Regs., Part II. and the Staff Manual respectively. Title pages will be prepared in manuscript.

Place	Date	Hour	Summary of Events and Information	Remarks and references to Appendices
Jn Hafulal	17.2.18		Capt PENNINGSON RHA joined & posted to 1st Brigade from the Base. Posted was	(a)(b) page (1)
	19.2.18		detailed for a "Flash letter" for today. There seems now to be ready to advance and a slight attack with tanks G.O.C. Division inspected the baker.	
	20.2.18 / 25.2.18		Normal training	
	26.2.18	11 am	27 Battery & 134 Battery Relieved respectively G. 28.5 Battery & 126 Battery. The two former latter marched to their new wagon lines in G. 22 d. ½ 60.	
	27.2.18	9 am	27 Battery & 134 Battery marched from their wagon lines to FOREMONT for the purpose of shoeing & calibrating their guns.	
	28.2.18	10 am	29th Brigade HQ wagon lines relieved to 32.Y.3.0 wagon lines in N.6.6. The latter marched to their new lines in G. 22 d 60. 15– 2nd Lt HOTSON RHA posted to 135(H) from D.A.C.	

General Summary for the Month

Whilst in action all batteries were in good positions and the men comfortably billeted accommodated at times. The O.P.s were good and gave a good field of view. At Mysyl was an Infantry brigade to keep watch came rather wasm but evening were to good. There were a great deal of the casualties were very slight whilst in the front area. As the Brigade was there for a more prolonged rest carried out "C.B." Brigade orders which included a great deal of Signal training chiefly Signalling, Visual & Gas drill for gun detachments Drift & Close Mostatry, Physical training, signalling between Battery & gun pits. Lectures by Officers, who were to keep map of the line some of the batteries had wisked out found from hospital. He knows of what looks like a very nice new little Sicilian orange tree.

Stuck to Capt. H. P. H. 1-3-18 in the absence of Lt Col...

4th Div.

WAR DIARY

Headquarters,

32nd BRIGADE, R.F.A.

M A R C H

1 9 1 8

4th Divn

WAR DIARY.

32nd. BRIGADE R.F.A.

MARCH, 1918.

Army Form C. 2118.

INTELLIGENCE SUMMARY.
(Erase heading not required.)

2nd Brigade RFA

Place	Date	Hour	Summary of Events and Information	Remarks and references to Appendices
In the field	1/3/18		Programme of training being carried out by 185 & 36 Batteries	FRANCE 57.3 NW / SW
	2/3/18		106 away at FRICOURT calibrating their guns.	20000
	3/3/18		27th & 134th Batt[er]ys returned to wagon lines at 3.30pm and 135 & 36 Batt[erie]s marched from their wagon lines to BUSNVILLERS en route to FRICOURT to calibrate their guns.	
	4/3/18		General cleaning up and training. Exercising of Gun teams returning mules &c.	
	12/3/18		Battery laying, map reading & lectures to Runners, Signrs & N.C.O's	
	18/3/18		A Mounted Exhibition was reviewed by G.O.C. & Division in the ARRAS race course, at 3pm.	
	14/5/18		Visual training during the evening period. Later practised [illegible] reinforcement positions & 2 emplacing positions in the vicinity of BOUCLAINC. 74204	
	15/3/18		Men viewed quiet places in the wood and the later showed signs of fatigue.	
	17/3/18		27 & 134 Bty[er]s sent 1 Officer & 420 R. other ranks per Bty to work in reinforced position to these [illegible] The work consisted of making dug-outs.	
	19/3/18		4H19.a. recce for a counter attack, the counter attacks Battn's were B.Cs & Batt Commanders acted to inform H.Q.Ds of the 75.131 & R.F.A. Guard SWA [illegible] a group of taking men & showing him the situation v likely position, in case	
	20/3/18		H.23. toilets the N[ew] positions were H.15.7. H.21.7. H.22.a and having 21/23 advanced sections in H.17.d H.20.a v H.22.3. Relief was ordered to the night 20/21	
	21/3/18		Enemy heavy bombardment commenced about 6.30 am on front of MONCHY along the 3rd Divisional. 2 Brigade received orders at 7.30am to join in to go into Action at 10.30 am under arrangements of the Group H.Q. Q.D.O. Batt's to the Rear of B.H.Q and the relief of the places with the Rear Brigade was completed at 9pm.	

WAR DIARY
or
INTELLIGENCE SUMMARY
(Erase heading not required.)

Army Form C. 2118.

Place	Date	Hour	Summary of Events and Information	Remarks and references to Appendices
	22.3.18		The enemy heavily shelled the our around behind, finishing track & road throughout the day. Our Artillery replied with vigorous harassing fire. Orders were issued at 1.15pm to withdraw 13th & 16th Batteries.	57.B NW & SW
	23.3.18		Infantry withdrew thro' lines posn of the Scarpe to the Second Polin. evacuating MONCHY to PREUX. During the night our artillery gun's shelled the numerous enemy concentrations. An attack was repulsed at dawn. Enemy heavily bombarded French breastworks on our front between 1.30am & 8am. By 8am the infantry & Cavalry were being pushed back through our trenches. During enemy renewed a attack engaged by our artillery at 6.30pm HEAVY BOMBARDMENT with Scarpe Valley & Vaux about 1hour was kept down along the outer edge of MONCHY-LE-PREUX & the Scarpe Valley.	
	24.3.18		Very severe shelling on Polin Scarpe. Enemy attacked TRIANGLE POSN on Polin Scarpe. BATTERY VALLEY & Nr SCARPE VALLEY Enemy shelled at 9am with vigorous Polin BATTLE TRIANGLE. H19. Battery shelled during the day, most of Battery waggon lines at ANZIN shelled with an 11gun. Our attr Polin killed 12 horses & wounded 15.	
	25.3.18		Our Artillery bombarded enemy front lines from 1am to 5.30am. Enemy anxiously action flying very low over our trenches. By 7.30pm attacking artillery to 1126 — 135 Battery to BATTERY L BAM & 76 Battery to SPIDER breastworks H208. All were concentrated by 10am. A heavy attack expected at dawn.	
	26.3.18		Light Engt except in harassing fire. Our artillery bombarded enemy lines from 5am to 5.30am. Enemy very quiet. No shelling except to destroy the enemy to rear Valley etc. aircraft very but active.	
	27.3.18		5.30 Enemy shelled our lines from BPN & direction of OPPY, got well up North H. the 1st Battalion Relieved at the Chinese at 11.15am. I received instruction to prepare Bays Night Posn	

WAR DIARY
or
INTELLIGENCE SUMMARY

Army Form C. 2118

Place	Date	Hour	Summary of Events and Information	Remarks and references to Appendices
	28.3.18	3 a.m.	A very heavy bombardment was first down by the enemy extending from ORPY, southwards, along the whole front. Practically every battery whether positions were heavily shelled with gas shell & H.E. All roads, bridges, communication trench were recipients of gaseous shells attention. Bois. du. Biez in particular. Though the H.Q.s. were heavily shelled. At 4.30 a.m. communication from H.Q.s. with Bns. Cut owing to the intense hostile barrage. Each battery in its own sphere fire on S.O.S. lines. their shelling lasted for 4 hours during which time the 86 Battery had the camouflage of the S.O.S. Gun pit set on fire and about 1500 charges destroyed & shells fire, & 135 Battery was under continual shellfire from a hostile 8" super battery, the 87 Battery sitting it out actually shelled to our support. Very little returned fire by the Railway Bridge on Head of the 87 Battery was fairly neutralised. Below 5.25 a.m. & 8.15 a.m. Bmbrs Lewis, Peters & Fowler, 5.9 4.2 Howitzer battery. At 5.15 a.m. 2nd Lt. RICHARDSON, N.C. & O.R. of the 86 Battery were killed and at 6.45 a.m. 2/Lt SCOTT 1/Lt 735 Battery wounded. At 9 a.m. the shelling by the enemy decreased in intensity undoubted, about commenced it having on our right — held the line from MOMMY to CAMBRAI. It was fired back in rather until the 8 light Manch of 108 Infantry Bgd. to rather slight. Artillery in our confusion with too held that of the line from A.23.3.b.b.10. North of the CORPS three retiring to position & our Infantry of EMERTEFFRIES, who were on rearward of two Batt.Jack guns 105 Band great steady revitalitation. At 7.30 a.m. He received warning of the enemy advancing (assisted) on trenches. 7.45 a.m. the detached N.C.O. got the gun into action, and fired but the rifle on the other. N.C.O. got the gun into action and fired but the rifle on the garden — I am being told 13 wounded, H himself worked by the enemy advancing, enemy this strong and eventin. About 10 a.m. as the enemy ground to advancing enemy this strong great eventin. About 10 a.m. as the enemy ground to Capt. N. The SHIPLEY withdrew to destroyed his gun withdrew his self-fund works, his gun which was an H.18 in form of the Channel work & proceeded to	578 SW N.W.

WAR DIARY
or
INTELLIGENCE SUMMARY.

(Erase heading not required.)

Army Form C. 2118.

Place	Date	Hour	Summary of Events and Information	Remarks and references to Appendices
	28.3.18 (cont)		his Lewis gun in H.18 - South of the Railway, when he found the enemy had advanced to within 100 yards of it. Being unable to shift it he took away the breech block, & buried them, & returned to H.19a with valuable information. At Map 134-135 was Coln were about to relieve the two platoons in H.19a. Before this was carried out orders were issued to the above parties to hold fast in their position, & H.19a was to be occupied by the infantry were falling back to this position. At 1.30 p.m. the infantry were leaving the infantry were holding the Army line retook to the bottom of Gya. At 6.15 p.m. the 70th infantry Brigade counter attack along the Railway & succeeded in forcing the enemy back to a distance of 500 yards. About 1000 hardened gradually about 7pm and was later not too heavily shelled throughout the retirement, but as yet saw shelled throughout the night. A good deal of machine gun the enemy were several slowly. Enemy attack chiefly on the right. Our retreat was cut during the preliminary bombardment. He remained to the Brigade in addition to those already sustained were four wounded. 2nd P/King-Mill wounded. 2nd Lt killed 16 wounded & 4 gun damage to get for. The Bn was withdrawn to the retirement Night Guard Lay among party exist Ben City Broclund from at one point wounded O.R. MRP Rank I killed.	078 W/446 Gus
	29.3.18		Enemy approached de Legendery . Ben arty engaged enemy on Orange Hill 24.184 advance to a portion in pp9 on gp o. 2nd Lts J.H.B.E to a portion in H.19a at 4.30pm. Day & night normal shells, enemy was again engaged by our artillery. MRPP.	
	30.3.18			
	31.3.18		Lewis shelled further. Ruthenium portion recomforted to GSOO. MRPR	

4th Divisional Artillery.

32nd BRIGADE R. F. A.

APRIL 1918.

WAR DIARY or INTELLIGENCE SUMMARY

Army Form C. 2118.

32nd Brigade R.H.A.

FRANCE

Place	Date	Hour	Summary of Events and Information	Remarks and references to Appendices
April 1st	1st		Throughout the day hostile artillery was quiet. Our artillery engaged movement north of SCARPE. Orders received that 32 Bde. was to move from field by MR of 1 Bde (N.W. of SCARPE to H.11.d.19.29) This necessitated all batteries moving forward. Postns. reconnoitred. H.11d 19.29. Orders for forward posn for 86 Battery & HQs were noted to postns H.18.3 90.45 & G.14.5 60.50 respectively.	
	2nd		Day & night quiet.	
			Move reported to above completed. 134 battery to H.4.d 60.55 + 135 battery to H.4.a 45.19. On section of 86 Battery advanced to H.18.5 70.30. It was completed. On enemy bombarded posns N & S of H.155 Battery + D of 86 Bryn without hindrance.	
	3rd		Reconnord. positns to 135 Battery & D of 86 Bryn & 82 Battery HQ.	
			Morning quiet. During the afternoon enemy systematically bombarded our Lus N.Y.L. (approx) especially PUDDING TRENCH. Our battery replied and engaged hostile incoming. Colors issued at 4.30pm to batteries to prepare to withstand a hostile attack at dawn.	
	4th		Morning quiet. Enemy movement in DEFENCE HILL engaged with MG's and counteracted. During the night harassing fire was carried on. Enemy approaches communications. Enemy shelled our front system of the Scarp. Enemy shelled the town and outskirts of town. No. for enemy approaches counter of MG harassing fire. Hostile fire was our artillery for throughout the day.	
	5th		Very quiet day & night. Orders received at 6pm that 32 Bde Bryat CYA was to relieve 32 Bde on the 9/6. Postns were reconnoitred up to the Bde Commander & 134 Bde CYA and this battery commanders. During night 9pm. Enemy shelled back areas lightly. The Bryad. had been relieved by 1/71st Bryad.	
	6th		Getting quiet. At 2am the Bryad had been relieved by 1/71st Bryad. Passing batted over guns at 8a. Bryn less moved during the morning to the GOVES and MONTENESCOURT (about 30 yards day R(R.N.R.) place). New Lus were dug in. Night posn & later officers mess, during the night a new flag in stables. Shelled 134 battery Mess-Sigs. about 16 shells arrived during night. Enemy RNG 45.19

Army Form C. 2118.

WAR DIARY
or
INTELLIGENCE SUMMARY.
(Erase heading not required.)

Place	Date	Hour	Summary of Events and Information	Remarks and references to Appendices
April	10th		Brigade & Battery Commanders reconnoitred positions just south of the CITADEL ARRAS to be positions of observation to cover the reserve line of ARRAS – (BLANGY sector). Positions were found in G.25 & 26 north of Ors at the CITADEL. Orders received at 12 noon by 2nd in Command to the effect that these positions had to be occupied with dumps for gun at each position by 2nd in Command. This was completed by 6pm. Guns remained at GOUVES & MONTENESCOURT.	FRANCE ARRAS. 57C N.E. 1/40,000
	11th		At 10am the Brigade came under the orders of the 15th Div. An OP was established in G.30.B. and Liaison Officer sent to 45th Inf. Brigade and to the Left Bde in the line. All communications were excellent as the Bns. through the tunnel caves of ARRAS & BLANGY. The guns of our line were laid at so as to cover the whole of the 15th Div. front which extended astride the CAMBRAI Road.	
	12th/17th 18		Brigade remained in position of observation. At 11.30am orders were received to the effect that the Brigade would proceed to be withdrawn to its wagon lines in the afternoon. This was confirmed at 12.30pm. All Batteries & H.Q.s arrived at their wagon lines at about 7pm when orders were received for the move to be continued to BRUAY. The march was commenced from wagon lines to BRUAY (1st Corps area) at 4.30pm, and arrived at 9am 19th inst. Horses were in fields & men in bivouacs.	LENS II. 1/40,000
	19th 20th		Remained in BRUAY awaiting further instructions. Our section for taking Relief on receiving the taking of the 251st Bde which was at the Divisional Infantry at LANNOY.	
	21st		Advance Section & MC.Qrs. covering the Divisional Infantry at LANNOY. Advance Section & MC.Qrs. completed the relief by 12 noon. The Relief was carried out without hindrance and the march was very quiet.	FRANCE 56 a S.E. 1/20,000

WAR DIARY or INTELLIGENCE SUMMARY

Army Form C. 2118.

Place	Date	Hour	Summary of Events and Information	Remarks and references to Appendices
Ofret	22		The Brigade supported an attack by the 11th Infantry Brigade from LA PANNERIE through PACAUT WOOD to original front line & just South of RIEZ-du-VINAGE. Zero hour was at 4.30am and the attack complete success. Batteries put down a creeping barrage of 30 minutes duration. The whole shelling in establishing Africa was all carried out from front & support areas - none of the batteries lay quiet. Our artillery harassed PACAUT WOOD and tracks leading to it.	FRANCE 36a SE 1 20·0·0
	23rd		2nd Battery of the Brigade assisted in supporting an attack by the 12th Inf. Bde to front of RIEZ-du-VINAGE. This again was successful. During the day enemy shelled the back areas around LANNOY with close attention for gun pits 4.2 & 5.9 cm shells.	
	24th		Our Artillery carried on day and night firing on enemy defences.	
	25th		Day normal. Our Batteries engaged various targets observed from OPs at BERNANCHON & HINGES ridge. Several direct hits on houses were obtained and the enemy shelling and engaged with success. 88th Battery were ordered to position 40 V.12.c.B.40. Very shelling heavily from 9 pm to 10 pm. Took a battery of 4.2 cm shells. Enemy artillery active along the OMMAL canal and back areas re LANNOY & CONNIEHEM. Our artillery continued to harass the enemy backs, roads & buildings.	
	26th		OPs moved to W.1.a.08.00. and the 89th Battery to V.12.c.90.40 where it was heavily shelled on arrival and throughout the night. Casualties were inflicted before the battery tired fire. The 87th & 88th observed all of this area and came under the orders of 22 Bde. In last was made the Right Group.	
	27th		134 a 135 v 86 Battery exchanged positions with A B & D batteries of the 281st Bde at V.12.b.90.70 - V.6.d.20.35 - V.5.d.20.15 respectively. Hostile artillery retaliation to our artillery continued it harassing fire.	

WAR DIARY
or
INTELLIGENCE SUMMARY.
(Erase heading not required.)

Army Form C. 2118.

Place	Date	Hour	Summary of Events and Information	Remarks and references to Appendices
April 9	28th		Day and night very quiet. Approach around GONNEHEM district of the Aumbay fire. Recce patrols around LA VALLEE & tracks to them reconnoitring By Battery moved me section to V12c.80.10 & So Battery one section to V12c.90.60. These two sections were included to do day and night firing for the Brigade - the other position was to be kept silent.	FRANCE 36a SE 1 20000
	29th		Harassing fire carried out on houses believed in Brigade Zone. Both artillery normal.	
	30		Nothing to report day and night quiet.	
			During the month the Brigade casualties were slight both in men & horses. The conditions under which personnel & horses had was varied considerably whilst in action in the AREAS the majority of dug outs were good, which in "position of observation" men & officers lived in houses just in rear of their positions. When the Brigade went in action for the LAWNOY area the guns were in hedges & under trees with the detachments in farm buildings in rear. Whilst during the month living in the open and were in very good condition. Reinforcements and turnouts posted to the Brigade were far inferior to those received during the previous month.	
			Decorations received :- 2nd Lieut E. H. JEFFRIES By Batty M.C.	
			Sergt. S. MOLSWORTHY 185 - " M.M.	
			No 740 " DAVIS 86 " M.M.	
			No 96132 L J. FERRIS 27 " M.M.	
			No 108172 Dr C. PROCTOR 86 " M.M.	
			No 181086 Gr E COOPER 134 " M.M.	
			No 69185 Bomb A ALLEN 135 " M.M.	
			No 42265 Cpl D GUNMARTIN 82 " Bar to M.M.	
			" " E LONGBOTTOM 86 " M.M.	

Steele Capt
for Lt Col 32 Bde R.F.A.
2/5/18

Army Form C. 2118.

WAR DIARY
or
INTELLIGENCE SUMMARY.
(Erase heading not required.)

32nd Brigade R.F.A.   No 38

Instructions regarding War Diaries and Intelligence Summaries are contained in F. S. Regs., Part II. and the Staff Manual respectively. Title pages will be prepared in manuscript.

Place	Date	Hour	Summary of Events and Information	Remarks and references to Appendices
In the field	May 1st		A very normal day. Our artillery carried out harassing fire concentrations on enemies lines with enemy replied feebly by harassing our lines occasionally.	FRANCE Sheet 36 c SE 1/20000
	May 2nd		Orders received that the 6th & 7th DJA were coming up to reinforce the Brigade Commanders Group & his Battery Commanders reconnoitered positions in VIV VIA in CENSE la VALLÉE. On coming into action they were to come under 32nd 133rd RFA for tactical purposes.	
	May 3rd		Nothing of any note. Galleys of 32nd & 36th RFA came into action during the enemy 32nd 133rd RFA heavily shelled by 77th during the enemy 134th 135th Batteries suffering slight damage. No casualties. Enemy action with his artillery & aeroplanes throughout day & night.	
	May 4th		Remaining Batteries & HQrs of 34th 36th RFA came into action. 32nd HQrs shelled & hit during the day. Shells falling also around the 134th 135th Batteries during the evening. Continued harassing fire day & night. Shelt of M. ENIN BANK occur.	
	May 5th		Many registering & counter-batteries during the night. Very shortly sent by FM field artillery if any aeroplane. Our artillery harassed Haven occupied Shed held by enemy in front of SHONE wood.	
	May 6th		Harassing normal. During the afternoon 2nd Lt Baly was hardly wounded with pieces of bullet & 2nd Lt McBrink was wounded. Enemy flying aircraft very active over valley position in consequence of which our men reel very active. At about 11h a heavy gas concentration was deposited in GROVE HUT.	
	May 7th		Day normal. An attack in depth was expected on the early morning. Our usual nightly concentrations was carried out on the known dispositions & concentrations in the forward area.	
	May 8th		A good deal of the day shelling in our V12 & V18 through the day. Our artillery shelled Sun Pa & called NE-A slight attack developed & shortly the flying & right through their flank retreated. Our artillery opened out opposite eight pains. Flying cE = p & 6 hrs. Some active. Shells with gas shells from right flank forced us to retire to be places of concern in a hostile attack.	

Army Form C. 2118.

WAR DIARY
or
INTELLIGENCE SUMMARY.
(Erase heading not required.)

Instructions regarding War Diaries and Intelligence Summaries are contained in F. S. Regs., Part II. and the Staff Manual respectively. Title pages will be prepared in manuscript.

Place	Date	Hour	Summary of Events and Information	Remarks and references to Appendices
In the field	May 10		Normal everyday with but possibly heavy the afternoon. There was an increase in hostile artillery activity in our V.3 + V.6 + V.12.C. Our batteries were mostly used to harass hostile batteries being up along our front. Lt. N.5ffr 13th Battery Nitr in V.12.C.50.30 was subjected to a gas bombardment lasting about 3 hours. Lt. Horgan + 3 ORs was slightly gassed. Aerial activity also normal in the flying weather.	France Sheet 36c S.E. 1/20000
	May 11		During the afternoon 13th Battery was position (V.12.B.95.45) was heavily shelled, personnel withdrew as guns was badly damaged + left 2 other was injured not of action. This Bty was carried out with hostile batteries. An order during the night forced out vigorous night fire.	
	May 12 May 13		CANAL BANK + HINGE'S were heavily shelled during the days + night. Our harass batteries were engaged by the enemy whilst hostile harassed front towards + Villa carried this vigorous night firing contained throughout Day both relation in the forward area. The Off Legal was short up by the enemy on the OP line and whilst the attacks was shut on battery from at present on the OP line. The OP was done at 11:45 pm and firing continued until 12 m. Rest of the night was dont.	
	May 14		Enemy aircraft active. GONNEHEM sheld throughout the day.	
	May 15 May 16		Normal. At 6:30 + 9:35 engaged enemy the day by our artillery with effect. A great deal of firing was carried out by the enemy + our artillery during the night.	
	May 18		Forward area suffered very little shelling. Our crew at Pont de Remembery wounded.	
	May 19		BURNETT Shelled with a long 50.15 gun. Nothing to report. 2/Lt BARROW joined 13th Battery from 4 DAC.	

WAR DIARY
or
INTELLIGENCE SUMMARY.

Army Form C. 2118.

Place	Date	Hour	Summary of Events and Information	Remarks and references to Appendices
In the field	May 19		All units of the Right Group were detailed during the afternoon. At 9pm a hostile bombing party was observed. VERTBOIS FARM was fired on and dispersed by an M. Battery. Dover Trench Mr. Sh. 36a during 6 in 9.8 7.30pm. M. BERANCHEN was also subjected to heavy shelling. SOS S/A commenced.	France Sh.36a Ref 1/20000
	May 20		Day very quiet. Relief of 6 in S.A.P. completed. The 206 Brigade relieved the 306 Brigade & came under the orders of 33 Brigade. During the night HINGES & our O.P. & Q. Bank shelled with gas shell. 3 Lieut. J.R. PINNETT being slight CP Officer in 706 S. 9.8 was gassed & evacuated.	
	May 21/22		Day quiet except for desultory shelling along the CANAL BANK & DROUVIN WOOD line activity continued as previous day.	
	May 23		H.Os shelling in the early morning with gas shell. GONNEHEM suspected of a very concentrated kind of gas shell. Our S/B balloon harassed our guns seen to be as this commenced a systematic destruction of all houses within this range.	
	May 24/25		Absolutely quiet. Own aeroplanes very active photographing. Gas was projected into DROUVIN WOOD during the night.	
	May 26		Enemy Relief took his battery & aircraft V5 & V6 suffered heavily during the night our battery carried out concentrations of fire tasks & quiet appeared then to.	
	May 27		Very very quiet. Sudden holds alternate bonds of about a day which considerably hindered our shooting. During the night the artillery cooperated with the Divis to Divisy. Day normal, no ideas around DROUVIN VILLAGE & CORNET MALO.	
	May 28		Day normal.	
	May 29		Enemy harassed back area the CANTRAINNE area largely larger lines, CENSE LA WALLEE. fired and very quiet. Aircraft of both sides active during day & night. Enemy night foot firing about normal, along the HINGES EDGE & along HARASSR. An about firm fell close to or out of a prop to DROUVIN WOOD shot was spoken.	
	May 30		Harassing quiet except for aeroplanes taking about byes. During the afternoon enemy aircraft appeared very active & flying low over back areas in the evening several artillery appeared in intense activity & 6.30pm HINGES was shelled for 3 hrs 4 pm F L area this. Harassed ballt defensive thought the night.	

Army Form C. 2118.

WAR DIARY
or
INTELLIGENCE SUMMARY.
(Erase heading not required.)

Place	Date	Hour	Summary of Events and Information	Remarks and references to Appendices
	May 31st		At 8.30 a.m. the scouts arrived before O.Pip. No further enemy advance. General balance of GONNEHEM falling practically the whole day. The Battery was in action in CAMPAGNE St with 82nd M.Gun covering the Evacuation of Locon (lightly wounded) to the line covered. Summary of the Month. Our casualties for the month were rough but good although they was at first very little guilt-fired pistols they had simply to avoid heavy & lifeness. Casualties as regards were booked by the aid of the tanks. The general health & spirit of the personnel of the Brigade was very good thanks and even with so great heat of fighting then general condition was better than had been in a long while. The casualties during the month were very small covering to belt. actually I cannot accounts for. A few wounded & passed through the Brigade which was to help deep & [illeg]. and passed through by the Drs, the majority of different diversion & man R.G.A. [illeg]. The type of General wound record caused	Home (Mister) [illeg] DR [illeg] (1) [illeg]

[signature] Capt.
Capt 20 Bde R.F.A. M.H.Qs
1-6-18

Army Form C. 2118.

VA Army 37

WAR DIARY
INTELLIGENCE SUMMARY
(Erase heading not required.)

32nd BRIGADE, R.F.A.

JUNE 1918.

Instructions regarding War Diaries and Intelligence Summaries are contained in F. S. Regs. Part II. and the Staff Manual respectively. Title pages will be prepared in manuscript.

Place	Date	Hour	Summary of Events and Information	Remarks and references to Appendices
BELLERIVE	1918 June 1		Hostile Arty. HINGES and trackways shelled. Canal bank W.16.c and a W.7.a.o.o.o and GONNEHEM shelled. Some Blue Cross Gas. Our Arty. T.M's and M.G's in Q.35.a.6.7. shelled. Heavy Q.5.5.6. of front on harassing bursts and approach Q.32.A. batteries fired on buildings 28.D and in Q.34.c.d. Harassing fire at night. Heavies shelled known Q.32.b. enemy Q.3.a.4. and battery positions round PARADIS.	Refer Map 1/20,000 Sheet 36.a S.E.
	2		2/Lieut H.P. de LOOZE 56th Battery was wounded. HINGES, Pond at HINGES W.4.C, W.3.d.46, W.4.c.34 shelled. E.A. very active. Our batteries harassed at night. Some Gas shell. Our batteries harassed at night Q.29.a.b.c Q.35.a.29.C. Hours fixed B.N.C.	
	3		Hostile Arty. Shelled HINGES, Les HARISOIRS, W.8.a, W.9.B. (concentration) shelled with Blue Cross. Instructions shoots carried out and Hoer Batteries engaged losing Q.3.d.4.o.9.o Harassing fire at night on Q.32.b. Our batteries shelled Q.11.a. Result houses burning and ammunition dump blown up. German wire cut ahead at LA PANNERIE Rd. Q.4.q.q.o.q.o.	
	4		Hostile Arty. slight. Harassing fire at night on back areas. 13u Wagon line shelled, 2 men injured. Our Arty engaged houses in Q.34.d and also registered at night hostile shoot Q.34.b.c.	
	5		Hostile fire inactive. Battery on bearing 36° from O.P. (W.9.b.5.6.) spotted. Heavies call on recruits effective. Our Arty. fired on Q.29.d.2.0.80. and Q.35.b.0.20. E.A. inactive. Our Arty. barraged line Q.26.0.1. O 27 d.6.4. 256 Bde were relieved by 504 Bde A.F.A. and came under command of 32 Bde forming Right Group 1st Divisional Artillery	
	6		Hostile Arty. E.A. active. Heavy fired Gas shell on PACAUT WOOD. HINGES shelled. lifting 100 yards every minute to line Q.28.b.y - Q.22.d.35.15. Harassing fire at night Q.3.a.4.d. Q.27.x. 21.d. 22.c.d. 29.d. 30.c. and 36.a. Heavy fired Gas shell on PACAUT WOOD.	
	7		Hostile Arty. HINGES shelled at irregular intervals. O.P. shelled. Heavies retaliated with a concentration. Hostile Batton in Q.11 a firing gas shell. My teach man spotted reported to Heavies who engaged it. Cawing 2 explosions. Some saddles distributed fire during night before normal. Our Art. harassed LE VERTOIL FARM W4. 29.a. 35.d. 36.a. Hours fired B.N.C.	

WAR DIARY or INTELLIGENCE SUMMARY

32nd BDE R.F.A.

Army Form C. 2118.

Place	Date	Hour	Summary of Events and Information	Remarks and references to Appendices
BELLERIVE	June 8		Hostile Arty quiet apparently. Our Arty harassed Q.34.d. 35.a. 34.b. Hostile fired called on enemy Q.34.d.70.85 and Q.29.b.	Refer to Map 1/20,000 Sheet 36.a S.E.
		11.24 p.m.	Heavy enemy bombardment left of Brigade Zone. Heavy shelling of our front. S.O.S. sent up on left	
		11.30 pm to 12 MN	Regt. greatly fired on S.O.S. lines at slow rate	
	9		Hostile inactive and very quiet.	
			Our Arty fired on harrage lines Q.28.c.60-W.5.d.39 lifting 100 yds every minute to L.c.a.3.6.a.21 - B.36.c.9.50. Harassing	
			Hostaressed at night Q.34.a.6.c.d. 33.b. 34a. 29.c.	
	10		Hostile Arty below normal, at night harassed le CAUROY, HINGES and Les HARISOIRS. (Gas and H.E)	
			Our Arty Q.29.a. 22.b. 23.c.d. 29.d.	
	11		Hostile Arty very quiet. At night intermittent fire	
			Our Arty during day harassed PACAUT WOOD and shelled farm Q.29.a.10.40. At night harassed Q.29.a.9.c.	
	12		Hostile Arty carried out registration on HATE FARM, Les HARISOIRS. Vaccubie W.3.c to W.9.b. HINGES at night. harassed HINGES and also used gas shells.	
			Our Arty. Heavy fires on houses Q.34.b.6.c and at night harassed Q.33.b. 34.a. 28.c. 33.b. 34a and 86c. Howitzers did very careful shoot on houses in Q.34 Central. Houses in Q.34.d.45.80 hit and direct	
			M.G.S.A.A. 4% bodied. Four houses were burnt and 7 explosions caused. 106 fires showed very effective	
	13		Hostile Arty quiet. Harassed le CAUROY and le VERTANNOY	
			Our Arty harassed Q.33.a.b.d. 28.c. 34.a.b.c.d.	
	14		Hostile Arty inactive. Canal Bank W.4.c.1. W.5.b shelled at 10.35. From Monument Gervaeux rau froui farm Q.24.a.5.4. to Q.24.a.5.6 during shoot of howies on Q.24.a. Several fires in CORNET MALO PACAUT and PARADIS	
		11.45 a.m.	In support of the attack by the 3rd Division on our right this Brigade fired down a creeping barrage in Q.34.d and Q.35.c. Lifts were made till zero + 32 when the guns remained on the Protection Barrage from Hartle zero + hour creeping barrage were put on at intervals beginning from the Protection Barrage and lifting leg. 100 yds to 800x, the last except moved towards the North. The Howies kept harage and lifting leg. 100 yds to zero + 32 mins and then engaged targets likely to shelter troops on	

Army Form C. 2118.

WAR DIARY
or
INTELLIGENCE SUMMARY.
(Erase heading not required.)

JUNE 1916   32nd BDE R.F.A.

Instructions regarding War Diaries and Intelligence Summaries are contained in F. S. Regs., Part II and the Staff Manual respectively. Title pages will be prepared in manuscript.

Place	Date	Hour	Summary of Events and Information	Remarks and references to Appendices
BELLERIVE	1916 June 14/15		Hour in above given. At 11.45 a.m. when having barrage came down a great number of coloured lights went up and evening reply started it immediately afterwards on the CANAL but was very scattered. Our subsequent bursts of fire from zero + 32 mins to zero + 4 mins were answered by scattered shelling of CANAL HINGES and vicinity of OP W9 b 56. At 5 a.m. the situation was normal. Parties of our Infantry were seen at Minned House at Q3 a d 8.3 and standing E. and W. apparently digging in. Subsequently we hear was from BOURKES FARM through Q3 a d 2.7 to Q3 a d 46.25.	Refer Map 1/20,000 Sheet 36 a S.E.
	15		Hostile Arty intermittent shelling during day on CANAL BANK and HINGES to TANNERIE Rd. Our Arty engaged in harassing fire performed system and at 7 p.m. our batteries co-operated in bombardment of Q3 c 60.30 when there was a TRENCH MORTAR. Enemy Very lights Q3 b 6.6 and Q3 d 2.3 and 3.5.	
	16		Hostile Arty active on battery area and on Road V6c - especially ranging during night CANAL BANK HINGES heavily shelled. Enemies estab. house Q25 c 9.1.5. burst in AVENTAN set on fire. Our arty harassed Q29 a c d 35.6 - 50 rounds RNC.	
	17		Hostile Arty shelled V16. Located at Q7 c 80.72. Our Howitzers silenced this battery firing. Rather more active during night CANAL BANK (W5 6-M4C) LES HARISARS heavily shelled at intervals. E.A. active flying but battery harassed rifles on PACAUT WOOD Q25c and N5 a and burns in Q25 a d, PACAUT and BOHEME rolls.	
	18		Hostile Arty deliberate mostly in forward areas at night CANAL BANK and HINGES harassed regions Q29, Q29. Our Arty harassed Q25 d and 3 u a Q3 ab cd and 35a. Our Howitzers active on PARADIS 3 fires in N26.	
	19	8 a.m.	Hostile Arty very quiet. Our Arty harassed Q35 b 29 b.d. 35 a 30c. 36 b 2c + d - 50 RNC A and C Batteries of 104 Bde AFA were transferred to 106 Bde our right. 104 D + B transferred under command of Right Group. Left Group transferred from Left Group to Right Group. S.O.S. Lines were altered.	
	20		Hostile Arty quiet during day single rounds at long intervals. Our Arty harassed Q3 a b d 29 a b e and Hachs Q28 a b c d. Large fire caused by burns in Q23 during night by Howitzer 6.15 p.m. (arty.2) 1 large fire caused at the PINETTE.	
	21 and 22		Hostile Arty very quiet decrease at night settled. Our Arty Q29 cc 36 a 35 b Q29 b, Q29 c 36 b 36 c, 29 d c Our Howitzers fired by FORWARD OBSERVATION Officers caused fire PINETTE. Work will be liable to Q3 w a	

WAR DIARY
or
INTELLIGENCE SUMMARY

(Erase heading not required.)

32nd BDE. R.F.A.

JUNE 1918

Army Form C. 2118.

Instructions regarding War Diaries and Intelligence Summaries are contained in F.S. Regs., Part II. and the Staff Manual respectively. Title pages will be prepared in manuscript.

Place	Date	Hour	Summary of Events and Information	Remarks and references to Appendices
BELLERIVE	1918 June 22		The Wagon lines were moved to BOURECQ and the Limber lines to the previous Wagon Lines in CANTRAINE. The Head Quarters Wagon Line was moved to 27th Luther Line in CANTRAINE.	Refs. Map 1/20,000 Sheet 36 A. S.E.
	23-24		Hostile Arty. inactive. Loc. HARISOIRS, CANAL BANK, and GORDON LINE HINGES, and O.P. registered. Our Arty. Instructional Shoots harassing fire and EA on (Q36.a.29 & c.85) shell hole (B34 D-A55c and B5a 0070. CORNET MALO Q29 a.c. BNC on (Q29a.3c.15, and 7500. Ammunition dump (Q34d.1665 x/c sof sur harass Sercoux area, hour (Q34C7065-Q34A.5525), Q18d.0070-5025). EA active our our front system at 10 pm (Z34) and CRESSEUR. on 24th hours fired on houses in Q34 b.d. 2/Lieut. L.T. WEBBER rejoined 135th Battery from Hospital.	
	25.26		Hostile Arty. below normal but harassing fire at night HINGES, CANAL BANK and LOO HARISOIRS. Our Arty. Instructional shoots and harassing fire at night on Q29.d (with BNC) 29 b, Ride in PACAUT WOOD and loc HARISOIRS. Our Arty. Instructional shoots (with BNC) 34 a EDGE of PACAUT WOOD W34 a 64c. Tracks in Q28 c.6 33.6 34 at.	
	27		Capt. E.P. CREAGH, R.A.M.C. MO fo bigade was accidentally injured. 36th Hostile Arty quiet. Ben vigorously harassed at night CANAL W4C Road W8C at Rookery Crossing and loc HARISOIRS. Our Arty Instructional shoots and engaged moving humo Q29 C1030 shell holes in G85 a and 29 b c, Ride in PACAUT WOOD and edge of wood 27 c d 96005. 50 BNe on Q2.9 and 23 d	
	28		2/Lt X McGERSIGNEY 135th Battery, worewed Diet at O.P. Hostile Arty quiet. Harassing fire on roads and track. 136 Battery shelled with gas one casualty. Our Arty Batteries fired a few rounds on SOS line. Instructional Shots. PACAUT WOOD Q83f 24a and Q30 c and Gas on Q30e. PACAUT WOOD Q83f 29a and 28c also engaged.	
	29-30		Hostile Arty, inactive. Ranged on Y6 d. X6. W6 v. Sixgus. followed by two MG H.E. harassin Battery frming from 19th hour O.P. (W.9.6.5.6). HINGES and W 9.6. (1·35Sz) shelled during night) a few losing g & shells Our Arty Registration, calibration and instructional shoots and harassing fire on Q82 b.30 a 28 c.d. 35.a.b 29 a.b.e.d 30 7d BNe on Q 30 a. 40.25. Vigorous Barrage on PACAUT L'EPINETTE, QUENTIN and CORNET MALO with good effect. Fire and large Enemy M.G. behind CORNET MALO and at LE CORNET VAN LOUPS. area fire in Q25 a Central.	

WAR DIARY or INTELLIGENCE SUMMARY

Army Form C. 2118.

32nd Bde R.F.A.

JUNE 1918

Summary of Events and Information

During the month gun batteries have been engaged in instructional shoots and registration and calibration by day, while the 86th I.F. Howrs did considerable damage to houses along the HINGES Road on the edge of PACAUT WOOD in (A.38.b. and 28.d. and also at A.34.a. 35. Hostile M.G. centres of activity was also shelled. At night concentrations were carried out, especially in the area shown in conjunction with the Infantry. M.G. bdes, centres of activity, houses, PACAUT WOOD, were harassed nightly, and when the wind was favourable, gas was frequently used. On the 14/15th hostiles put down a vicious barrage in support of the 3rd Division stunt, two and on the night of the 5th our S.O.S. signal went up, and our batteries fired on S.O.S. lines observed. Our batteries were slightly shelled on two occasions, and the 130th Battery wagon line had casualties to horses with hostile shelling. The casualties to personnel were slight (1) to horses rather frequently called on when enemy guns were spotted and the neutralization was effective. The batteries were very successful in putting up dumps and carrying fires. The hostile artillery was comparatively quiet, they had no out situation to our guns and wks. However, enemy concentrations routines shoots, last situations and creatures seated fire and occasionally, single rounds at intervals. There was also a good deal of registration. Their various places were engaged and lately were not causing their irritation as never ensure. After the situation on 10/11/15 the situation was very settled and no movement of May observed considerable movement. The bounds has been waiting well into fireside in addition to taking up to his S.O.S. line.

The conditions of living owing to the good weather have been very good. The health of the troops has been very good, but a scattering of the usually has been the outbreak of 3 day fever, about one eighth of the Brigade having gone sick with it.

The horses and in good conditions and the wagon-lines at CANTRAINE were very good. The Remounts are a good lot, and the reinforcements of horses have been mostly very old, I have few extra seek to do for average.

Major W.B. MACKIE rejoined 8 June, being out Major C.F. MACKAY lately 130th Battery proceeded M.C. very good, but a scatter of the night has been the outbreak of 3 day fever. Lt TALBOT was the same D.C.M. and the R.E. TTON 2 pok Bty received the D.C.M. R.F.A.

H. Bound a 32nd Bde R.F.A.

WAR DIARY.

32nd. Brigade, R.F.A.

July, 1918.

Army Form C. 2118.

WAR DIARY
or
INTELLIGENCE SUMMARY.
(Erase heading not required.)

32nd Bde R.F.A.

JULY 1918

Place	Date	Hour	Summary of Events and Information	Remarks and references to Appendices
BELLER IVE	1918 July 1.	1.	Hostile Arty. Quiet vigorous harassing fire bought. Large Hows probably 8 in. firing on L'ECLEME from R.y.c. 65.80. 11 p.m. CANAL BANK, LES HARISOIRS and Mt BERNENCHON were shelled with 105 and 150 mm. HINGES GONNEHEM and V6d also shelled between 6.30 and 10.30 p.m. E.A. very active over PARAUT WOOD	Reference Map 1/20,000 36 SE.
			Our Arty. Some 8 in engaged by our batteries with good result. Large dump exploded. Our 6pdrs and 4.5 Hows shelled tracks O.28e.9 and targets Q.27d and shellholes Q.34a, Q.29a.s.e. also engaged. Hows fired bursts of gas on O.29a, Q.30a and O.29.C.6. Instructional shoot carried out.	
			On 27th June both 2nd Lt S. CAMPBELL M.C. R.A.M.C. attached for temporary duty during absence through an accident of Capt. E.P. CREAGH R.A.M.C.	
	2.	6am	Some rounds very close to 135 Battery but target probably sector of 6 in. Hows	
		—	Hostile Arty. Very quiet harassing throughout usual W.B.C. shelled at half hour intervals. 11.35 p.m. Heavy bombardment on left of divisional front. Enemy search aircraft up tried green lights to late a.m. red and green a.a. rd. Gas shelling nil. E.A. active slight	
			Our Arty. Registration and instructional shoots. At night harassed Q.30d.6.0, O.29a, O.27.6, O.23.C. Hows on O.33.8, 30.6. 23.3. 23.C. hours and buildings.	
	3.	—	Hostile Arty. Rather at night harassing fire towards front line W.4 and O.34c CANAL BANK at 4.10 a.m. (4th) LES HARISOIRS shelled with H.E. and gas. Flashes of guns observed - M.G. guns engaged by our teams. Observed 2 Seaplanes seen missing East from Bellue in O.29d 20.40	
			Our Arty. harassed Q.29h and Q.30a (Houses) tracks between Q.28.C. and V.29d. Fire on house and cutroads O.36a O.29d and cut Q.26.b.20 to 50.40 and on house V.26.d.	
	4.		Hostile Arty. Active Harassing fire HINGES and CANAL BANK W.3.6. Heavy bombardment on left of divisional front	
			Our Arty. Registration carried on Rds. Q.34a nd 28.e 27.27e. Gas on O.36.8 28.C.a.	

Army Form C. 2118.

WAR DIARY or INTELLIGENCE SUMMARY.

(Erase heading not required.)

JULY 1918   **37th Bde R.F.A.**   Page 2

Instructions regarding War Diaries and Intelligence Summaries are contained in F.S. Regs., Part II. and the Staff Manual respectively. Title pages will be prepared in manuscript.

Place	Date 1918	Hour	Summary of Events and Information	Remarks and references to Appendices
BELLERIVE	July 4		2 Lieut J.E. GOODBODY posted to 27th Battery from 4th D.A.C.	Refer Maps 1/20,000 36 A. S.E.
	5		Hostile Arty. Quiet. Harassing fire not so heavy. HINGES shelling early half hour. S.W. (dud holes) on CANAL BANK W4c. Our Arty. Instructional shoots and registration. Harassed O35a (shell holes) and O27c and O35a (shell holes) at request of Infantry fired on shellholes O33a 65-85 – 87-60-00, Shellhole in O33a and O27c disengaged.	
	6	9:30 am	S.O.S. on O30a 45.28 30.00. Raid carried out by Yorkshire Fusiliers (1 Bn. of 36 Bde. I.R.) as enemy posts in O34c 50.71 and O34c 50.65. The Artillery barrage (rifle) was heavy, and located Battery operations were carried out in attached Order. The enemy's reply was some heavy shelling of our forward system for a short time from 9:45 am to 10:25 am. One 10.5 howr. was with rally short burst on farm in Q.34 b 20.20 and also on O34 a 40.40. Our counter barrage, neutralisation and counter Battery work was very successful. At night HINGES and CANAL BANK shelled	Right Group after 4 p.m. 7/2 4 p.m. 7/5 2.XII Bde. Counter battery order No. 26 of 3.7.18 3. H.A. VIII Bde Instructions No. 20 5-7-18
			Our Arty. Our Batteries took part in above operation. At night harassed track roads and crossroads. Our Arty. engaged buildings and cutboxes.	
	7	9:40 am	2 Lt G.H. HOLLAND 27th Bty posted to 29th Bde. R.F.A. Seroual. E.A. machine	
			Hostile Arty. Quiet vigorous during night. Registration on W.9 b.6.8. V.6d shelled with two salvoes at about 15 mins interval. Post in W1 and HINGES shelled 10:55 to 11.5 enemy arty. was keenly bombarding enemy line North of PACAUT and Battery City appeared to retaliate with harassing fire, reply disturbed LES HARISOIRS, CANAL in W.3 a,b and 16th BERNENCHON shelled altogether with M.G. fire E.A. active 9. 9:45 unusual activity E.A. flew low over our lines engaging them with M.C. fire 12:35 am 8th E.A. dropped 9 heavy bombs on Q.32 C.	
			Our Arty. Harassing fire in view of suspected relief on line of TURBEAUTE Farm carried on all night	
	8		Hostile Arty. Normal at night vigorous HINGES Mt BERNENCHON LES HARISOIRS W9 a,r c W2d W3 a,b were harassed	
			Our Arty. Normal. Deep real shelling during day. Harassed HINGES M.T. BERNENCHON at night all along front (F.C.Coy) R.F.A. during night. N. EDGE of PACAUT WOOD and Noush shelled 60 rounds B.M. in Q.38 b 0.0 55	

Army Form C. 2118.

WAR DIARY
or
INTELLIGENCE SUMMARY.
(Erase heading not required.)

32nd Bde. R.F.A.   JULY 1918   Page 3

Place	Date	Hour	Summary of Events and Information	Remarks and references to Appendices
BELLERVE	1918 July 9		Hostile Arty. During day apparently registered V.12.d. area W.7.a.0.0. with air bursts. Light firing below normal. HINGES and Mt. BERNENCHON shelled. HINGES shelled with gas.	Rifle Strength 1/20,000 36ª S.E.
		9.35 a.m.	Much shooting near LESTREM. Large farm at B.2.34.00.15 caught fire. Our Arty. harassed O.29.d. Roads and Tracks in PACAUT WOOD edge of WOOD W.27.c. 50 to Q.27.a.24. New fires on heure O.33.6.70.60 and Targets in Q.29.b.s.a.	
	10		Hostile Arty. quieter than usual. Intermittent shelling of HINGES during night. Our Arty. harassed roads and retouses Q.34.d.4.6 area. Heure on town in this area. Also harassed roads and edge of wood over heure at Q.33.6.70.60.	
	11		Hostile Arty. below normal. Between 2.4 a.m. (13)A area shot on W.9 and W.14 central. Support Line CANAL BANK area. Le HARISOIRS shelled. Large fire in R.19.C. Our Arty. Prene bursts on rds. O.33.6 (27)A and on E DGE of WOOD Q.27.c.1.d. Roles and houses engaged.	
	12		Hostile Arty. very quiet. Air bursts at W.7.a. Our Arty. engaged tracks and still hopes in Q.23.d. and road Q.23.a. bursts on Q.23.a. & buildings in whole area. Coffee in Q.30.d.70.90. New fires on buildings in whole area.	
	13		Hostile Arty. Normal. GONNEHEM shelled deliberate fire. Old night each sell with A.V. Sun and CANAL BANK W.4.c. front and Supt. Line shelled. GONNEHEM and road Q.36.d.80.90 harassed about 20 Saddles. Our Arty. Heure harassed O.33.l.b.s.a. Heure on Le WERTBOIS FARM. Heure Bridges Q.23.e.5.3.7.0 and road junction Q.23.c. and a shelled.	
	14		Hostile Arty. Our O.P. in W.9.6. shelled at intervals. Registration of house W.9.6.55. CANAL Bank at 4.6.66 and W.3.6. Probably calibration. GONNEHEM HINGE CANAL BANK shelled. at intervals. Some car shells in W.8.6 and road V.12.6. Our Arty. Prene retoures and house Q.34.a and Q.29.e, 28.a.	
	15		Hostile Arty. area W.9.a. probably receiving. HINGES air bursts registration. Our Arty. Ex HARISOIR shelled in PACAUT WOOD. Our He Bursts a fires on STEAM MILL PARADIS and PARAUT our aeroplanes engaged targets in HINGES sector.	

WAR DIARY or INTELLIGENCE SUMMARY

Army Form C. 2118.

32nd BDE R.F.A. 4

Place	Date	Hour	Summary of Events and Information	Remarks and references to Appendices
BELLERIVE	1918 July 18		Hostile Arty. Quiet. Hpopm harassing fire at night. Airspher Gds 105 HE fell on the HARBONS Refs Maps appeared to be checking registration. M7a and V12 B LEVERTANNY Road Junction, 40,000 Q31 c1 d CANAL were shelled. 36 A.G.E. Our Arty. Fired an SOS lives to hit shellfire also Q27 c+d 23 c+d and 29 a F.A. abud.	
	"		Hostile Arty. No shelling in forenoon. Towards turning day. At night MT BERNENCHON Reffent line CAPAS Road shelled in Q35 b+d 36 a, 23 c, 28 b, 34 a. Our Arty. fired shellfire needs answer to harass.	4th Divisional
	18	2.30 a.m.	A party of 5 Officers and 300 O.R of 2nd Dukes of Wellington and Redwig Regt carried out a raid against enemy position in PACAUT WOOD about Q34 c Q 2 and Q33 b and d, the raid was completely successful. 29 Prisoners and 3 machine guns being captured. The batteries of the Regt Group took part as an arborite 3 A of 2nd Div Arty Order No 12? The barrage lifted to the Infantry advanced round the wood and a protective barrage was formed beyond and on the flanks of the objective. Mortars to machine guns being also dealt with. The barrage was most excellent. It appeared to me aeroplane observers well defined and accurate. The German barrage came down about zero +4 mins on his own fell lights for support but PACAUT WOOD and RIEZ touch our howit kept. The German barrage becomes appreciably when up stopped hours and lifted on to HINGES RIDGE. Prisoners stated they were completely surprised. A may of enemy shells fell on his own shell bets.	Artillery Order No 12 dated 12th July 1918 and relative map (2) for 18/7/18 and Y5 Mu-lan barrage
			Hostile Arty. at night normal. Trench system W9 b central our back area were shelled. Our Arty. Heavies very active on enemy back areas all day. PARADIS STEAM MILL and EPINETTE. At night our batteries did usual harassing fire and fired 50 B.M.C on Q32 e. Our aeroplanes were very active all day.	

Army Form C. 2118.

WAR DIARY
or
INTELLIGENCE SUMMARY.
(Erase heading not required.)

32nd BDE RFA 5

JULY 1915

Place	Date	Hour	Summary of Events and Information	Remarks and references to Appendices
BELLERIVE	1915 July 19		Hostile Arty. Normal 9-10 am 80 odd 10.5 mm on W.7.b. YAOUT Line and Supports of Right Bygade HINGES and vicinity shelled intermittently during night	Refer Map 1/40,000 36a S.E.
			Our Arty. ride and road W.0.34.a.28.c.41 29.d 30.a 23.e 28.b Mow fired 50 BNC on 50° zeros of Q.28.e.80.00. Our planes booked PACAUT area	
	20		Hostile Arty normal V.5.b. cross roads near HINGES shelled. By night HINGES intermittently shelled.	
			Our Arty. 6 gun front-line from La PANNERIE to PACAUT WOOD by bursts of fire intermixed with usual harassing fire. Six shots of ranging time and varying targets each night. Roads and outskirts areas and shell holes were engaged.	
	21		Hostile arty normal. HINGES CANAL BANK W.9.a.b. shelled. Probable registration of V.6.a Considerable movement about house O.29.d.20.95. Our planes very active.	
			Our Arty. Special harassing fire in anticipation of evening ship. All mean roads to trenches by PACAUT WOOD was engaged. Trench bridges shell holes and roads received attention.	
	22		Hostile arty. On nights 21/22 22/23 certain unwersmes displayed. Increased activity. Harassing fire on our front and intermediate area.	
			Our Arty. shell holes and trench and webway in O.34.d. trench network and roads were harassed. Train seen going from behind LESTREM in N.E. direction.	
	23-31		Hostile arty. normal. Occasional registration. The usual harassing fire on trench spots. Aeroplane CANAL BANK and to HARBOURS.	
			Our Arty. continued this increased harassing fire on the day after they was taken were of great value as any Photographs coming in the day after they was taken were of great value as any fresh work in trenches could be immediately engaged.	

WAR DIARY
or INTELLIGENCE SUMMARY

Army Form C. 2118.

32nd BDE. R.F.A.

JULY 1918

Summary of Events and Information

During the month the hostile Arty was fairly quiet. They occasionally brought up roving pieces but even then were engaged by our Heavies. In this area our Counter Battery work appears very successful. Registration by hostile Arty was noticeable. They had the usual area shoots and varied it a little by sharp bursts and unremittent shelling. None of our batteries were shelled except 135th Battery who got some rounds over near the target being a 6 in Howr near Méon.

Our Arty carried out instructional shoots and registration by day and did some very varied and specially lately some very severe harassing fire at night. The barrages for the raids on the 6th and 18th were the principal events of the month.

The conditions of living in the batteries were excellent. The gun positions had thoroughly fortified cellars or concrete shelters for the men. The turkey-hens at CANTRAINE were comfortable and the Wagon Lines at BOURECQ Wagon battle tents were very comfortable in the dry hot weather. The food in the lines was very good with plenty of variety of fruit and vegetables. The attacks of "3 days fever" was pretty severe. Well over 50% were down with it. The N.C.O.s were off their feed. Also reinforcements were good and the remounts were satisfactory.

A. Savage Lt.
for Lt Col. Commdg 32 Bde CFA

1st Aug 1918

Army Form C. 2118.

WAR DIARY
or
INTELLIGENCE SUMMARY.
(Erase heading not required.)

32nd BDE R.F.A. Vol 4

August 1918

Place	Date	Hour	Summary of Events and Information	Remarks and references to Appendices
BAUE RIVE	1918 Aug 1		Preparatory to a withdrawal about 5th August the enemy commenced on this date to withdraw. He gave whilst doing so he made a series of slow concentrations east & west H.V. guns against each area. By the 4th there were very few guns west of the LAWE River. Our batteries engaged communications the rd TUBÉAUT River the houses beyond in Q29d PARADIS and various M.G. nests	Ref Maps 1/20,000 36A S.E.
	1		Hostile Arty. Quick bursts on HINGES, CANAL BANK Q31 and 32, and W3b and nests in W1a	
			Our Arty. including 50a Battery and 466 Battery which went up the Regd/Croch heard bursts 5 H.V. nights on Rds in PARADIS WOOD, Roads Q31b and 23c and steel work in Q29c and also the North of PACAUT WOOD Q28a and Q27d	
	2		Hostile Arty. CANAL BANK and HINGES intensified and our concentration. Our Arty. Rds Q3a and 28c bridges over TURBEAUTE Q29 a bc roads by BOHEME and PARADIS and North of PACAUT Wood etc. On the night 2/3 12th Squadron Flying Division who obtained lately of the netherview 135 Battery H.V. gun at night and also registration of HINGES from 4 new positions	
	3		Hostile Arty. W3a c v d scattered. Our Arty. from B.M.C. on Q25c 7010-70 90 to Q3y 50 90 Rd Bridges and PACAUT Wood and North tempt engaged with lovely effect as our 3rd 135 Battery had a direct hit by a stray round on one gun. the battery dug in on two shells near Henin	
	4		Hostile Arty. quiet on the forward front. He sent one on 3rd	

WAR DIARY
or
INTELLIGENCE SUMMARY.

Army Form C. 2118.

August 1918 32nd BDE RFA

Place	Date	Hour	Summary of Events and Information	Remarks and references to Appendices
BELLEVUE Aug 4th			Our Arty carried out concentrations on Hostile Btys in forward zone and the first special attention to enemy communications behind the line in anticipation of a relief	1/20,000
	5		Hostile Arty very quiet during day but active from 8.30 p.m. onwards. Frequent concentrations on CANAL BANK and HINGES. Black took the form of barrages on	
	6		fired during the night. PACAUT WOOD also shelled heavily. There was arty guns in back area and showed but little nervousness by the enemy. Considerable movement seen at Q27d 2550. A/10 p.m. a dump was exploded by our Heavies behind CORNET MALO. Our Arty concentrated with frequent bursts of fire during night on roads, bridges and shelled areas. Nervous night. Hostile Arty harassed battery area and back areas but quiet on forward areas. H.A. active at night harassing back areas. Movement seen in Q29a but dispersed by our guns. Our Arty continued their bursts but at different times each night	
	7 and 8		As the infantry advanced our batteries got the front line each night. From the Liaison Officer who was with the Battalion Commander interviewed in charge of the advance Battalions and we fired on machine gun emplacement and on posts held by the enemy. Hostile Arty active on forward areas and H.V. guns on back areas HINGES WOOD HOUSE W.9.E Q34ave ug O28g hole shells. Our Arty fired on Q23d Q36a and road Q30a d	

Army Form C. 2118.

WAR DIARY
or
INTELLIGENCE SUMMARY.

(Erase heading not required.)

32nd Bde R.F.A.   3

August 1918

Place	Date	Hour	Summary of Events and Information	Remarks and references to Appendices
BELLERIVE	1918 Aug	9-14	Mostly Bty quiet. Our arty fired on line O29c4540 - O33c9030, house O30c1010 - Q3d S090. Line Q23d 8530 - 3575 Line Q23d 8530 - 3575. Hostile arty shelled hules u O29d 23d and 30c and engaged. Our heavy arty active on TACAUT VILLAGE BOHEME, PARADIS, QUENTIN heard bombing HINGES CENSE LA VALLEE and each areas.	Refer May 1/20,000 /36A SE
	16 15d		Major C.T. McKAY M.C. comdg 134 Battery left to take over command of N/152 R.H.A. Capt C.T. HUTCHISON M.C. 27th Bty appointed Major of 136th Bty. Capt A.V. BROWN 29th Bde R.F.A. appointed Captain of 27 Bty R.F.A. Hostile arty below normal CULVERT FARM O29d 23 HINGES CANAL BANK shelled our arty fired on line O29b 6075 - O23d 1530: Road O30a.2520 - O30.6060 Roads 100 yds radius from O30a 4530 - O30a O30b and road O 30 to b O 30d nowell shelled O515: Road O30 c - O30a - O30b and road O 30 to b O 30d nowell shelled	
	16.21		Very little to report. Our batteries had moved forward for the S.O.S. line and engaged	
ERNY ST JULIEN	23 24		Bruges, PARADIS and O29d Stockfontaine hostel action Q9135 etc.	HAZEBROUCK LENS MA
	25		The Brigade came out of action and marched to ERNY ST JULIEN for training but orders came to march the next day instead.	
HERNICOURT	26		Marched to HERNICOURT. 37th Battery fighter to D anti-aircraft Bty.	LENS 1/40000 /51 3
ESTERRE-au-CAUCHIE	27		Left HERNICOURT 8.30 pm arrived ESTERRE-au-CAUCHIE 5 am	
ANZIN (ARRAS)			Marched to ANZIN	
BOIS de VERT	28		Came into action at BOIS de VERT	

WAR DIARY or INTELLIGENCE SUMMARY

Army Form C. 2118.

32nd Bde RFA

Place	Date	Hour	Summary of Events and Information	Remarks and references to Appendices
Bois du VERT O.9.c 80.95	1918 Aug 28		August 1918	Refer Map 1/40,000 51.B
		3.pm	Brigade Commander reconnoitred positions in O.15 and 9	
		5.pm	Brigade Commander met Battery Commanders at FEUCHY CHAPEL	
		5.pm	Brigade marched to rendezvous in H.33.c and d	
		12 midnight	All Batteries in action S. of BOIS du VERT. Wagon lines near FEUCHY CHAPEL in H.33 and N.3	
	29		Batteries registered Hostile batteries & observed bursts principally with H.V. guns on various points chiefly on CAMBRAI ROAD and BOIRY ROAD. 86th Battery commenced cutting wire on ROEUX-QUEANT line. Round P.2.6 central	
	30		32nd Brigade supported 11th Infantry Brigade in attack towards DROCOURT-QUEANT line at 4.pm. 86th Battery moved forward to O.10.d.8.1. and continued cutting wire. 18 pdr batteries moved evening opened.	
	31		Wire cutting continued fired two S.O.S's about 6.pm. Supported 11th Infantry Bde in an attack. Put down a creeping barrage and shelter on DROCOURT QUEANT LINE at P.2.6.7. while Infy kept a line H.9 killed 4.2. H.V. 86th killed with 4.2 H.V. and had one man killed and four wounded. Remaining 3 batteries of Brigade moved forward to positions in O.11.c and O.16. Sgt 3 — Eng'. (?) Lyne benefits under open sights revolution at about 6 hrs and the commanded with 120° C. and 6 hrs. S L Owens Lt Col Comdg 32 Bde RFA

Army Form C. 2118.

WAR DIARY
or
INTELLIGENCE SUMMARY.

(Erase heading not required.)

32nd BDE R.F.A

August 1918

Place	Date	Hour	Summary of Events and Information	Remarks and references to Appendices
HERNICOURT	Aug 26		Bde at HERNICOURT under command of Major W.B. MACKIE, M.C. vice Lt. Col. T.R.F.A. BLOCK DSO being on leave. All guns of the Brigade sent to PETEWAWA range to be calibrated.	Refer Appx. Y on no 2 Engs.
ESTRÉE CAUCHIE	26/27		Bde marched at night to VILLERS-AU-BOIS area to join Canadian Corps. Starting point St POL Square 10 h.m. Billetted at ESTRÉE CAUCHIE	
	27		Marched off at 8 h.m. to ANZIN	
ANZIN	28		Brigade ordered into action that night positions suggested near PETLARO S. (MONCHY) Brigade formed part of Right Artillery Group under Lt.Col. POSTON, DSO R.F.A. 29th Bde R.F.A. Brigade ordered to rendezvous at ETRUN CHAPEL Crossroads at 4 p.m. As a result of the day's operations the Brigade Commanders found it impossible, all moving forward and to positions suggested owing the fact that advanced orders to reconnoitre positions near BOIS du VERT. i.e. of Square 05 not between 02 and 05 and Square 05. Owing to the lateness of the hour and owing to the most dire circumstances was very hampered. 1 Bde rendezvous all batteries in action without any casualties. Bde HQ here at O.m.C.65: 27 Bty O's A.15. 136 Bt.16 d-a.31.15.4. Morning. Appx. S 1 2	Appx. X on no 31

OG c m. Se Bty 09c39 Wagon Lines established near FERNOY CHAPEL Cross Rds M31

Army Form C. 2118.

WAR DIARY
or
INTELLIGENCE SUMMARY.
(Erase heading not required.)

3rd Bde. R.F.A.

August 1918

Place	Date	Hour	Summary of Events and Information	Remarks and references to Appendices
Bois de Vert	1918 Aug 29		As Wagon lines watering was very difficult the 4th Divisional Boundary was North, road line dividing squares J and P south ARRAS–CAMBRAI ROAD. Infantry – 10th and 11th Infantry Brigades in the line 13th in reserve Artillery Right Group supported right Brigade the 11th	Ref. Maps 1/20,000 51 b S.W. 51 c S.E. 4th DA Order No 106 d/28/8
	29		Batteries registered. 81st Bty commenced cutting wire in DROCOURT QUÉANT line in P.16 and 27.a	
	29/30		At night Brigade carried out harassing fire as ordered, chiefly cutting wire. Infantry advanced their line without artillery support, confluence REMY and HAUCOURT	
	30		Section of 81st Bty moved forward to On.C.8.1 in the afternoon and endeavoured were cutting in square P.21.a Infantry attacked and captured junction of two Brigade expected this attack with a creeping barrage 86th Battery moved forward to reinforce anthem at 6 h.a.	
	30/31	4 hm	Harassing fire as ordered.	

WAR DIARY or INTELLIGENCE SUMMARY

Army Form C. 2118.

32nd Bde R.F.A.

August 1915

Place	Date	Hour	Summary of Events and Information	Remarks and references to Appendices
Bois de Vert	1915 Aug 31		8c Bty continued wire cutting. Infantry withdrew on part of line captured yesterday owing to heavy M.G. fire	Refer Bde Instr No. 500 5/9 (6 W.) 5/8 S.E.
		5.45pm	Line re-established by Infantry supported by barrage by Brigade. Barrage of Brigade moved forward to the following positions:- 27th Bty O 18 4 56, 13th Bty O 11 6 3070, 13th Bty O 11 C 78 – not now there one Battery being out of action at a time	4th Div Artillery Instr No 117 of 31/8
	Sept 1		12th Infantry Brigade relieved 11th Brigade on left	
			Lt Col BOWES D.S.O. took over command of the Brigade at 4 P.M., continued wire cutting	
	1/2		10th British Brigade relieved by 4th Canadian Division and British divisional line had next attack on one Brigade front (ie 12th I.B.) on a frontage of 1500 yards including village of FRAINE and retaining (later from 5 am 2. W.	4 Div Instr Gen Instr Instructions No. at 1 9.
			4th Divisional Boundaries were:- NORTH, ST NICE. Road. SOUTH, Road line between square P13 and P19 for about 1500 from A 00 thence on a track line through Q 7 central to Veloire lane.	

Army Form C. 2118.

WAR DIARY
or
INTELLIGENCE SUMMARY.

(Erase heading not required.)

32nd Bde R.F.A.

SEPTEMBER 1918.

Place	Date	Hour	Summary of Events and Information	Remarks and references to Appendices
	Sept 1/2		Artillery. (4th British Div Arty, 29th and 35th Bdes) Right Group came under orders of 4th Canadian Div Arty until completion of the creeping barrage his Barrage Map A. 32nd Brigade Zone allotted in between E and W trees through P14 & 0010 and through P30 & 0050. This supported attack on DROCOURT-QUÉANT line [Barrage Map A. 23 a.]	4th Instructions to 4th C.D.A. Instructions No. 2 (1) 1/9 Barrage Map Canadian Def A
	2	5 am	Zero hour. Brigade supported attack on DROCOURT-(QUÉANT line till Zero + 150 minutes with creeping barrage (Barrage Map AB), 4th DA 135, 35 Bde OP/172) Brigade supported attack by 4th Canadian Division. 27th Battery and 135th Battery dusted the 600 ft front [zone in line through P14 0010 and through P30 & 0050 into two lanes. 134 Battery supporting up 2nd echelon front and 81st Battery barrage (and storm 100° E of 1st & Bde Batteries covering lanes] 27th and 135th Batteries. 134 Battery detailed to deal with wireless calls (4th DA Order 138 Am 1) After the capture of the Red line, the 11th Brigade were to pass through the leading Brigade (the 12th) supported by 32nd Group Brigade RFA.	4th DA Order No 136 24/1/9 32 Bde R.F.A. O.P/173 1/9

Army Form C. 2118.

WAR DIARY
or
INTELLIGENCE SUMMARY.
(Erase heading not required.)

32nd Bde R.F.A

Place	Date 1915	Hour	Summary of Events and Information	Remarks and references to Appendices
	September 1915			5
	2 Sept	8 am	Right Group (79th, 33rd and 52 (How) Bde RFA) again supported 4th British Division under command of Right Group on completion of Barrage tasks with H.Q at VIS en ARTOIS O.H.a.7	Ref on the y/28,29,30 /31 Aug V on 1.9.15
			The Right Group Commander kept in touch with the 52nd Bde RFA who advanced at 11 am with the 10th Infantry Brigade	4th Div I.O. Order No 159 A 17½
		6.30am	Batteries harnessed up ready to move off at 15 minutes notice to move (Brigade orders). On reported counter-attack Brigade fired on fixed targets duly, PROSPECT FARM O.9.d.2.7	
	3.		Brigade under orders to move forward at 15 minutes notice after 9.30 am (4th D.A. B-24/508 para 1) to support attack by 11th and 12th Brigades - Nord 1.B Carron Battalion leaves in reserve. This was cancelled owing to German harass retired	4 D.A B/24/548 para 5 9 2/9
			Wagon lines ordered to move up to Battries but met by C.R.A. on the move up and ordered to return	
			Brigade relieved during the afternoon by 1st Divisional Artillery and moved to billets in TILLOY and TILLOY O'SAVY	
	4			

Army Form C. 2118.

WAR DIARY
or
INTELLIGENCE SUMMARY.

(Erase heading not required.)

33rd Bde R.F.A.

Place	Date	Hour	Summary of Events and Information	Remarks and references to Appendices
	1918 August Sept 3.		Casualties to personnel horses and equipment 4 OR's killed 25 wounded 17 Horses killed 30 wounded One Gun carriage temporarily out of action Battery positions never came under direct fire, casualties were caused by wounds etc From an Artillery point of view the situation showed the apparent lack of direct observation at the hand of the German Gunners. Prior to the attack our guns had good observation into ground & towards & from the MOEUVRES DROCOURT P.S.A. on the ARRAS CAMBRAI ROAD and further on O.g. and S. Movement of whatever nature was practically continuous all day with hostile Artillery fire was slight and apparently by map on selected areas. Hence casualties & opportunities of infantry traffic and inflicting casualties were missed. The performance of Forward reconnaissance by Brigade and Battery commanders had encountered its own from Infantry Brigade. it was difficult to obtain reliable information concerning our own Infantry. It was extremely difficult for a Brigade Commander to combine the duties of Group Commander and Brigade Commander as a group battle requires to be in fair close to the Infantry Brigade Hqtrs with the Reconnoitring Officer Platoon and knows sufficient close to Brigade and Battery position to be able to influence the Situation.	

WAR DIARY
or
INTELLIGENCE SUMMARY.

Army Form C. 2118.

37th BDE R.F.A.

Sept. 1915

Place	Date	Hour	Summary of Events and Information	Remarks and references to Appendices
SAVY	1915 Sept			
	4-10th		Batteries engaged in training special attention being paid to open warfare, engaging MG's and close co-operation with Infantry.	1/100,000 LENS
	11th		Major W. B. MACKIE M.C. 86th Bty in command of Brigade while Lt Col C.E.S. BOWER D.S.O. went on leave.	
	6th		2/Lt E.W. TAYLOR joined Brigade and posted to 27th Battery.	
	16th		Lieut G.W. PENNY 4th D.A.C. joined 135 Bty in place of Lieut GREENWOOD to 4th D.A.C.	
	17th		Lieut A.V. COCKLE M.C. 27th Bty posted as Captain to 128th Bty R.F.A.	1/20,000
	19th		Brigade came into action S. of SENSEE RIVER, relieving 11th Division (heavy Bde) and Bus Brigade RFA 86 Siege Arty (2 x 2" Bde R.F.A.) 135 Bty and 2 Hows 86th Bty came under Right Group (Lt Col W.T. POSTON D.S.O.Cmdg 27th Bty and 4 Hows 86th Bty Left Group (Lt Col S.F. GOSLING D.S.O. R.F.A.) grouped with 77th (Army) Bde R.F.A. 56th Division on our right. 46th on our left, 46th relieves later by 51st Division.	51 B.N.W. N.E. S.E. S.W.
	23rd		86th Bty detached section at T9 d 5060 came under command of 9.C. Left Group	
	30th		135 Bty came under command of O.C. Left Group	
			Major W.B. MACKIE M.C. Brigade Commander since the 11th Lt Col BOWER returns as C.R.A. on his return from leave.	
			Position of Batteries as follows. 27th O1 c 4050 (behind Ord 5010 (4 guns)) 135th O1 a 4 8 One 1060 (1 Section) 135th O1 c 3025 O.65 3504 (1Section) 86th Ord 4030 Pgd 5060 (1Section)	

Brigade HQ. O7 d 670

Army Form C. 2118.

WAR DIARY
or
INTELLIGENCE SUMMARY.
(Erase heading not required.)

33rd Bde R.F.A.

Sept. 1915

Place	Date	Hour	Summary of Events and Information	Remarks and references to Appendices
MONCHY	Sept		Operations consisted of cutting wire by day and keeping lanes open at night North of River Sensée. The front is largely flooded & so the S.A.S. (line of this (centre) division) were confined to a few bridges that are passable over the reeds leading to them. The Brigade was prepared to move forward for 'peaceful penetration' but the floods have held things up.	57 B N.W. S.W. S.E. N.E.
	Sept 20		16 Adn Batteries fired on the following gaps in enemy wire to keep them open: J.21.d.00.90, J.28.c.80.50, J.28.a.45.30, J.28.a.35.35, J.21.d.60.20, J.21.d.60.20 J.21.a.25.50, J.21.d.35.60. Registered Road Junction J.21.c.6.3. Hostile Arty. O.S. area shelled 150 rnds H.E. SAILLY (S.E.) BOIRY shelled LONG WOOD (O.S) and J.36.c shelled with gas shells	
	21		Registered gaps in wire. Fired on above gaps. Hostile Arty fairly normal 105 shells H.V fired levels S.of BOIS du VERT. Fired at gaps at night	
	22		BOIRY Tssd. 62 MUNCHY CAMBRAI Rd. O.12.b (with H.V.) shelled	
	23		11 Gun Hostile battery 10" fire from J.36.d.55 shelled O.S.A. J.31.d and 36.e BOIRY and Bois du VERT shelled 86th Battery did wire-cutting on above gaps. 15Adn shelled their dummy night	
	24		Hostile Arty very slight 8.40 pm. 12 Lyddite shrapnel near O.P.A. Two fell in 86 Bty Wagon Lines. 20 Horses killed and 20 evacuated.	

WAR DIARY
or
INTELLIGENCE SUMMARY

Army Form C. 2118.

Sep/1/1915   32 Bde R.F.A.   9

Place	Date	Hour	Summary of Events and Information	Remarks and references to Appendices
MONCHY	Sept 1915 24	6 am	Knew several shots on J.16.d and J.27.b. J.30.b and K.25.d. Valley in J.23.a.	51 B Hqrs S.E. N.E. S.W. N.W.
		1.15 pm	Also fired 30 rds on J.30 and J.31	
			50th Battery forward section fired 150 rounds on J.27.b. 3080 and J.31.a 3060 cutting wire.	
			151 Bde kept their gaps open at night and also the gaps detailed on p.8. fired 150 rds.	
	25		150 rounds fired by 86 Bty forward section on J.22.c.1030, J.27.80.70 and J.28.a.80.25	
			151 Bde fired 150 rounds on these gaps during night.	
			Hostile Arty very quiet. Movement 3.5 pm 30 men in twos and threes walked South over MONT. NOTRE DAME. Suspected OPs at T.15.a 6055 and T.15.a 7082.	4th D.A. B/51/561
	26		Practically no hostile Arty. 12 midnight heavy bombardment to the NORTH.	
			Our arty 86 Bty fired 150 rds on wire from T.15.a 8025 to T.16.a 6070 also J.22.d 3550. 50 rds fired on 106 those reported in J.23.a.	
			151 Bde fired 150 rds during night on their gaps.	
	27	5.35 am	This Brigade carried out bombardments as ordered 4th DA. B/4/51/561 awaiting attack on our right astride ARRAS CAMBRAI Road and (19)	B a/25 4th 4th D.A. B 4/51/56/4 19 d 27/9 32 Bde No OPs
			Smoke producers were discharged in O.13 - Q.15 (RECORD) by a patrol from the Brigade under Lieut TURNER 134 Bty and Lieut JEFFRIES	
			27th Bty. It was very successful and secured several useful purposes in the attack on our right. The wind was just right and the screen	
			was absolutely impenetrable to observation.	

WAR DIARY or INTELLIGENCE SUMMARY

Army Form C. 2118.

33rd Bde R.F.A.

Sept 1918

Place	Date	Hour	Summary of Events and Information	Remarks and references to Appendices
MONCHY	Sept 27		From the heights on our left of the movement of our guns on our right and the advance of our Infantry North of where the Enbrasée of the CANAL du NORD. The area worked very heavily. There was one casualty – one man killed.	Refer to Maps 51B S.E. N.E. S.W. N.W. 1/40,000
		At 3hr 4.45 hrs and 6.15 hrs 27th and 134 Battys fired creeping barrage in cooperation with Left Group – part of the "Chinese attack" Yr area shelled was J31c 90 to J31e 65 35 to J31b 50 10 to J25d 5090	
			The cutting 80th Battery cut were at J27d 1560 and J28a 7040 130 rds. Negro Young 27th and 13th Btys fired 50.90 on J31d and J28a 86 Bty fired 50.90 on north J21d 0060 to J21b 4000, J27b 2060 to J21d 9060 Road Junction J27d 5095	
	28		BOIRY J21 central, J31 J36a shelled The cutting 86 Bty fired 150 rds on ware in J22c 6050 and J25a 1590 86 Bty fired 20 rds on dug outs in J15d 4530 and 50 rounds on Near cutting Quarry J22b 48 and J21b 48 27 and 13 Bty fired 150 rds each on trenches J21d and J28a (Left Counter Batten J3)	Left 5 very O. for No 5 9/28/18
	29 30		When Brigade carried out concentration as ordered on M.G. post N.27 E.10 33 and cutlows N.27 E.25.50 in support of 11 Brigade operation for the Kings Div. to establish bridge head at J.37 c 24. 30th Bty did more cutting and 13.1.27 Bty fired 4.30 rounds each to night on trenches J21d J25a and cutting J15c and J21a	Left 5 very O. for No 5 9/28/18

30th Sept 1918

A.J. Rogers Lt Col
OC 33 Bde RFA

Army Form C. 2118.

WAR DIARY
or
INTELLIGENCE SUMMARY.
(Erase heading not required.)

32nd Bde RFA   October 1918

Place	Date	Hour	Summary of Events and Information	Remarks and references to Appendices
MONCHY	5/10	1-6	The Brigade was commanded by Major W. B. MACKIE M.C. R.F.A. 82nd Battery R.F.A. The flooded part of both of the SENSEE formed an obstacle. SOS lines were on the bridge and place where the flood was narrowest. Each Battery cut wire for two belts over the lanes by night and did harassing fire during the day in Battery. Hostile shelling was quiet. Three batteries were carried out in J32d J25d J27e J27b J28e J21d J21b J21a. 150 rounds per day. Night firing on Roads J21 27bd Quarry J27 MG post J27e 1052 DEOCOURT line J21d. QUEANT line J21d. Considerable movement seen and engaged by Batteries and batteries opened fire on SOS line. On night 5/6 SOS signal went up.	5/ 8 NW SW NE SE (1/2050)
	6.		Brigade served by 4th Canadian Brigade R.F.A. 2nd Canadian Division. One section per Battery (18 pdrs) went out to train with the Infantry Brigade. 27th with 11th K.R.R. 131 & 1135 with 12 R.R. The Brigade (less 3 above sections relieved 4 Brigade Canadian R.F.A. and came under the 2nd Canadian Division and later the 4th Division. The battery wagon lines in J25a W30a X19c and a Bde HQ to J25g.	
	7. 8/9		15/6's encountered positions. Col W. B ROWN 77 Battery proceeded to B4/08 and his Bde to Protective barrage line. 6 batteries came into action to N.W. of CAMBRAI and at 5am carried out barrage ordered on northern half of line B14e 5.6 - 13 1/c central B9408 and his Bde to Protective Barrage line.	Artillery ordered No 5 by 6 of 2nd B.R.O.

WAR DIARY or INTELLIGENCE SUMMARY

Army Form C. 2118.

Place: CAMBRAI
Month: October 1918
Unit: 32nd Brigade RFA Page 2

Date	Hour	Summary of Events and Information	Remarks and references to Appendices
Oct 9		Batteries moved up to position in S.29 (MORENCHIES). The Zone was from T.15.b to NAVES. Northern Boundary Road T.15.b to T.19.a. S. Boundary Road T.27.a.26 to T.34.a. Lt Col C.E. BOWER D.S.O. who had been acting C.R.A. 4th Division resumed command of the Bgde.	37A SW 1/20000 Right Group Operation Orders No 77
10		The Brigade took part in attack ordered (Right Group Operation Orders No.5). The commanders, signallers and others were given to be ready to move at short notice & keep touch & to be left with wagon lines. Harassing fire carried out. Batteries ordered to move section forward to S.16 and S.24 and batteries later moved to T.19 and T.20 & ordered to T.21.C.0.4. Railway (inclusive). The Brigade were now engaged in moving warfare and there were considerable casualties to wagons, owing to a few shells getting amongst wagon lines in the shelter. Capt Allis, 160th Battery wounded, Sgt Honeychurch, 135 HQ, 2 Horses killed, 7 wounded. 49th Division took over this part of the line & Infantry of 2nd Canadian Division. 32nd Brigade came under command of Lieut Colonel W. FLUCEY D.S.O commanding 245th Bde R.F.A.	Right Group Operation Orders No 75 2/10/18 49th Div Art Ordr 153 and 154 2/10/18
10/11			
11		Bde commander and B.C.s went forward to reconnoitre positions in U.7 and 8. Bgte of Right Group 49th D/A. On reaching river E.12.C.41.N. our wire was seen returning from the cross in D.2 & 3. Later reports showed enemy had used tanks. Right Group commander ordered advance of batteries to cross 135 Battery led ahead, moved and came into action T.27.6.30.00. Later 134 Bty moved to T.27.6.00.10. and 27th to T.21.9.20.80 where being ordered to take up orders by (Batty CTN 80) Coy during night orders received from Right Group (3rd Batty 8) to fire barrage from 30X in front of Infantry to objective (3000X in front of Railway) through 06 to 028	245 Bde OO No 8 0/11 Oct 1918
11/12			
12	5am	Brigade Commander and B.Cs went forward to select positions in U.13. 6am 56 Battery moved to V.13.6.20 and 134 Bty to U.13.4070.	

Army Form C. 2118.

WAR DIARY
or
INTELLIGENCE SUMMARY.

(Erase heading not required.)

32 Bde RFA

3

Place	Date	Hour	Summary of Events and Information	Remarks and references to Appendices
NAVES	Oct 1918		Remaining batteries were to move forward at 9am.	Ref Weh 57 d S.W. 1/20,000
		10·30am	Orders received from Group that enemy had retired and patrols were pushing on to final objective AVESNES le SEC and VILLERS-en-CAUCHIES. Attack cancelled. Bde Commander and B.C's again went forward to select positions in T.14 and T.10. H.Q. ordered to move up at 10.45am to V.18.d.4.0.10. Infantry reported on objective at 12 noon. R.F.Bty moved to V.14.d.80.60-13.50 V.10.c.40.10-13.5 to V.14.a.30.20. 86th to V.10.c.70.60 and came into action at 3pm on V.2, V.9. Later was stated Infantry patrols were pushing high ground in V.2, V.9. The various night had been very quiet. HV guns on MAVES VIELES en-CAUCHIE Road during night Infantry attempted to push forward and consolidate across river in P.20 and P.26.a. S.O.S line 300x in advance and harassing fire carried out.
		13	During night orders were received that Infantry were to attack a gun and advance to line through P.8-15 and 23.
		5am	Brigade Commander and B.C's went forward to select position in valley at O.6.6.d (HQ at O.6.c.46). All batteries moved forward at 5am to a position of readiness. All batteries in action at 7am having first got through the village of VILLERS before heavy shelling commenced. Enemy plastered villages throughout the day. All batteries ready to open enfilading barrage. Infantry believed to be short of the Railway HASPRES-SAULZOIR but a none even.

Army Form C. 2118.

WAR DIARY
or
INTELLIGENCE SUMMARY.
(Erase heading not required.)

32 Bde RFA

October 1918

Place	Date	Hour	Summary of Events and Information	Remarks and references to Appendices
VILLERS en CAUCHIE	Oct 13.		in P 20 c and P 26 a. Our barrage opened at 9 a.m. and from the shelling it appeared that enemy were resisting strongly. Infantry attacked at 9.30 a.m.	Refer Map 1/20,000 57 A SW SE and NE
		10am	Wounded showed our troops in SAUIZOIR and later shots were that our troops were across the LA SELLE River. As visibility cleared it was noticed that our batteries were under direct observation from high ground N.W.	
			Batteries were in SOS lines at 10.30 a.m.	
		12 noon	Enemy preparing to counterattack with tanks. Every order barrage at slow rate for 1 hour but this Brigade had not enough ammunition (about 60 rds/gun) Supply was difficult owing to enemy observation	
		2pm	Our aici reported P.33 central. P.3's central to O.24 and 17 central. Prisoners stated enemy were to attack 7.30 pm	
			13.5.15 aici to withdraw to V.11 & central.	
		3pm	Right section ordered our batteries to withdraw. All batteries moved away to positions without a casualty in spite of severe hostile shelling.	
		5.30pm	Batteries in action in V.11 and 14 and H.Q. at RIEUX Our line had not advanced on Railway between HASPRES and SAUIZOIR were heavily shelled with M.G.s	
	14.		Batteries increased ammunition to 200 rds/g. Hostile arty quiet. Section of 13th and 135 reserve batteries at 3 p.m.	Casualties 1 officer 60% wounded 1 horse killed 3 wounded

Army Form C. 2118.

WAR DIARY
or
INTELLIGENCE SUMMARY.

(Erase heading not required.)   32 KAC 3FA   5

Place	Date	Hour	Summary of Events and Information	Remarks and references to Appendices
RIEUX	1918 Oct	14	Infantry established bridgeheads over river LA SELLE in front of SAUZOIR. SOS flares fired out. 18 pdrs fired on railway during night.	Refer MAP 57 4 SW NE SE
		15	Harassing fire on railway and approaches. Battery area shelled. Heavier night 29th Bty, rather heavily. Relative 12 mm and 2 an casualties 3 killed 3 wounded. 135 Yeager Coy killed 2 killed 2 wounded and 6 how killed. Enemy aircraft much above normal.	
		16	32nd Bde to become left group in the line with 52 AFAB 2nd, 197th and 16th Btys. Bde commanded by Lt Col CE & BONAR DSO. Offensive patrols to reconnoitre. Avre & the bridgehead in the John and 57th Majors C McBALLENTIN 27th Battery left for ammunition Col. E UK CLAY ORCLE. M.C. assumed command of 29 Bty.	
		17.	Bde commanding in left group reconnoitred positions 32nd Uncertain 57th VIII. 147 D3ed, 27th O39, 8tds. O34 Lieut Allen to cover HACPEG.	
		18	11th Infantry brigade received orders to attack north 2 Battalion in line and 2 in rear.	

Army Form C. 2118.

WAR DIARY
or
INTELLIGENCE SUMMARY.
(Erase heading not required.)

32nd Bde R.F.A.

Oct 1918

Place	Date	Hour	Summary of Events and Information	Remarks and references to Appendices
Rieux	Oct 19	10	Orders for attack postponed on account of enemy's withdrawal. Orders cancelled and batteries ordered to move up to position at 21.d railway.	Ref map 51st N.E.
		11	Enemy in touch with Infy on high ground in O.2.	
	20		Further orders re attack on Haspres. At 15 o'clock batteries ordered to reconnoitre position in O.30 and to occupy them at dawn the following day. H.Q's moved to Rieux.	
	21		Brigade moved at 16.30 to position in O.30 & O.40.80 — in action by 17.30. At 14.30 batteries reconnoitre positions in 014. H.Q's moved to Haspres.	
	22		32nd Bde H.Q. billets destroyed by hostile shell-fire — two men wounded. Preparation made for an attack by 10th & 11th Inf. brigades on the following day for high ground west of Monchaux.	

Army Form C. 2118.

WAR DIARY
or
INTELLIGENCE SUMMARY.
(Erase heading not required.)

Oct 1916 32nd Bde. R.F.A.

Place	Date	Hour	Summary of Events and Information	Remarks and references to Appendices
Harfleur	23		Cleaning on our left attacked successfully. Enemy artillery on our front normal. Orders received from 4th D.A. that division would attack at 4 in conjunction with 51st Division on left and 61st Division on right. 52nd Bde. R.F.A. (Left Group) was to support 51st Brigade (11th Hy Bde). 29th Bde. R.F.A. (Right Group) to support 8th Brigade (10th Hy Bde). Two batteries from 11th Division (B 56 & B 59) attached to 51st group. All batteries East of the Selle received guns and maintained ammunition to 500 rds per gun. Reported at 20.30 that enemy had retired half and out patrols. Enemy reported to be holding village of Menchive.	Ref. Map 51 N.E.

WAR DIARY
or
INTELLIGENCE SUMMARY.

Army Form C. 2118.

32nd Bde. R.F.A.

Oct 1916

Place	Date	Hour	Summary of Events and Information	Remarks and references to Appendices
Haspres	24		Barrage came down & forward Inf. attacked. Whole of first objective gained at 6.30 am. Second objective reached at 7 am. 15th Bde R.F.A. ordered to reconnoitre positions in P.9.a.b.c. 32nd Bde. R.F.A. to be prepared to move to positions in 83.d. at short notice. At 12.30pm 135 Battery section ordered forward to J.35.c.d. At 12.45pm 135 section ordered forward to 83.d. and to be followed by remainder. Received verbal orders from D.A that at end of day Left Group would only consist of 18th, 52nd and 32.D Brigades. Remainder to go East on to DOUCHY-HASPRES Valley. 1.57pm 13H & 135 Batteries moved forward to positions in P.3. 3pm Orders received that advance was to be continued the following day & Captain QUERNAINS and CONSTABLE to reconnoitre a line East of trolleys. Batteries ordered to make up to 357 obs per gun by dawn 25th inst. 3.30pm 52nd Bde. ordered to 8.6 to positions in P.3. and J.33. 11pm Orders for following days operations received. Enemy artillery fire throughout the day very mild - scant harassing rations used 77mm & 105mm. Night very quiet. Our infantry attacked 8th objective gained up to time & pressed in close support of infantry.	Map M.26 57.H.N.E. 22000
Oct. 25th			11.30am 135 Battery ordered...	

WAR DIARY or INTELLIGENCE SUMMARY

Army Form C. 2118.

Place	Date	Hour	Summary of Events and Information	Remarks and references to Appendices
	Oct 24 (cont)	12 noon	Battery secured N heads of J36 & J36 M/Pr established at PLM 4.47 M/Pr	5H9 NE 1/20000
		3.30pm	Infantry reported dropping shells of enemy batteries. Enemy shelling a bit heavy but very quiet during rest of afternoon.	
		4.30pm	Enemy tanks attacked line on left flank to back of high ground around M7 HOW. caused 136 Battery to come under direct observation and machine gun fire. Battery remained silent but shot turn at withdraw to J36 d	
		8pm	Active received from 4 LFA that infantry now of Essuine abed	
	Oct 26"	10 am	at 26" inst.	
			Active for attack secured at 1 am. 18th & 22.30m retired forward of P.B. and J55. at 11pm 25 inst. and 10 hr Troops for gun at 11pm by dawn	
		10 am	Barrage started. First report 11am showed Infantry held up by machine gun fire. 11.30am reported Infantry advancing 12 noon Infantry report back objective gt Battery near RDM (map ref) KJ near support of Infantry front counterattack by enemy launched at 4.30pm at 18/B all had a great deal of success in front of our light except during evening. Attack stopped. Enemy shelling for light except during evening.	
			Considerable enemy barrage ("normal") was very heavy shortly before & during an attack along ENNEMIE line. This was heavy harassed by our artillery. Situation regained up to 7pm when enemy attack was found to assist our base to an left also were being actively prepared for. & FC Battery RFA	
	Oct 27"	11am	One aeroplane sighted, taken above there were engaged G FC Battery RFA	

WAR DIARY or INTELLIGENCE SUMMARY

Army Form C. 2118.

Place	Date	Hour	Summary of Events and Information	Remarks and references to Appendices
	Oct 28		2 pm 18th Bde moved forward to posn in K.32.a. & 84 Bde within 2000 yds to own posn in T.36. all in action by 5 pm. Our artillery continued harassed fire of RHONELLE and high ground beyond to East. All night firing cancelled in order to allow infantry a rest. Poor enemy aeroplane very active over forward areas during early morning. 58 & 59 Bdes. came into action on 18 Bde. 32.13a. 11.15 am 86 Baty engaged MG at Hberon ey afflicting 32.13a. 11/pm 90 Batty engaged K.33 a.9.0 Co. Light eny artly morning very quiet. 4 pm to 6 pm heavy hostile down barrage on R.26 a.5.6 and QUERNAING. Cancelled operation show 11TH HOUR that B.C & Capt. Finch by the enemy. Enemy's comms not harassed throughout day and night.	Maps 57c.N.E. 1/20000
	Oct 29		Seen 9.6 am enemy. but down heavy orientated bombardment on QUERNAING with yellow cross gas shells. Day in general quiet. Hostility bad. 52 & 32 Bdes fired on gun for baby of 56 & 59 Bdes.	
	Oct 30		moved forward to posn H.36 & H.9. Sug B.s. came into harass fire. 9 pm enemy's fauvb reported movings north from ESTRELLA of the by defended to star from a section to Sund pivot a second a K.32. 835.9. Puffpsnt of infantry in the attack in the 15th. Div. moved to R.22. Reg 11. at 4 pm. 8.30 pm all balloon reported in action in south front. H.q.W. very quiet	
	Oct 31st			

WAR DIARY or INTELLIGENCE SUMMARY.

(Erase heading not required.)

Place	Date	Hour	Summary of Events and Information	Remarks and references to Appendices
			During the month of October. The 32nd Brigade took part in the open fighting around CAMBRAI and onwards. He accommodation for men and horses was chiefly in stables, billets or dug out sheds. Care also to be considered in the matter of the fighting very slight to up of November. Casualties very. Major 10.3 Master M.C. and Lt McRoberton killed on the 15th of November. The wagon lines of A & B batteries were pretty cars and a heavy shell gun fire especially 13th Battery who had to leave on two occasions. Horseflesh losses were chiefly men who had been shot or wounded and had been led back. Remounts on the whole were very few but look ed & in a fair condition.	

Shields Capt
for OC 32 Bde RFA

WAR DIARY OR INTELLIGENCE SUMMARY

32 B⁽ᵈᵉ⁾ R.F.A.

November 1918

Place	Date	Hour	Summary of Events and Information	Remarks and references to Appendices
F	1/11/18		In the early morning enemy heavily shelled QUESNARING and battery positions (Major McMaster M.C. wounded & Lieut McCartan killed) Several casualties amongst ORs. Battery licked off. 5am barrage put down in support of infantry attack. Enemy retaliation was at first slight and support had then died down about 7.15am and then onwards was very erratic. 6.30am O.P. reported attack going well & several hundred prisoners seen coming in. His report was confirmed by the Infantry at 7.30am. 8.30am high ground N of H.24 captured. Soon Artillery obj⁽ᵉˢ⁾ of PRESSOIR taken by an Infantry patrol. 9.15am on ridge in H.12. 10.15am enemy counter attack on the front L.S.R put down but enemy supported by Infantry in troop both S8, 57 & 58 C.R's continued slow but unsteady retreat. Situation was such that 10.30am doubts reported by air observers in L.20.b & H.19.d. On chiefs from Salient had offices through KB and Quentin Road K/S. Enemy batteries seen firing from PRESSOIR. A new enemy O.P was engaged. O.Big-Search of prisoners full and no tracks not and a very fine [?]. By the 5/6th army L.Mar K more (general) at 4pm ??h suspected Capt Mitchell M.C sent the maps. Then infantry from 9am to 4pm. 9pm Left O.P. orders to further attack some but were repelled at 8.30am to order not from H.29.0 7/10 6.30a. And the attack to this time were repelled later from H.29.0 5.30pm that. Barrage put down are 8 orders & reported very effective. Enemy barrage put out reserve from S??m firemen?? seen but rangers latter.	4/ex Hosp 7/11/18 51ˢᵗ and 51.
	2/11/18			

WAR DIARY
or
INTELLIGENCE SUMMARY.
(Erase heading not required.)

Army Form C. 2118.

Instructions regarding War Diaries and Intelligence Summaries are contained in F. S. Regs., Part II. and the Staff Manual respectively. Title pages will be prepared in manuscript.

Place	Date	Hour	Summary of Events and Information	Remarks and references to Appendices
	2/11/18		Little difficulty to be entertained by ML in forcing the crossing here covered by Lt Gen'l Rawly. 1 Coy of 2 Coy Hampshire 2LS Brigade & Battery came on (Second) Brontore in K.B. & K.2g appeared to have forward. Light coy L.G. teams ascended to dominate, give covered SUZZANVING with M.G. & A.T. Gun.	
	3/11/18		4.30 am Lt Gen'l Gray, Brins perform 2 Coy of above from H.BN Sam Command of Gen'l passed O 59 Brigade Battn command, supply commenced supplying measures as H.15 & H.24. It was rarded messages ped from BHQ Bn Major saying army had ordered H. BHQ detached to from up. of BHQ remain in prior position. Coastal position order. 9.15 am message rec'd to you three from the front reported in CELLES. 9 hrs C.D Bn carefully carry out being would come under Han Grond Gas messages from B.N. The Corps dated O Brigade order, and could serve forward Battery of Regiments road. The two confirmed by Recon. Men onward, tries to the first command RATITES. Raised most of day. MB received at SUZZAVING.	
	5/11/18		Further rested in the day. Coys received Bn take occurred to trackle order and to swing it at forward thro F.20 e 50 70	

WAR DIARY
or
INTELLIGENCE SUMMARY

Army Form C. 2118.

Place	Date	Hour	Summary of Events and Information	Remarks and references to Appendices
	6/11/18		Old Cable entered & changed over at General Headquarters at general's departure. Many ran at day break had 5 pm cars ready and ordered Brigade to turn out at 36 BURG and to report to 36 BYO. Batteries moved off at 9.30 p.m. Owing to bad roads and bad roads from wagon lines crossroads (number of different cars, E Batty lost 4 hours to clear the wagon lines. Advance party went to find road found guard post of 36 BOURG which took party to about South to desired to stay night in Camiers, D Battery arrived at 1130 — Brown stat. Had breakfast. Ali Gatten ran by Campfel. 36 BYO ordered Bde to get the day's rest till afterward to serve in the East. Bdes from 36 BYO used own artillery Bde to move to Ed of Mers AMIELE. Batteries marched at 1615 am and took on advance posts at Gare to report to 36 BYO at 1 BRUAY.	
	7/11/18 8/11/18		Fair, good accommodation. Went to the right Cavalry Div infantry arm and to meet the Brigade to 1st Lt ROMAC. Brigade continued & artillery position	
	9/11/18		proceeded at 9 am to 36 BYO, taken Villiard at 10 am, good billets found and at billets. Low troops hospitable. Body of Column marched in at 12 noon.	

Army Form C. 2118.

WAR DIARY
or
INTELLIGENCE SUMMARY.
(Erase heading not required.)

Place	Date	Hour	Summary of Events and Information	Remarks and references to Appendices
	9/4/18		Words now to the offer to push grain field, then to bases & cauply lanes.	
	10/4/18		At 10 am Bde moved to COLON, advance parties issued to take up at PITGAM. Advanced troops but at rise were got such cover taken avoided to at 2pm beside incident to machinery, roads good	
	11/4/18		Orders recd from 56 Bde to march to (NEUVE) E. PETIT at 6 am. Batty Victor (particular) at 9.30 am, believe ordered to now off at 11.30 am. the order to advance at Colon come at 10.30 am — a long sport. settled that the Germans broke Germany had been signed.	
	12/4/18		Remained at COLON & commenced clearing up	
	13/4/18		Bde moved to FLEURBAIX Chateau	
14/4/18			Batten. Remained at COLON and continued clearing up and started	
15/4/18			fronts in the afternoon	
	16/4/18		13 B. Battery moved to longs farm Cage 1690	
	20/4/18		86 Battery moved to form just back of Headquarters	
			All Batteries received orders as from 10 a.m. & Network of the 51st being employed by the Div.	

Army Form C. 2118.

WAR DIARY
or
INTELLIGENCE SUMMARY.
(Erase heading not required.)

Place	Date	Hour	Summary of Events and Information	Remarks and references to Appendices
	21/10/18 to 30/10/18		Battalion continued cleaning up and training. As horses got tired C.O.'s and Staff Officers Coys of Infantry worked Football and other sports were held daily.

During the month the Brigade and Divisional Coys depts of Inspection, mostly men who had returned after being wounded or sick. They have had to be cast and at the beginning of the month a large amount was Rated Remounts, the Remounts sent to Isphaaven had mostly arrived, some very poor and in bad type while others were so poor, or in indifferent health condition to the Brigade according to Infantry. Very Foot front in were very slight, the influenza epidemic claimed wipes of spreading during the latter part of the month owing to lack of many NCO's.

Richst. Cpl.
for O.C. 3. B.L.H. F/A | |

Army Form C. 2118.

WAR DIARY
or
INTELLIGENCE SUMMARY.
(Erase heading not required.)

December 1918   32 Brigade R.F.A.

Place	Date	Hour	Summary of Events and Information	Remarks and references to Appendices
CORON K(2) 1535	1918 Dec 1		A Brigade march past was to be held but was cancelled. Recruits resumed. Exchange of horses made so as to have our Battery with Black horses with Keys 54.	Refer Maps 1/100,000 VALENCIENNES
	2		Brigade marched to BOUSSOIT (BO 1055) MAURAGE (BO 2550) STREPY (BO 4055) H.Q. being in BOUSSOIT 27 and 28 "KP" in MAURAGE and 132 in STREPY All the horses now got under cover in large barns. We were not very well comfortable being billeted in a large number of houses in the villages even the inhabitants our great trouble. There is plenty of amusement for the men. Football and all forms of games were organised. The Brigade football XI was busier in the Lucas Cup for the Division. Very good fields were secured and sufficient asked for. Education treated great difficulties as the Brigade were pretty scattered for grouping the classes and limited materials and Charts were issued. We held a recruiting team. Carets have been organised and suitable class rooms secured but we are not yet supplied any text books. A recreation room has been opened and Father's Keith C.F. has been giving general lectures. The decoration of houses and demolitions hospital was and two teams were has been carried out - upwards of 50 spring from the Brigade.	Refer Maps 1/100,000 NAMUR
	To 31			

Army Form C. 2118.

WAR DIARY
or
INTELLIGENCE SUMMARY.

(Erase heading not required.)

33 Brigade R.F.A.

November 1918

Date	Hour	Summary of Events and Information	Remarks and references to Appendices
1916			
19		Batteries moved to ST SYMPHORIEN & MAURAGE and STEPPY and reported for a few days. The horses who were badly in need were got into a well covered factory and were most comfortable.	
20		Batteries returned to their former billets at MAURAGE and STEPPY, began inspection by the Corps Commander on the march at Villers Chislain. Morning the month batteries have carried out training according to schemes laid down. The country is not suitable to advance daily service to early what exercises were but small fields were secured and it has been carried out. The interchange of officers between batteries and the hunting and reconnaissance of rabbits and hares has been vigorously carried out.	
25		Christmas Day was quietly enjoyed by the men. The divisional train managed the difficulties in a wild weather fit way and the large supply of plum pudding and turkeys and good fare and men very much appreciated. We are informed reinforcements have been set to Lembecq.	
31st Dec 1918			A E Cowan Lieut Col, R.A. comdg 33rd Brigade R.F.A.

4th Division

War Diaries
32nd Bde R.F.A
Royal F. Artillery

Jan-Feb 1919

Army Form C. 2118.

WAR DIARY
or
INTELLIGENCE SUMMARY.
(Erase heading not required.)

32nd Bde. R.F.A.

Place	Date	Hour	Summary of Events and Information	Remarks and references to Appendices
BOUSSOIT	January 1919		Bde H.Q. at CHATEAU BOUSSOIT L6a37 (Sheet 45) 27th Bty MAURAGE M2a00 (Sheet 45) 15th Bty STREPY M3600 155th Bty MAURAGE M2a92 86th Bty TRIVIERES N12a50 Major F.I. GRIFFITH-WILLIAMS R.F.A. commanding 155th Battery received the D.S.O and Military Cross with Bar. Major H.B. MACKIE formerly commanding 86th Bty received the bar to the M.C. Capt. A.V. COCKBURN M.C., 27th Bty received a "mention". Lieut. J.I. AUSTIN received the M.C. On demobilisation the following Officers were dispatched to England 1. Major M.P.M. MILNE 86th Bty 19 Jany 1919 2. Qr-Mr JENKINS Capt 32nd Bde 22 Jany 1919 3. 2/Lt Y MARSH 134 Bty 20 Jany 1919 4. A.N.M. DEMPSTER 86 Bty 1st Feb 1919 5. J.R.A. BURNASH signed attest 2 sides 2nd Sept 1919 6. 2/Lt J BARNES 27 Battery 29th Dec 1918 16 4 O.Rs were dispatched during the month 40 Y Horses A.B.C. and D were dispatched to base during the month 11 D Horses were sent for destruction Efforts were made to keep the instruction of 1 men to 5 horses over this balance about the average	Regl Strength for 4th and 46 1/40,000

WAR DIARY or INTELLIGENCE SUMMARY

Army Form C. 2118.

Place	Date	Hour	Summary of Events and Information	Remarks and references to Appendices
BOUSSOIT	Jany 1919		**Training.** Drills and weekly inspections have been kept up. The Brigade Commander instituted a Battery Competition similar to the Left up in Peace Time. The C.R.A. Brig. B. Bowes D.S.O. presented a Loch Each Battery to keep each week the cup three times in succession to retain the cup. Although winning the cup three times in succession the cup was to be open to the X Battery in each match. The 60 Arty cup was also played for by Batteries and HQ. Horse cross country races were instituted. As going to Landrecies the Brigade could not enter a team for the divisional competition being four horses from the Brigade took part in races competitions. The Brigade pulled in the semi-final of the divisional tug o' war. **Education and recreation.** Training conducted in various clubs etc was a libeary instituted. The horses were all under cover and the men were in most comfortable billets and the care of horses have been very good.	

A.G. Roome Lt
F.O.C. 3 Xdo RFA

Army Form C. 2118.

WAR DIARY
or
INTELLIGENCE SUMMARY.
(Erase heading not required.)

32nd Brigade R.F.A.

February 1919

Place	Date	Hour	Summary of Events and Information	Remarks and references to Appendices
BOUSSOIT	1919 Feby 1		Changes in command	Refer Maps Nos 4 & 5 and 6 1/40,000
			1. Major E.L.G. Griffith-Williams D.S.O. M.C. commdg 135 Battery in command of Bde. Brigade RFA from 1st February 1919 during Lt Col C.E.S. Bower's absence on leave.	
			2. Capt A. METAXA commanded 135 Battery vice Major E.L.G. GRIFFITH WILLIAMS.	
			3. Lt/W G.F. WOODROFFE in command of 134 Battery from 20-2-19 whilst Major F.T. VACHELL was on leave.	
			4. Capt J.L. LOWE T.M.B. posted to 27th Battery RFA on disbandment of 4 Div T.M. posted to 135th Battery RFA	
			5. 2/Lt L.H. ALDRIDGE T.M.B. posted to 135th Battery RFA	
			6. Lieut A.G. CAIRNS appointed Adjutant (a/Capt) from 24-1-19 vice a/Capt J.E. NICHOLS demobilised (auth:- First Army A/04b/727.A-22 Feb 1919)	
			2. LOCATIONS	
			Bde H.Q. Chateau BOUSSOIT L6 a37 (Sheet 43)	
			27th Bty MAURAGE M2 a00 (Sheet 46)	
			134 Bty STREPY M3 b00 (" ")	
			135 Bty MAURAGE M2 a00 (" ")	
			86th Bty TRIVIERES M12 a32	
			3. Demobilization	
			2 officers Lieut (a/Capt) J.E. NICHOLS Lieut H.A. BURWASH	
			O.R.s 25	
			Horses 121	
			At 28th February Strength of horses and mules 397 "X" 108 Mules 45. "Y" 10 "Z" 234	

WAR DIARY
or
INTELLIGENCE SUMMARY.
(Erase heading not required.)

February 1919   32nd Brigade R.F.A.

Army Form C. 2118.

Place	Date	Hour	Summary of Events and Information	Remarks and references to Appendices
ROUSSOIT	1919 Feb		4. *Education* About 10 attending Blacksmith's shops.	
			5. *Entertainments* "RAMMERS" dissolved owing to demobilization. Gave a successful matinée. Took a week from 29th Brigade concert Party, in aid of R.A. Benevolent Fund. Numerous small dances organized. No W.O.S.I's lecture much appreciated.	
			6. *Sport* Col. B.S. BOWER's Bath provided a sensational finish. 85th Battery proved runners up with one loss one draw. 132 Battery after defeating 86th Battery in the latter's last match had two matches to play and had to win both to win the Cup. They lost one and drew one. The Div. Arty cup matches were also play'd but not yet finished. 86th Battery are in a prominent position.	
			7. *Casualties* Very few casualties to men or horses. The health of the Troops has been very good.	
			8. The billets are very comfortable. The demobilization of horses has been the principal item of interest.	
			9. Honours M.M. Farrier Staff Sergt LINTERN A.E. 134558 BARROW R. 86553 BIBBINS H. 27765 BLANKS N. 174181 WOLFENDEN W.E. 85127	
	3rd March 1919.		A.G. Barnes Capt for O.C. 32 Bde R.F.A.	

4th Division
War Diaries
34th Brigade R.F.A.

August to December
1914

To 7 Division

Aug. 1914

121/806

WAR DIARY 121/806

37th Brigade R.F.A.
4th Division
Volume I.
4 – 30.8.14

Army Form C. 2118.

WAR DIARY
or
INTELLIGENCE SUMMARY

(Erase heading not required.)

37th Brigade Royal Field Artillery

Hour, Date, Place	Summary of Events and Information	Remarks and References to Appendices
4-9/14 6.45p	Orders to mobilize	
" 7 pm	Bgde orders issued	
" 7.45 pm	Letters to Herbert hospital, Reading, Hospital Staties Yorktown	
	+ from Adjt re Ruppert's mare	
4"-8/14 9.40 pm	(2) H.K. Deacon attached to Bde for service	
5"-9/14 9 am	Received Sunday Signal Party for B239 Am Col issues Lecture for conveyor equipment	
5" 9.30 am	Roley RAMC & 2 prisoners to Rd. F.A. Battn	
5" 10.45 "	2nd Lieut Telegrams. Am Cooper's + " (9. officers reverse to camp)	
5" 12 Noon	Letter issued. Send Spier to Blum + 4.A.B. Chefs tyres atlas	
5" 12.40 pm	4 Hess detail to check time tables	
6" 11 am	Inspection of horses	
5" 2.30 pm	Movement rate of Officers leaving the fate meet the Brigade	
6" 2.30 pm	" " " " " p.m.	
5" 3 pm	List to Fit + Pd Records of number of horses required to complete	

Army Form C. 2118.

WAR DIARY
or
INTELLIGENCE SUMMARY

(Erase heading not required.)

37th Brigade RFA

Hour, Date, Place	Summary of Events and Information	Remarks and References to Appendices
August		
5th 4.30	"Progress" reported to Genl Babington. Normal with exception of projecting scar on L-arm.	
6th 8.30 am	Officers to complete arrived. 2/Lt Johnstone (to 31" Battery) 2/Lt Troughton (for 37"BDe details). Capt Fraser RAMC 37"BDe M.O. 2/Lt Walker D.V.C. 37 Bde V.O.	
6th 2.30 pm	Stores issued to 4" Bat & Bde Am Col.	
6th 6 pm	A.0.7 Horses required from Staff Capt L.ofC.BA. Uriconditions weed for "A unit not to be reduced to the bare tomorrow laid down in note below.	
6th 5.15 pm	A.S.C. Reservists (9) joined	
6th 5 pm	3 Reservists from R.O.L. depot Jn.	
6th 6 pm	Conducting party for Preston left.	
6th 10.30 pm	Ammunition Column & Baggage formed for pay etc	
7th 9 am	245 Reservists arrive from R.O.L. depot	
7th ?		
7th 4.30 pm	Report (progress) 50 reservists not arrived from R.O.L. depot	
7th 6 pm	Entire regiment over power strictures.	
	1 Reservist joined from 20.L. depot.	

Army Form C. 2118.

WAR DIARY
or
INTELLIGENCE SUMMARY
(Erase heading not required.)

Instructions regarding War Diaries and Intelligence Summaries are contained in F.S. Regs., Part II. and the Staff Manual respectively. Title pages will be prepared in manuscript.

37th Brigade R.F.A.

Hour, Date, Place	Summary of Events and Information	Remarks and References to Appendices
Woolwich		
7th 9.30 pm	Order received confirming verbal orders to Col Bathcombe to hold horses 35th Battery in readiness to transfer immediately to 32nd Brig. R.F.A.	
7th 9.40 pm	Orders issued to 35th Batt. R.F.A. hold horses in readiness to transfer to 32nd Brigade R.F.A.	
8th 8 pm	Statement called for in Sept 4" gun ret. as to extra credit of new posts to L.S.A.H.Q.	
8th 5.20 am	150 Recruits arrived from No 2 Depot Preston.	
7th 10.50pm	Order from War Office : per Brig Maj. All surplus officers on completion of mobilization to be sent to Woolwich Reserve Brigade.	
8th 11.0 am	Order from 4" D.A. to hold 1 Battery in readiness to move on receipt of orders. When movement of Battery ordered, has been effected. When movement of this Battery is ordered to report No of Battery to 4" D.A. Horses no previous to be allotted to Battery first. Com. Col'. but.	
8th 11.50 am	Orders from 4 D.A. Indents for January Rations or earlier to be made out on A.B.55. dated & signed by an officer.	
8th 4 pm	37th Brigade R.F.A. completed up to strength in Horses and men during the day.	
8th 5.0pm	55th Battery confirms to Bestock permanently in anticipation of orders to move.	

Army Form C. 2118.

WAR DIARY
or
INTELLIGENCE SUMMARY

(Erase heading not required.)

37th Brigade RFA

Hour, Date, Place	Summary of Events and Information	Remarks and References to Appendices
8th Watford 8.15 pm 6 pm	Progress normal. Except for A.F. B 64 not complete (not yet issued/a report) 37th Bgd's return	
9d. 7 am	Orders received from 4th D.A. No personal effects or others ranks horses or equipment in excess of War Establishment is to be taken with units from place of mobilization.	Issued to Batteries
9h	During the afternoon the Batteries paraded in field service order and were inspected by the O.C. 37th Bde to be sworn in per P.O, 4th D.A.	
10d	Routine. Batteries on field service marching order paraded & gun drill	
11d	Routine.	
12d	Routine.	
13d	Routine.	
14d 15d	Routine Routine	
16d	Routine. Orders received from Bgd for 1/c Drivers & E.C. Attaugh Gar. Cy. to be in readiness to move to Harwich on 18th Sept.	
17d. 8.30 am.	Orders from 4th D.A. re move to Harwich and replacement of casualties.	
	army horses.	

Army Form C. 2118.

WAR DIARY
or
INTELLIGENCE SUMMARY
(Erase heading not required.)

37th Brigade RFA

Hour, Date, Place	Summary of Events and Information	Remarks and References to Appendices
Woolwich 17th	Preparation for move to Harrow.	
18"		
19th Camp (A "Bur) Harrow	Marched from Woolwich to Camp Gothic Hill nr Harrow. Still and Camp routine.	
20"	" " At 10.20 pm orders (see memo) through 12 Brigade area commander for the 37th Brigade RFA to entrain according to time table received, on the night of 21st/22nd Bryant & clay L 22 D	
21st Camp Harrow	Orders re entrainment distributed to Batteries & Amn Col. 37th Battery entrained at 10.30 pm.	
22nd 2nd Sep	Remainder of 37th F.C. Brigade entrained at Park Royal Stat Brigade arrived at South SOUTHAMPTON + Embarked.	
23rd	Brigade arrived at Bout BOULOGNE and proceeded to Pontoon Rest Camp No 1.	
24th Camp Boulogne.	Battrie entraining for the front.	

181 Position and to M

37th Brigade RHA

Army Form C. 2118.

WAR DIARY
OR
INTELLIGENCE SUMMARY
(Erase heading not required.)

Instructions regarding War Diaries and Intelligence Summaries are contained in F. S. Regs., Part II. and the Staff Manual respectively. Title pages will be prepared in manuscript.

Hour, Date, Place	Summary of Events and Information	Remarks and References to Appendices
August—		
25th. 7 am	Bivouacked at FRENAY. Marched to MONTIGNY, thence to Bivouac in LIGNY.	
26th 500 SW of HAUCOURT	Left bivouac 10 am. Brigade came into action pursuing N but did not fire in the morning. Changed position at Quiveley and took up position of SELIGNY. 31" & 55" Batteries fired at enemy's Artillery & Infantry during the afternoon, effect of fire could not be noticed (being woodlands) there the Batteries were repeatedly shelled, especially shelled fire for some hours, but little visible effect. Shells nearly all were of 3.1". Was slightly wounded & some horses. 35th Battery did not fire from this position. One was ordered at about 2 pm to take up a position in rear to cover retirement. While on the move on road S.P. posters, they were shelled, & Lt. Braw killed & wounded. I have since received wounded. They also shelled one ammn' waggon. 32nd Brigade Battries covered retirement of 32nd Brigade	

Army Form C. 2118.

WAR DIARY
or
INTELLIGENCE SUMMARY

(Erase heading not required.)

31th Brigade O&a

Hour, Date, Place	Summary of Events and Information	Remarks and References to Appendices
26th	Brigade retired at 6.30 pm to VENDHUILE arriving 11.30 pm.	
27th	March continued 5.30 am to POISEL arriving 9.30 am. Some pause and night march to VOYENNES arriving 7 am, 28th, carrying large numbers of infantry on the curriages. During day 2. 27th Battalion in billets in several portions but 20 Senior. 8de ordered to cover retirement of 3rd Div through HAMS. Infantry an hour after arrival. Battalion did not come into action. T.A. very tired. 2.30 pm retired to MURANCOURT arriving 7 pm.	
29th	Marched for NOYON 9 am arriving 11 pm (long halt during afternoon). Troops watched combat between 2 aeroplanes. (Troops all in good health + spirits) thrown night of 29/30. Bridge over OISE was destroyed.	
30th	Left LESCLOYES 2 am. Marched via BRIEULTE CHATEAU LA CHENOYE arriving 7 pm. Arrangements	

Sept. 1914

181/1063

WAR DIARY.

37th Brigade R.F.A.

4th Division

Volume II.

31.8 — 30.9.14

WAR DIARY
or
INTELLIGENCE SUMMARY

(Erase heading not required.)

Army Form C. 2118.

Instructions regarding War Diaries and Intelligence Summaries are contained in F.S. Regs., Part II. and the Staff Manual respectively. Title pages will be prepared in manuscript.

Hour, Date, Place	Summary of Events and Information	Remarks and References to Appendices
31/-	Paraded at 2 am. arrangement for march very bad, all troops late and in wrong places, via FONTENOYE, through forest of CANPIEGNE via SAINT-IMES. to Platoon S. of ST. VAAST.	
1st	Reveillez at 5 am. Very thick mist. At 5.50 am heavy firing heard to South away S.E. towards NERY. Brig. Harmans'd H? to S. moved away at 6.10 a.m. Firing caused heavy damage among Queens Bays & L Battery, who were caught while providing horses & Battery guns abandoned, but recovered one hour later. and 8 German horse artillery guns supp.d Captured. Remnants of Queens Bays formed (about 40) I never recover with refugees from 3rd & 5th D.G.'s. B'de Returns to BARON and came into action against our own Cavalry, but did not fire. Returns for night- S. of BARON arriving 8 p.m. Moved 2 p.m. to DAMMARTIN arrived 9.30 am while on by Germans on march news received that Pontz had been cut up by Germans (Cameron)	

WAR DIARY or INTELLIGENCE SUMMARY

Army Form C. 2118.

(Erase heading not required.)

Hour, Date, Place	Summary of Events and Information	Remarks and References to Appendices
2ⁿᵈ Cont.	At Brooming horse and cattle pass about, 1 man wounded while on horse patrol by an air cropola.	
3ʳᵈ	Marched at 1 am for LAGNY. Changed temporarily on the town, & then moved to JOSSIGNY.	
4ᵗʰ	Marched to FERRIERES, bivouacked at 11 pm order to march again at 2.30 am.	
5	2.30 am Marched to BRIE expect to rest here come days.	
6ᵗʰ	No rest up. BRIE at 3.30 AM. Marched back to FERRIERES watered there. thence to JOSSIGNY thence from thence towards LAGNY. Thence to ROMAINVILLIERS & bivouacked	
7ᵗʰ	At Midday marched through VOULANGIS to MAISONCELLES which German had just quitted village pillaged.	

WAR DIARY or INTELLIGENCE SUMMARY

(Erase heading not required.)

Army Form C. 2118.

Instructions regarding War Diaries and Intelligence Summaries are contained in F.S. Regs., Part II. and the Staff Manual respectively. Title pages will be prepared in manuscript.

Hour, Date, Place	Summary of Events and Information	Remarks and References to Appendices
8th September.	The Brigade moved early in the day from MAISONCELLES to point ¾ mile North of PETIT COURRIB. At 11 AM 35th Battery came into action firing towards TOURRE, range long, a fringe which turned out the observers, effect of the hostility unknown. At midday, the Brigade advanced to positions 1S and SH of JOUARRE, close to the town. 3rd Battery observing from the Church tower. 61st Battery crossed marsh West of the town and joined other General Wilson's Brigade across the bridge. 35th Battery did not fire. 9 PM 1.30 Brigade bivouac'd to bivouac ½ mile SE of LE Gd CLAIRET. 35th Battery did not fire during the day.	
9th September. 9.15 am 10 am 10.45am	3rd and 35th Batteries at 5am occupied positions on east evening of hill and fired at intervals during the morning at enemy's infantry N of the river MARNE. Our information received from our infantry who were held up in LA FERTE. 35th Battery fired at machine guns and snipers on quarry N of river. 35th Battery were ordered to VENTEUIL C". 3rd and 35th Batteries fired at enemy infantry retiring from LA FERTE, and continued to fire at any bodies of troops seen N of river until mid-day.	

WAR DIARY
or
INTELLIGENCE SUMMARY
(Erase heading not required.)

Army Form C. 2118.

Hour, Date, Place	Summary of Events and Information	Remarks and References to Appendices
9th September.	During the afternoon all batteries of Div'l Horse Arty at LA FERTE, from which time was being directed on the Infantry Bridge who were trying to cross the Bridge. Effect on the Shelling fire was turned on to returning Infantry on the MONTREUIL road.	
6 p.m.	55th Battery ordered to join Col. Ross-Johnson 14th Bde @ 3 a.m. to avoid crossing D/12th Army Brig. at LE SAUSSOY. 3rd + 35th Batteries bivouacked at JOUARRE.	
7 p.m.		
10th September	3rd + 35th Batteries occupied positions tomorrow evening at 4.30 a.m. At 7.30 a.m. 55th Battery marched to LE SAUSSOY and crossed the MARNE here. A show hall made and march resumed through ST AULDE to COULOMB and bivouacked. 55th Battery rejoined.	
11th September	Marched at 5.15 a.m. bivouacked 7.30 a.m. at MARIZY LE MARD. No supplies were received by the Brigade on this day. 35th Battery detached during afternoon to join 14th Brigade in Advanced Guard.	

Army Form C. 2118.

WAR DIARY
or
INTELLIGENCE SUMMARY
(Erase heading not required.)

Hour, Date, Place	Summary of Events and Information	Remarks and References to Appendices
12th September	Advance at dawn to ROSIERE arriving in afternoon, a long halt was made here, just before dark orders were received to return through village and bivouac, this movement caused much confusion, with the result that only one battery (55th) was able to reach its proper position, the roads all being blocked with other artillery units, ambulances &c. Very heavy rain fell during the night.	
13th September	Marched at 8am towards ACY. On arrival at 10.11AY orders received to move into a position of readiness. Halt here till 4pm, thence through ACY. 55th Battery to position in new cover south of DEMOISELLE. This Battery fired during the a/noon at Infantry in direction of MAUBEUGE Road, on VREGNY Ridge, and at 4pm at Guns at Pt. 137, and South [off?] V in SHIVRES at about 5pm. At 4.5pm 31st Battery took up position just south of JURY, but did not fire. 37st & 55th Batteries bivouacked on their positions. 35th Battery also with 14th Brigade	

Army Form C. 2118.

WAR DIARY
or
INTELLIGENCE SUMMARY
(Erase heading not required.)

Instructions regarding War Diaries and Intelligence Summaries are contained in F. S. Regs., Part II. and the Staff Manual respectively. Title pages will be prepared in manuscript.

Hour, Date, Place	Summary of Events and Information	Remarks and References to Appendices
14th September	Brigade and 55th Battery crossed the AISNE at VENIZEL at 5 a.m. 55th Camp 15th in position ½ mile N.W. of LA MONTAGNE Fm. and engaged guns at Pt. 132. Soud Sergeant observing from Infantry firing line to N.W. gave good information while under fire from field and machine guns. At 7 a.m. 36th Battery came into action on the right of 55th against Pt. 132.	
15th September	35th Battery rejoined during the morning at BUCY LE LONG but did not come into position till late in the evening when sent back to position at LE MESNIL 1 mile S.E. of VENIZEL. 31st and 55th Batteries in position as on 14th. During the morning both batteries fired at guns at Pt. 132, later four guns of 31st Battery were turned on to guns towards the N.E. 55th Battery again engaged the fire of his battery from an advanced position. Four guns of the 31st Battery observed the fire of four guns from a position N.W. of LA MONTAGNE Fm.	

Army Form C. 2118.

WAR DIARY
or
INTELLIGENCE SUMMARY

(Erase heading not required.)

Hour, Date, Place	Summary of Events and Information	Remarks and References to Appendices
15th September	under heavy fire from where he observed being blown up by a shell just after he left. He directed the fire of the battery guns with great skill, one of the enemy's observing stations and a wagon (?) being blown up. At about 2 pm the enemy's aeroplane came over the position and signalled. Shortly after this the batteries were subjected to a heavy fire from heavy guns (21 centimetre mortars) 40 to 50 shells falling among the batteries in from five to ten minutes. During this firing the 30 Battery lost 16 killed 12 wounded and 33 horses (one 30% of personnel with the firing battery), one shell falling among the men, who had been moved under cover into a sunken road, killed 12 and wounded 9 men. The names of the following Officers and men are mentioned for gallant conduct under fire at this time:-	

WAR DIARY
or
INTELLIGENCE SUMMARY

Army Form C. 2118.

Hour, Date, Place | **Summary of Events and Information** | **Remarks and References to Appendices**

Sablières

3/d Battery:—
For relieving, dressing and removing wounded under heavy fire:— 2/Lieut J.A. Johnston, 2nd Lieut E. Simpson, No 2310 Sgt Dawson, No 51255 Cpl Sweet (since promoted Sgt) No 67707 Gunner Mostyn, No 65724 Gunner Cox.

Lieut Batts as stated previously.

For displaying remarkable coolness in extricating horses under fire:— No 55704 Dr L mallory, No 73555 Dr Butcher, No 33744 Dr Roberts, No 55696 Dr Haddock, No 70927 Dr Cunha, No 58122 2/L Chamberlain, No 5366 Gnr Blackwell *

* This man is brought to special notice for repeatedly returning to the Battery under fire and bringing away wounded, including the Battery QMS, horses and limbers.

55th Battery:—
Captain J.R. Colvill, for gallant conduct in collecting men and horses under heavy fire.

WAR DIARY or INTELLIGENCE SUMMARY

Army Form C. 2118.

Hour, Date, Place	Summary of Events and Information	Remarks and References to Appendices
15th September	**15th Battery:—** Of first Aid. Parties, dressing, collecting and removing wounded men, chiefly of 20th Battery, under heavy fire. No 2563 BQMS J.R.Cotton, No 22153 Far Sgt Morel, both these men showed great gallantry in assisting Capt Colville. The following men of 15th Battery also showed great courage and did splendid work under heavy fire:— No 55116 Cpl E. Goodhead, No 59167 Bdr C.E. Thomas, No 56779 Dvr D. Trimble, No 14441 Gr. W.G. Cox., No 38170 Gr R. Hales, No 78950 Gr. A. Orbell, No 51694 Dr. O. Jones, No 55352 Dr. D. Parris, No 69567 Dvr. F.G. Steele (age 16). After these two batteries were getting to have their guns and take cover teams were collected and remade in BUCY LE LONG. The batteries were brought out of action about 7.30 pm and taken to position 300 yards	

Army Form C. 2118.

WAR DIARY
or
INTELLIGENCE SUMMARY
(Erase heading not required.)

Instructions regarding War Diaries and Intelligence Summaries are contained in F. S. Regs., Part II. and the Staff Manual respectively. Title pages will be prepared in manuscript.

Hour, Date, Place	Summary of Events and Information	Remarks and References to Appendices
15th September	N.E. of VENIZEL Bridge, where they bivouacked for the night. At 8 am on 15th the telephone cart was sent up to MONTAGNE Fm. Owing to a breakdown at observing station near MONTAGNE Fm. Owing to a block on the road Wag: Bdy k car was delayed and came under shrapnel fire. The Nol. Car (telephone) being hit, also one Shoeing Smith and a Driver of the Brigade Amm. Column who were with the wagons replenishing ammunition. The telephone line was got into position without loss of time by the remainder of the detachment.	
16th September	31st and 55th Batteries in action 800 x NE of VENIZEL Bridge. During morning, both batteries fired at enemy's guns towards PONT ROUGE, but observation of aeroplane unsatisfactory. A few of the enemy's shrapnel burst near the Batteries during the day, but no damage was done.	

WAR DIARY
or
INTELLIGENCE SUMMARY
(Erase heading not required.)

Army Form C. 2118.

Hour, Date, Place	Summary of Events and Information	Remarks and References to Appendices
17th September	31st & 35th Batteries entrenched during the day, and fired a few shots towards PONT ROUGE in the afternoon. Few brownings, 35th Battery, slightly wounded in left hand in the evening, returns to England. 35th Battery also at LE MESNIL.	
18th,19th & 20th September	Same position. Batteries entrenching. Ground under water, men moved into barges as night or never able firing. 35th Battery as before. Supplies and mails coming regularly.	
21st	The Average Day position.	
22nd	31" 55" Battery shelled enemy's position near PONT ROUGE very well. Point of fierce day that burst of guns unknown.	
23rd	Baltin (31 6") fired at 5 km into about of to own breakfast French attack a PERRIERE + E The attack was not carried out.	

Army Form C. 2118.

WAR DIARY
or
INTELLIGENCE SUMMARY.
(Erase heading not required.)

Hour, Date, Place	Summary of Events and Information	Remarks and references to Appendices.
23rd Cont.	Enemy at ghost midday on A & B flanks went [into] action. [illegible] was starving [illegible] out B.S.Y. T + T.E.R. (950 6M) Mr J [illegible] that I manage battery.	
24th	Major Gill arrived at [illegible] who took over I at "Bar O.P."	
25th	Unto aircraft on B (?) and 53rd Howitzer attacked	
26th	at 2 pm 24 [illegible] batteries fell [illegible] if you [illegible] fire at TRUE RIDGE to support forward attack on our left.	
27th	3" 6th fires at times with increased rate to treat the men in zero today [illegible] heavily. fired at ... 55 Battery have to [illegible] [illegible] cover the [illegible] of the Battery was accounted by fragment of shell.	

Army Form C. 2118.

WAR DIARY
or
INTELLIGENCE SUMMARY.
(Erase heading not required.)

Instructions regarding War Diaries and Intelligence Summaries are contained in F.S. Regs., Part II. and the Staff Manual respectively. Title pages will be prepared in manuscript.

Hour, Date, Place	Summary of Events and Information	Remarks and references to Appendices
27th	Stationer reported Lay V.O. amongst German's LEFTOY (Confirmation)	
28th	Brigade ordered to join in from at P. 172 of the trench line with shelves from Ebau. Arnoury out of and in focus. Brigade H.Q. move into hour west South of VENIZEL bridge, Signal Co.'s also in other house. New position to South reconnoitred march the afternoon.	
29th	Nothing done today except preparing new position reconnoitred 28th.	
30th	31st and 55th Batteries opened in envious from 3 p.m. in target A and beyond BAUBEUGE ROAD in support of French attack on Upr. PERRIERE Fm – CUFFIES. Result of fire unknown. The attack seems not to have been pushed home or little firing was heard from the West. 35th Battery firing during the day towards CHIVRES.	

121/1818

37th Brigade R+H.
4th Division
1—31.10.14

Army Form C. 2118.

WAR DIARY
or
INTELLIGENCE SUMMARY
(Erase heading not required.)

36th Brigade R.F.A.

Hour, Date, Place	Summary of Events and Information	Remarks and References to Appendices
October 1st.	Position of batteries unchanged. No further ones taken during the day. One man of Suzanne(?) slightly wounded. 2nd Lieut Anthony's section detailed to engage hostile sniper machine gun and trenches N. of Group. Section did not fire to-day.	
Night of 1st–2nd	55th Battery moves to STE MARGUERITE.	
2nd.	Some fire near 31st Battery during the day. No damage to battery. Detached section of 31st Battery under Lieut Simpson with the 2nd French Flank Detachment drove enemy from trench and put two machine guns out of action. Fire from Germans on to enemy occupying mill. Several fires lit inside the enemy being driven out. The section then engaged enemy and machine guns in buildings at railway station, all the Frenchmen being hit and the enemy driven out. Lieut Anthony	

Army Form C. 2118.

WAR DIARY
or
INTELLIGENCE SUMMARY

(Erase heading not required.)

37th Brigade RFA

Hour, Date, Place	Summary of Events and Information	Remarks and References to Appendices
October 2nd	Received the Special thanks of French Commander. Special report of the action of this action was sent to the G.O.C. IIIrd Army Corps. 37th Bgy being assembled round the whole of front. Division.	
Night of 2nd/3rd	35th Battery moved to BUCY-LE-LONG.	
3rd	35th and 55th Batteries firing at enemy's guns.	
6.30 pm	35th Battery moved to position above the River AISNE ½ mile SE of VENIZEL.	
4th	35th and 55th Batteries firing at enemy's guns. Headquarters moved to LA CARRIERE. The enemy shelled message near 55th Battery, one man being slightly wounded.	
5th Hors.	35th Batteries shelled CHIVRES, three German aeroplanes flew over batteries during the day.	

WAR DIARY or INTELLIGENCE SUMMARY.

Army Form C. 2118.

37th Brigade R.F.A.

Hour, Date, Place	Summary of Events and Information	Remarks and references to Appendices
Oct. 6th	35th and 55th Batteries crossed to S. side of River AISNE after dark, coming into position on left of 31st Battery.	
7th	Brigade marches into billets at SEPTMONTS, coming under command of G.O.C. 11th Infantry Brigade.	
8th 8.am.	55th Battery moved back to another near LA CARRIÈRE. Remainder of Brigade moved to CHAORISE. Brigade Ammunition Column rejoined. 55th Battery rejoined after dark.	
9th	Halted in CHAORISE.	
Night of 9th-10th	Brigade marched to VILLERS COTTEREST halting at 3 a.m. on 10th just outside the town (French Army Headquarters in town).	
10th 2pm	Brigade marched to MORIENVAL.	

Army Form C. 2118.

WAR DIARY
or
INTELLIGENCE SUMMARY.
(Erase heading not required.)

34th Brigade RA

Hour, Date, Place	Summary of Events and Information	Remarks and references to Appendices
October		
11th / 8 am	Brigade marched to COMPIEGNE. Brigade Ammunition Column entrained. Headquarters and 31st Battery entrained.	
2 pm	35th Battery entrained.	
6 pm		
10 pm	55th Battery entrained	
12th Noon	Brigade Headquarters and 31st Battery arrived ARCQUES, and marched to billets at ferme NE of HAZEBROUCK arriving 6.30 pm. 35th, 55th and Ammunition Column detrained at HAZEBROUCK, arriving in billets at 9.30 pm. 12 midnight, and 11 am.	
13th 9 am	Brigade marched to FOUR CROIX and billeted there. Afternoon 35th and 55th Batteries moved up to FLETRE, coming into action in support ½ mile NE of village. 55th Battery in support of attack on HTE PORTE F?, 35th Battery against FONTAINE HOUCK.	

Army Form C 2118.

WAR DIARY
or
INTELLIGENCE SUMMARY.
(Erase heading not required.)

31th Brigade H.J.

Date, Place Hour	Summary of Events and Information	Remarks and references to Appendices
October 13th	but infantry attack was unsuccessful. 101st Battery in action from S.W. of FRETRE-LATE on the enemy, but did not fire. Batteries billeted in farms near their positions. Ammn Columns remained at ROUGE CROIX.	
14th	Brigade ordered to move at 7am, but did not march till 8.30am arriving at BAILLEUL 6.30am. Brigade billeted in farms N.W. of town.	
15th	101st Battery detailed with advance guard under orders of Lieut-Colonel Stockdale, 55th and 55th Batteries remained in billets.	
16th	101st Battery moved to L.A. MENEGATE, also under Lieut-Colonel Stockdale. Remainder of Brigade stayed in billets.	

Army Form C 2118.

5th Brigade RFA

WAR DIARY
or
INTELLIGENCE SUMMARY
(Erase heading not required.)

Hour. Date. Place	Summary of Events and Information	Remarks and References to Appendices
17th Oct 1914	35th Battery moved to NIEPPE, 55th Battery remained in BAILLEUL. 31st Battery in billets at LA MENEGATE. Lieut-Colonel Bathsfords commanding 3rd, 35th and 125th Batteries (taking over from Lieut-Colonel Stondale) in afternoon. 125th Battery rejoined its own Brigade.	
18th 8.0am 6.am	55th 35th Batteries to form 43rd direct orders moved to French Div Arty. 31st Battery moved to LE BIZET coming under batteries supporting 10th Infantry Brigade attack on FRELINGHIEN. 55th Battery moves to HOUPLINES about midday, coming into action on left of 31st Battery, 31st Battery obtaining from Church Known. Shelled out, 31st did not 35th Batteries firing at trenches about LA FLOT. One gun of 55th Battery under Lieut A.J. Heron with Seaforth Highlanders to destroy houses on FRELINGHIEN ??oad. 35th and 55th Batteries	

Army Form C 2118.

37th Brigade RFA

WAR DIARY
or
INTELLIGENCE SUMMARY
(Erase heading not required.)

Hour, Date, Place	Summary of Events and Information	Remarks and References to Appendices
18th	Batteries billeted in HOUPLINES, leaving guns in action.	
19th 9.30 am	36th and 55th Batteries again firing in direction of LA FALOT. Infantry support few rounds. Detached gun doing good work.	
9 am	One Section of Battery ordered to join B/2RFA to be under Colonel Butler, Lancashire Fusiliers.	
3 pm	Remainder of 31st Battery sent to join detached Section. 55th Battery firing during the day on enemy trenches and guns. Headquarters and 65th Battery billets in HOUPLINES.	

WAR DIARY
or
INTELLIGENCE SUMMARY

(Erase heading not required.)

Army Form C 2118.

Hour, Date, Place	Summary of Events and Information	Remarks and References to Appendices
October 20th.	Headquarters at house North end of HOUPLINES; village heavily shelled all the morning, in evening moved back to HOUPLINES Station. 85th Battery's position unchanged:- firing at enemy's trenches and guns. 89 Battery in action E. of LE BIZET, did not fire. 35th Battery continued to engage enemy in FRELINGHIEN.	
21st	85th Battery's position unchanged, in action against bridge and village of FRELINGHIEN. Observation from LA RUAGE. 13th Battery moved to about 63 in action North of LA HUTTE. Shelled WHERETON and enemy's infantry attacking LE CHEER and ST YVES. 35th Battery firing on enemy in FRELINGHIEN.	

WAR DIARY or INTELLIGENCE SUMMARY

(Erase heading not required.)

Army Form C. 2118.

Hour, Date, Place	Summary of Events and Information	Remarks and References to Appendices
Oct/14 22nd	53rd, 54th(Heavy) and 55th Batterys: positions unchanged. 36th Battery fired on enemy's guns and infantry positions, knocking most enemy's rifles, chiefly enemy's position in front of our trenches (no an Observation station at WES. 35th Battery's position unchanged, firing on FRELINGHIEN.	
23rd	55th Battery fired on FRELINGHIEN & hund. also various gun fire and infantry targets. The Battery 30 in Leus. 36th Battery in action marched to WYTSCHAETE in action against OOSTAVERNE in support of 2nd Cavalry Division, fired on Battery at HOUTHEM with 1 certain observation hit, and certain manoeuvres in action against FRELINGHIEN.	
24th	55th Battery fired on enemy's battery and columns of cycling scouts in FRELINGHIEN. 33rd Battery, position observed by Field gale, shelled houses reported to contain machine in	

Army Form C 2118.

WAR DIARY
or
INTELLIGENCE SUMMARY
(Erase heading not required.)

Instructions regarding War Diaries and Intelligence Summaries are contained in F. S. Regs., Part II. and the Staff Manual respectively. Title pages will be prepared in manuscript.

Hour, Date, Place	Summary of Events and Information	Remarks and References to Appendices
October 24th (Continued)	Enemy & Somersets light infantry. Direct hits on two houses, three set on fire. 35th Battery returned to LE BIZET and section detached to 54th Battery at CHAPELLE D'ARMENTIERES.	
25th	55th Battery fired at village Minches and general observation by aeroplane; attacked gun teams & field hdqs just east and south west of FRELINGHIEN bridge. 25th Battery 2 sections in action against FRELINGHIEN and enemy trenches at Pont Ballots forward within 800 ft of enemy to harass enemy checking the 6″ gun against houses from which our infantry were being worried. So early had a few rounds at night to stop enemy's infantry fire.	

WAR DIARY
or
INTELLIGENCE SUMMARY

(Erase heading not required.)

Army Form C. 2118.

Instructions regarding War Diaries and Intelligence Summaries are contained in F. S. Regs., Part II. and the Staff Manual respectively. Title pages will be prepared in manuscript.

Hour, Date, Place	Summary of Events and Information	Remarks and References to Appendices
Jeffer 26/16	55th Battery shelled FREINGHIEN heavily. After our infantry had been forced to withdraw owing to enemy shell fire, Rued Houses gun withdrawn from Seafarers, this gun under afternoon opened to beat down occasional M.G. whilst was that regiment. 35th Battery located hostile heavy howitzer in NE TOURQUET which was apparently silenced by our gun under Lieut Phillips. Remainder of battery engaged enemy who advanced into FREINGHIEN. 3rd Battery howitzer unchanged fire round only time.	

Army Form C. 2118.

WAR DIARY
or
INTELLIGENCE SUMMARY

(Erase heading not required.)

Instructions regarding War Diaries and Intelligence Summaries are contained in F. S. Regs., Part II. and the Staff Manual respectively. Title pages will be prepared in manuscript.

Hour, Date, Place	Summary of Events and Information	Remarks and References to Appendices
27/4. April	Little firing during the day. 3rd Battery shelled by enemy's howitzers casualties 1 active bombardier assistant to hospital with severe shock. 36th Battery firing on FRELINGHIEN.	
28th	35th Battery firing on FRELINGHIEN. Watched guns of 55th Battery fired a few shots at houses from which Snipers were being employed.	
29th	Attack on Eleventh Infantry Brigade made during the day. 1st & 5th Batteries in action against this attack.	
30th	Very little firing during the day. 39th Battery fired in the afternoon on enemy's guns which were shelling Royal Warwickshire Regt's trenches.	

Army Form C. 2118.

WAR DIARY
or
INTELLIGENCE SUMMARY

(Erase heading not required.)

Instructions regarding War Diaries and Intelligence Summaries are contained in F. S. Regs., Part II. and the Staff Manual respectively. Title pages will be prepared in manuscript.

Hour, Date, Place.	Summary of Events and Information	Remarks and References to Appendices
Oetten 3/31	An attack expected today north of River Lys. About mid day enemy fired a few shell towards 39th Battery.	

COPY.

From O.C. 31st Battery R.F.A. to Commanding 37th Bde. R.F.A. -

The advanced section of my battery was in action at CHATEAU west of BUCY at 5.30 am. this morning and telephonic communication with 2nd Lieut. Simpson (who was in the French trenches in the ravine close to MAUBEUGE road about 500 yards S.W. of PERRIERE Farm) was established by 5.55 am. Owing to the mist it was impossible to open fire until 10.30 am. The guns were originally laid out by compass bearing, which was worked out from large scale map, and which proved to be within one degree of where expected. 2nd Lieut. Simpson first engaged enemy's trench containing maxim at S.W. end.

He very soon succeeded in putting four Lyddite shells in the trench and three were within 10 yards of the maxim, and caused the Germans to evacuate it. Then in accordance with orders from 4th Divisional Artillery, and with instructions previously received from the Colonel of the Zouaves in CROUY, the advanced French trench near the MOULIN de PONTFAURE having been evacuated by the French, 2nd Lieut. Simpson proceeded to switch his fire on to the Moulin and adjoining houses, assisted by observation by a French officer, who was in telephone communication with the French colonel at CROUY.

To show how necessary it was that this advanced French trench should have been evacuated before fire was opened on the mill, I may mention that even while shelling the first objective (150x from the mill) pieces of our Lyddite were falling in the French trench, fortunately without injuring anyone. The result of the fire on the mill was two direct hits, and six within 3 or 4 yards. The French reported that the fire was "encadré" and the enemy "se sauvent pas toutes les fenêtres and toutes les portes" into a largish house near the level crossing. A small house at the level crossing next to the largish house was reported to contain two maxims. 2nd Liuet. Simpson then switched his fire on to these two houses. The first two rounds burst in the small house at the level crossing, and the French report every other shell to have hit one of the houses in the vicinity. The French colonel reported by telephone "(des cries terrible et des pertes que doivent être enormes)". Owing to both French and our own telephone wires being constantly cut by the enemy's shrapnel fire at close range, the whole of this occupied from 10.30 am. till dusk (6.0 pm). I should like to add that the task though excellently accomplished by 2nd Lieut. Simpson was performed under circumstances which rendered it extremely difficult. During the whole day he was under rifle fire and maxim fire, reported by the French 250 metres distant, and under shrapnel fire at not more than 1000 yards...........

3/10/14.

$\frac{121}{2671}$

4th Division.

37th Bde. R.F.A.

Vol IV 1–30.11.14

Army Form C 2118.

WAR DIARY
or
INTELLIGENCE SUMMARY

(Erase heading not required.)

14th Brigade R.F.A.

Hour, Date, Place	Summary of Events and Information	Remarks and References to Appendices
1st November		
2nd	2 Guns of 25th Battery moved to Guns 68. 2 Guns remaining in LE BIZET	
3rd	Headquarters moved to R.A. 13 Wulverghem Farm at back of 8' PETIT PONT. Batteries as before. North artillery Group in 13.5th, 36 and 25th Batteries, also 4th Siege Battery	
4th	Weather very misty. No firing about 6' Point 63. 30th Battery firing on trenches South of MESSINES. 25th Battery firing at guns N.E. of MESSINES.	

Army Form C. 2118.

WAR DIARY
or
INTELLIGENCE SUMMARY
(Erase heading not required.)

Instructions regarding War Diaries and Intelligence Summaries are contained in F. S. Regs., Part II. and the Staff Manual respectively. Title pages will be prepared in manuscript.

Hour, Date, Place	Summary of Events and Information	Remarks and References to Appendices
6th November 5th	Guns in to supporting trench attack on MESSINES. Attack not pressed home	
6th	Same as 5th	
Night 6th-7th	Germans attacked on PLOEGSTEERT wood, and gained footing on eastern edge of wood and in houses North of LE GHEER	
7th	35th firing at guns N.E. of MESSINES also supporting trench	
8th	6th Siege Battery fired. Naval outbreak of French attack on MESSINES with no real results	
9th	French attack remains in same position. Front and East of MESSINES and to outposts in the rear	

WAR DIARY
or
INTELLIGENCE SUMMARY

(Erase heading not required.)

Army Form C. 2118.

Hour, Date, Place	Summary of Events and Information	Remarks and References to Appendices
9th November (Contd) Night of 9-10th	manner from Point 63. Our Infantry attacked Germans in their trenches on eastern edge of PLOEGSTEERT WOOD. This attack did not succeed in dislodging the enemy, owing to well-placed machine guns and the ? of barbed wire. Guns ?? fired all night to prevent enemy bringing up reinforcements. Some firing in a westerly end of PLOEGSTEERT WOOD by guns batteries at 63.	
10th		
11th	Lieut Colonel Rattle came to leave the Brigade to take over duties of Commandant at BAILLEUL. Batteries did not fire during the day. Enemy shelling about GUNY to byte Manage Ferme. (One alarm of S.O.S.)	

WAR DIARY
or
INTELLIGENCE SUMMARY

(Erase heading not required.)

Army Form C 2118.

Hour, Date, Place	Summary of Events and Information	Remarks and References to Appendices
April November 11th	Battery detached to LE BIZET. In the evening it fires of one of the Battery sent to billets in NIEPPE to rest. Supporting French attack on MESSINES as usual.	
12th	Headquarters moved to NIEPPE to intervene. 37th Brigade Headquarters under Major Colonel McCarthy take over North Artillery Group at 6.5". Lieut Colonel E.W. Spedding assumes command of 3rd Brigade RFA. Detached section & Stop returned battery at NIEPPE.	

WAR DIARY
or
INTELLIGENCE SUMMARY

(Erase heading not required.)

Hour, Date, Place	Summary of Events and Information	Remarks and References to Appendices
April 1914		
14th	Headquarters and 31st Battery resting in NIEPPE. Ammunition Column commence training under 31st Battery. 2 Lieut. O.B. Reynolds transferred to Ammunition Column.	
15th		
16th	Situation unchanged	
17th	Situation unchanged	
18th	55th Battery arrive in NIEPPE Kroch. 31st Battery relieve 35th Battery in the trenches.	
19th	Gun 68. 135th Battery arrive in NIEPPE to reset. One section 31st Battery also in NIEPPE under 2/Lt. A. Chesterton.	

Army Form C. 2118.

WAR DIARY
or
INTELLIGENCE SUMMARY
(Erase heading not required.)

Hour, Date, Place	Summary of Events and Information	Remarks and References to Appendices
19/11 November (Continued)		
At 10h (Continued)	At 11.30 Coy detached section 3/es Artillery moved from NIEPPE to PLOEGSTEERT. Major Roesel to England on 10 days leave. Headquarters, 85th and 55th Batteries in NIEPPE. 3/es Battery at Point 63	
20th.		
3/er	Maj. Gill to England on 10 days leave. Headquarters, 85th & 55th Batteries in NIEPPE.	

WAR DIARY
or
INTELLIGENCE SUMMARY

(Erase heading not required.)

Army Form C. 2118.

Hour, Date, Place	Summary of Events and Information	Remarks and References to Appendices

1914 Oldreacher

22nd — Headquarters takes over command of Centre Artillery Group at LE SIZE F, relieving 14th Brigade RFA Headquarters. Batteries in Centre Artillery Group:— 39th, 88th and 1 gun of 5th Siege. No firing during the day.

23rd — No firing. All quiet.

Army Form 2118.

WAR DIARY
or
INTELLIGENCE SUMMARY

(Erase heading not required.)

Hour, Date, Place	Summary of Events and Information	Remarks and References to Appendices
10h November		
24th	Situation unchanged.	
25th	6" Howitzers fired 16 rounds at enemy's trenches East of the Railway near LE TOUQUET Station	Attached from 4th Siege Battery.
26th	6" Howitzer fired 4 lyddite at FRELINGHIEN Bridge. Girder broken.	
27th	FRELINGHIEN Bridge reported repaired. This report untrue, but bridge still available for foot traffic. 6" Howitzer reported to have had one direct hit.	
28th	55th Battery and "B" subsection Brigade Ammunition Column moved from NIEPPE to SAILLY to join 4th Brigade A.F.A. 4th Division H.A. (Dorset) (this move is of temporary nature only). Few German H.E. field-gun shell fell in LE BIZET to-day.	

Army Form C. 2118.

WAR DIARY
or
INTELLIGENCE SUMMARY

(Erase heading not required.)

Instructions regarding War Diaries and Intelligence Summaries are contained in F. S. Regs., Part II. and the Staff Manual respectively. Title pages will be prepared in manuscript.

Hour, Date, Place	Summary of Events and Information	Remarks and References to Appendices
10th November 1914		
9.14	During morning hostile cavalry reported moving north to South on WARNETON - PONT ROUGE road. 88 guns fired on this road (29th Battery 88th Battery, 2-5 Battery, Section 36th Battery and 6" Howitzer). Few enemy's shell falling near LE BIZET Church during the afternoon, most of which did not burst.	
30th	Situation unchanged.	

121/3889

4th Division.

37th Bde R.F.A.

Vol V. 1 - 31.12.14

WAR DIARY or INTELLIGENCE SUMMARY

35th Brigade RFA

Hour, Date, Place	Summary of Events and Information	Remarks and References to Appendices
1914 December		
1st	25th Battery in action at Point 63 in relief of 2/of Battery which moved 15 kilos to NIEPPE. Enemy's trenches shelled during the day by howitzers and heavies (Lentic Arty Group).	
2nd	Situation unchanged.	
3rd	One Section 25th Battery registering from NORTH of BRIQUETERIE during the morning. Situation unchanged. Nothing to report.	
4th		
5th	Orders received to hand over Lentre Arty Group to 14th Bde RFA and establish on the situation unchanged.	
6th	Little shelling of German trenches and columns observed. Situation unchanged. Lentre Arty Group Centre Arty Group headquarters.	
7th	Taken over by 14th Bde RFA headquarters. 35th Bde RFA moved 15 kilos to NIEPPE.	

WAR DIARY
or
INTELLIGENCE SUMMARY.
(Erase heading not required.)

Army Form C. 2118.

Hour, Date, Place	Summary of Events and Information	Remarks and references to Appendices
1914 December 9th to 10th	Situation unchanged. In billets at NIEPPE.	
11th	104 How Battery R.G.A. attaches to Brigade and arrives in billets at NIEPPE.	
12th	Situation unchanged.	
Night of 12th-13th	Following reliefs took place. Detached section of 38th Battery at PLOEGSTEERT relieved by section of 104 How Battery, and rejoins its battery. 31st Battery took 1 Section to position in action East of LE BIZET.	

Army Form C. 2118.

WAR DIARY
or
INTELLIGENCE SUMMARY
(Erase heading not required.)

Hour, Date, Place	Summary of Events and Information	Remarks and References to Appendices
3rd	Battery under command of 2/M(Bn)-3SA 1-10A Bombed Hd Rtn Siege. The battery's registering enemy trenches S.W. of MESSINES during the day. (Hov. Battery moved into action as ordered (a today)	
4th	Battery under L. Colonel Seeding on outpost of attack on enemy's line between WYTSCHAETE and PETITE DOUVE Fm. Hov. Battery hung on BOIS DE WYTSCHAETE and 6A Siege against PETITE DOUVE Fm and trenches near 35A Battery and Hd Siege watching the line PONT ROUGE to this South of GAPAARD cross roads to prevent being made against (Rt. 11th Infantry Brigade) our reinforcements being brought up to E. MESSINES. Fire of guns on WYTSCHAETE Wood observed from Mount KEMMEL This fire very accurate the infantry attack made some progress capturing enemy's trenches	

Army Form C. 2118.

WAR DIARY
or
INTELLIGENCE SUMMARY

(Erase heading not required.)

Instructions regarding War Diaries and Intelligence Summaries are contained in F. S. Regs., Part II. and the Staff Manual respectively. Title pages will be prepared in manuscript.

Hour, Date, Place	Summary of Events and Information	Remarks and References to Appendices
19th December 14th (contd)	on East (West Edge of PETIT BOIS. Very few enemy's guns replied to our bombardment.	G.S.

Army Form C. 2118.

WAR DIARY
or
INTELLIGENCE SUMMARY.

(Erase heading not required.)

Instructions regarding War Diaries and Intelligence Summaries are contained in F.S. Regs., Part II. and the Staff Manual respectively. Title pages will be prepared in manuscript.

Hour, Date, Place	Summary of Events and Information	Remarks and references to Appendices
10p.m. December 15th	Three bursts of fire during the day – objectives same as those on 14th. Situation unchanged.	(A)
16th	Situation unchanged. Little firing during the day, except two bursts of fire, one at mid-day, one in the afternoon.	(B)
17th	Very little firing during the day. Two rounds E. of PLOEGSTEERT wood fired by Siege Battery	(C)
18th	Three bursts of fire during the day from 35th Battery. 40th Hows Battery in direction of WYTSCHAETE wood. Preparations being made for Infantry attack E. of PLOEGSTEERT wood.	(D)
9p.m.	Headquarters at 11th Infantry Brigade Report centre. 4th 7th Siege Batteries and 4th June 35th Battery commanded by Major EASTEET under orders of Lt-Col	(E)

WAR DIARY
or
INTELLIGENCE SUMMARY.
(Erase heading not required.)

Army Form C. 2118.

Hour, Date, Place	Summary of Events and Information	Remarks and references to Appendices
10/M December 19th (cont'd)	SPEDDING, in support of attack by 11th Inf. Brig. (remainder of 35th Battery under orders of North Artillery Group. Batteries firing by bursts of 15 minutes until 2.30 pm. Rate of fire of which increasing up to time of infantry attack. At 2.30 pm the fire of all guns directed on to enemy's reserve trenches, fortified houses, and machine guns. Comrades advance gained some ground, but Comrades unable to advance owing to shell of a siege battery falling in their trenches. The line at our point of attack was straightened out to some extent. Fire of siege batteries observed from ST. YVES, that of field howitzers	

Army Form C. 2118.

WAR DIARY
or
INTELLIGENCE SUMMARY.
(Erase heading not required.)

Instructions regarding War Diaries and Intelligence Summaries are contained in F.S. Regs., Part II. and the Staff Manual respectively. Title pages will be prepared in manuscript.

Hour, Date, Place	Summary of Events and Information	Remarks and references to Appendices
19th December 19th (Cont)	from LE GHEER. Firing ceases at dusk. (2) Lieutenant BOARD joins Brigade Ammunition Column	
20th	55th Battery, MAJOR KOEBEL, 35th Battery, LIEUTENANT-COLONEL CARTWRIGHT, orders to proceed to England for duty. Headquarters in same position as 19th during day. Situation unchanged.	
21st	Headquarters in NIEPPE. LT.COL. CARTWRIGHT and MAJOR KOEBEL proceed to England. MAJORS HARTLAND-MAHON and COLVILLE take over command of 81st and 55th Batteries respectively	
22nd	35th Battery to resting billets in NIEPPE. H group 3rd Battery take over 35th Battery's position at Point 63 and detached section with Centre Arty Group West of PLOEGSTEERT	

WAR DIARY
or
INTELLIGENCE SUMMARY.
(Erase heading not required.)

Army Form C. 2118.

Hour, Date, Place	Summary of Events and Information	Remarks and references to Appendices
1914 December		
23rd to 27th	Situation unchanged.	
28th	MAJOR D.H. GILL 31st Battery, invalided.	
29th	MAJOR M. HARTLAND-MAHON takes over command of 31st Battery. MAJOR STEET of 35th Battery invalided.	
30th	Lieut J.A. JOHNSTONE 31st Battery, invalided and sent to BASE. Lieut SIMPSON took over command of detached section 31st Battery, in place of Lieut JOHNSTONE. Battery Sergeant-Major AMOS, FETHERSTON, SAMMAYS, promoted 2nd Lieuts and effect from 15th Decr 1914, and left for BASE 30th militant	
31st	Situation unchanged	

4th Division

War Diaries

37th Bde. R.F.A. to IV. Corps
7-2-15

January + February
1915

121/4262

4th Division

37th Bde. R.F.A.

Vol VII. 1 – 31.1.15

Army Form C. 2118.

WAR DIARY
or
INTELLIGENCE SUMMARY.

(Erase heading not required.)

37th Brigade R.F.A.

Instructions regarding War Diaries and Intelligence Summaries are contained in F.S. Regs., Part II. and the Staff Manual respectively. Title pages will be prepared in manuscript.

Hour, Date, Place	Summary of Events and Information	Remarks and references to Appendices
1915		
January 1st NIEPPE	H.Q. 37th Brigade moved to NIEPPE	
2nd "	2nd Lieut James & 28th Battery joined. Were posted to 31st Battery. Rt.	
	31st Battery report three premature bursts from guns of Wilchita Section (W.J. ROECSTERS) shells still at front. Some 400 yards in front of the guns. The last two however been reported by No 1 before loading, no satisfactory explanation given.	
	O.P. 31st Battery reports irregular burning bursts of fuzes, owing to stems of different lots being issued together and not having been sorted in the Battery. From now on to be impossible to keep lots together, in order that there at one lot, only one lot fired from a Battery at a time. When a new lot comes into use the O.C. or observer officer should be informed.	

WAR DIARY
or
INTELLIGENCE SUMMARY.
(Erase heading not required.)

Army Form C. 2118.

Hour, Date, Place	Summary of Events and Information	Remarks and references to Appendices
3ᵈ NIEPPE	Nothing doing.	
Night of 3ʳᵈ/4ᵗʰ	35ᵗʰ Battery moved into action at 6.15, in relief of 31ˢᵗ Battery which moved to NIEPPE to rest.	
4ᵗʰ	Nothing doing.	
5ᵗʰ	H.Q. ordered to move to LE BIZET tomorrow to "Bryns" H.Q.	
6ᵗʰ 6ᵃᵐ	Capt Butler Stoney (Orderly Officer) goes to and joins 13ᵗʰ Battery.	
6ᵗʰ LE BIZET	H.Q. between 14ᵗʰ Bde H.Q. at LE BIZET.	
7ᵗʰ	Nothing doing. Lt Hess posted to R.H.A.	
8ᵗʰ		
9ᵗʰ	39ᵗʰ Battery position shelled near River LYS from moved slightly tonight 9ᵗʰ/10ᵗʰ to positions near Couvent at BIZET. Lt Bates joins R.H.A.	

Army Form C. 2118.

WAR DIARY
or
INTELLIGENCE SUMMARY.
(Erase heading not required.)

Instructions regarding War Diaries and Intelligence Summaries are contained in F.S. Regs., Part II. and the Staff Manual respectively. Title pages will be prepared in manuscript.

Hour, Date, Place	Summary of Events and Information	Remarks and references to Appendices
10ᵗʰ LE BIZET	2/Lt. SIMPSON (31ˢᵗ Batty) posted to R.H.A.	
11"	2/Lt. KERR (58ᵗʰ Batty) joins R.H.A.	
	LE BIZET and 5ᵗʰ LE TOURET shelled during the day. No damage done. 39" Battery, 6 "How" & 31" Heavy Battery replied to enemy fire by shelling trenches and posts of FRELINGHIEN VILLAGE. Q.M.S. (act. R.S.M.) LUER of/w 2/Lieut with effect from the 11ᵗʰ June 1915.	
12"	All quiet except for a few shells falling over 68" Battery NE of LE BIZET. 2/Lieut POWER joins and is posted to 31ˢᵗ Battery.	

Army Form C. 2118.

WAR DIARY
or
INTELLIGENCE SUMMARY.
(Erase heading not required.)

Instructions regarding War Diaries and Intelligence Summaries are contained in F. S. Regs., Part II. and the Staff Manual respectively. Title pages will be prepared in manuscript.

Hour, Date, Place	Summary of Events and Information	Remarks and references to Appendices
13" LE BIZET	A few shell (fired) at 65 Battery. No man wounded.	QM
14"	Batteries shoot LE BIZET shelled FRELINGHIEN Brewery in afternoon, with good effect. A few shots also put LE TOUQUET redoubt out hostile searched for 31st Heavy Battery for 2 and no damage.	
15"	31st Heavies shelled in afternoon. Shell very near. Battery to change position. By Simpson leaves to join RHA.	QM
16"		QM
17"		
18"	H.Q. 37 Brigade moves to NIEPPE. 14"8" H.Q. to LE BIZET. 31" Battery returns 35" at h"63. 35" Batt. to NIEPPE	

Army Form C. 2118.

WAR DIARY
or
INTELLIGENCE SUMMARY.
(Erase heading not required.)

Instructions regarding War Diaries and Intelligence Summaries are contained in F.S. Regs., Part II. and the Staff Manual respectively. Title pages will be prepared in manuscript.

Hour, Date, Place	Summary of Events and Information	Remarks and references to Appendices
19ᵗʰ MIEPPE		
20 "		
21 "		
22 "		
23 "		
24 "		
25 "	H.Q. Telephone under Cpl Hodgson (Signaller). Others engaged in construction on telephone & cable layout. Also 2 men of 15ᵗʰ Battery	05
26 "	As on 25ᵗʰ. 2/Lt Wilde & 2/Lt Wylie join Brigade and posted 2/Lt Wilde to Divisional Signals. 2/Lt Wylie to 15ᵗʰ Battery.	05
27 "	" Telephone course	05
28 "	"	
29 "	"	
30 "	" — nothing doing	05
31 "	nothing doing	

121/4664

4th Division

37th Bde. R.F.A.

War Diary 1 – 28.2.15

To Fourth Army Corps Feb. 17th

A2
A96

Army Form C.2118.

WAR DIARY
or
INTELLIGENCE SUMMARY.
Headquarters. 11th Bridge 9th [Brigade]
(Erase heading not required.)

Hour, Date, Place	Summary of Events and Information	Remarks and references to Appendices
February 1915		
1st ARMENTIERES	No change.	
2nd "	" "	
3rd "	H.Q. move to farm near 11 Inf. Brig. H.Q. 2 miles W. of PLOEGSTEERT	
4th PLOEGSTEERT	Relocation uneventful. Group.(Howitzer) 31" 3s: F.H. Battery 4"& 6" Siege Batteries. H.Q. shelled by enemy howitzer from direction of LES ECLUSES. (see pg. unread). Enemy aeroplanes observing, not lights over farm and observing fire. No endeavour [?] given in action.	R.F.
5th	No change. 31st F.H. By. & 6" Siege fired a few rounds in morning and afternoon in retaliation.	
6th	No change. 31st F.How. & 6" Siege fired in morning.	
7th	No Change.	
8th	" "	
9th	" "	
10th	" "	
11th	" "	

Army Form C. 2118.

WAR DIARY
or
INTELLIGENCE SUMMARY.
(Erase heading not required.)

Instructions regarding War Diaries and Intelligence Summaries are contained in F.S. Regs., Part II. and the Staff Manual respectively. Title pages will be prepared in manuscript.

Hour, Date, Place	Summary of Events and Information	Remarks and references to Appendices
12"	No Change. 2/Lt. Smith Jones 35th Battery.	
13"	" 2/Lt. Newman Jones 31st Battery	
14"	" (Newer forces heads to scout during night 14th-15th)	
15"	" Received orders for Brigade to move to join 1st Corps.	
16"	Sunday over Hazebrouck group to Maj HAINES 36 S.G. Battery	
17"	37th Brigade R.F.A. (less 55th Battery with 7th Division) moves from 1st Division to join 1st Corps. Brigade marched from NIEPPE at 19.30 a.m. On arrival N.S.P. S/E of LAVENTIE in afternoon of 17th Octr. one mile S.W. of LAVENTIE. 35th Battery move to billets in LA GORGUE, also HE. Q es. Amm Column Billetium in area 1 mile NE of SAILLY.	to Billets
18"	Lieut Boone comes 37" Bde Amm Col. and remains until L'Pierson. Lieut Newman posted from att" 31" Battery to Amm Column. 31st Battery now into action 1 mile S.W. of LAVENTIE in relief of 37th Battery. HQ, 35th Battery and Amm Column remain in Billets	

Army Form C. 2118.

WAR DIARY
or
INTELLIGENCE SUMMARY.
(Erase heading not required.)

Instructions regarding War Diaries and Intelligence Summaries are contained in F.S. Regs., Part II. and the Staff Manual respectively. Title pages will be prepared in manuscript.

Hour, Date, Place	Summary of Events and Information	Remarks and references to Appendices
19th	2.5" Battery now in action 500" South of Croix Barbee. Army position in RIEZ BAILLEUL. Relieved by 37 Bde H.A.	
20	"mm" Column moves to 1 Section N⁰⁴ MONDE, 1 section to FOSSE	
21st	Brig H.Q. open to billets in RIEZ BAILLEUL. Position Gun lines at Le Baudrie and Ghoselte	
22		
23		
24	The firing all Column improving position and teleph observing stations.	
25		
26		
27		
28		

4th Division
War Diaries
127th (How) Bde. R.F.A.
Formed 6-8-15.

August to 31st December
1915

K
May 1916

7th Division

D/7378

127th Bde R + A
full
Aug 8 to Oct. 15

WAR DIARY
INTELLIGENCE SUMMARY.
(Erase heading not required.)
Summary of Events and Information

12 T.H. Brigade R.F.A.

Place	Date	Hour	Summary of Events and Information	Remarks and references to Appendices
BAILLY-MAILLET	1915 6th August		12.7 (Howitzer) Brigade R.F.A. consisting of 86th and 128th (How) Batteries, formed with effect from the 6th August 1915. Batteries to remain attached, for tactical purposes, to the 14th and 29th Brigades for the present. Bt. Lt. Col. H.H. Seligmann assumes command of the Brigade. (From 'J' Battery R.H.A.) Capt. J. N. Thomson posted as acting Adjutant (pending confirmation from H.Q. 42 Division) 2/Lieut. Bouffey posted as orderly officer. (From 128 Battery R.F.A.)	4 D.A. orders 8/8/15
"	11th	8pm	127 Brigade becomes a Tactical unit. (86th and 128th Batteries) and for tactical purposes Left Section 16 Siege Battery (6 inch Howr.) is attached to Theen Positions of Batteries as follows:- 86 Battery - F. 20 B 1.9 128 Battery - F. 15 A 5.0 - 2 guns only in action other emplacements not prepared 16 Siege - F. 20 D 3.8	French Plan Directed Sheet 2 - Hébuterne
"	12th		Quiet Night. Day cloudy with rain showers. Instructions regarding Zones and registration issued to batteries. 86th Battery } Carried out registration on new Zones. 128th Battery } 16 Siege Section Registered important communication trench. Aeroplane tried to range 86th Battery in evening with wireless but instrument was out of order. In the evening the 4 guns of 128 Battery now in position registered their normal Zones	

Army Form C. 2118.

WAR DIARY
or
INTELLIGENCE SUMMARY.
(Erase heading not required.)

Place	Date	Hour	Summary of Events and Information	Remarks and references to Appendices
MAILLY- MAILLET	Aug, 1915 13th		Quiet night. - Cloudy day with slight showers. 86th Battery did not fire. - 128 Battery did not fire as good observing station for new gun not yet prepared. - 16 Siege Battery shelled BEAUCOURT in retaliation to hostile shelling of MAILLY.	39th Division Order 2
-"-	14th	4.40p.m.	Quiet night - cloudy day. Enemy shelled AUCHONVILLERS with small field guns and later shelled MAILLY. 128 By retaliated on BEAUMONT with good effect. A gun of 128 By accidentally fired on back from enemy position wounding 2 staff & putting the gun out of action.	
-"-	15th	12.30pm	Quiet night. - Cloudy day. A few field gun shells fell in MAILLY - MAILLET. 16 Siege and 86 By retaliated on BEAUCOURT with excellent effect. 128 Battery continued registration	
-"-	16th		Registration by 128 Bty. on BEAUCOURT & THIEPVAL	
-"-	17th		Registration by 6" Siege - Large fire in MIRAUMONT	
-"-	18th		Registration by 86 Bty of "Y" Ravine - 128 Bty fire on BEAUMONT as retaliation for shelling of AUCHONVILLER. A very heavy explosion was heard in the German lines - Thin period	

WAR DIARY
or
INTELLIGENCE SUMMARY.

(Erase heading not required.)

Army Form C. 2118.

Place	Date	Hour	Summary of Events and Information	Remarks and references to Appendices
	18"		To be a premature in the bore of a large German Trench Mortar	
	19"		At the request of O.C. 32 nd Bde — 16 Siege retaliated on Pt 394 & 86 Pkt on ST PIERRE.	
	20"		Germans employing large trench mortar against the Redan — 86 Bty retaliated. Heavy trench mortar in its vicinity & retaliated on item. German snowman balloon is up nearly very fine day. You can see from the left ground SE of MIRAUMONT when on the ground. It is plainly visible. also its winding engine & the men who work it.	
	21"		German trench mortar very active here Pt 326 — MAILLY shells with light field guns. Retaliation on BEAUCOURT, with 4.5" & 6" Howitzers. Enemy 8"/H howr KZ 14 B15	
	22"		Attempt to register the 96 Bty on cave shelters not successful owing to weather	
	23"		Trench mortars active again, 86 Bty replied & shelling ceased. German balloon seen partially deflated.	

Army Form C. 2118.

WAR DIARY
or
INTELLIGENCE SUMMARY.
(Erase heading not required.)

Instructions regarding War Diaries and Intelligence Summaries are contained in F. S. Regs., Part II. and the Staff Manual respectively. Title pages will be prepared in manuscript.

Place	Date	Hour	Summary of Events and Information	Remarks and references to Appendices
	24th		More snipers + machine gun firing last night than usual in front of the news of the Naval action in the Gulf of Riga they started again to the Germans. Reputation of 18th Rifle	
	26th		6 Siege fires 12 rounds into Kewshi near 345. an establishment to French hunters. — The front covered by the Division. Every time extended to the North by about 1000 x . the 36 Bty (plans) a section in action in a Wood F15A 7.3. in order to reach the Northern limit. The two batteries of the Brigade are now covering a front of 7000 x and have about 65 points registered. (not including the section 6" Siege Hows.)	
	28th		The 16" Siege fires 16 rounds near pt 322. — They are at present getting soft Coroïté and Baliscite cartridges, the former are shot erratic & make close and accurate shooting impossible.	
	29th		The 86th Bty in conjunction with the 60 prs shot at pt 926 where there are large numbers of Dugouts and which is probably a ration distributing centre. The 16" Siege had a shot unsuccessful shot at the German trench near pt 328, the suspected portion of a torpedo gun.	

Army Form C. 2118.

WAR DIARY
or
INTELLIGENCE SUMMARY.
(Erase heading not required.)

Instructions regarding War Diaries and Intelligence Summaries are contained in F. S. Regs., Part II. and the Staff Manual respectively. Title pages will be prepared in manuscript.

Place	Date	Hour	Summary of Events and Information	Remarks and references to Appendices
	29th (cont.)		Coals containing flack & bombs & sausages etc were seen to fly high into the air, a most inspiring sight	
	30.		Rather more activity on the part of the German artillery than usual was noticed in the 11th Bde area. A few 5.9" HNs still around. Up to date there have been very few here.	
	31st		Aircraft from tearing taken by the German Spionenbahr balloon shew that it is about 12500 + 7500 from our guns + 80 out of reach. If anything but a 6" gun or a clear day it is possible to see it on the ground. A considerable amount of work is going on near pt 926 which was well shelled on the 29th	
Sept	1st		For the last three days a certain amount of anxiety has been caused by the German mining operations near pt 333. Last night they were heard tamping the charge. — Early this morning we exploded a counter mine which effectually put a stop to these operations. German's retaliation with field guns on our trenches	

WAR DIARY
or
INTELLIGENCE SUMMARY.

(Erase heading not required.)

Army Form C. 2118.

Instructions regarding War Diaries and Intelligence Summaries are contained in F. S. Regs., Part II. and the Staff Manual respectively. Title pages will be prepared in manuscript.

Place	Date	Hour	Summary of Events and Information	Remarks and references to Appendices
	2nd		Great activity on the part of the enemy's trench mortars between SERRE & the REDAN. Shelled points 333, 514, 314, 312 & 928 which latter is believed to be a Bn. HQ. A horse in ST PIERRE DIVION which worries our Rifle Brigade snipers was shot.	
	3rd		Fired at a motor lorry enforcement near pt 316 & the reported bunker of a torpedo gun near pt 515 with the OB 314. Considerable damage done to enemy's trenches.	
	4th		Owing to the arrival of some wagons with teams of white horses also with lorries at MAILLY MAILLET Stn. on a clear day & in full view of the enemy in observation balloon, a considerable number of shell (77 m/m) were put near the Stn. Several returning wounded. The shelling was observed by the Balloon & observers sent to the Bty. by wireless. Some of the enemy's being caught by our window. No 5·3 B. _____ Serrurier Hindenwood the station in target put up near pt 947.	

2353 Wt. W2514/1454 700,000 5/15 D.D.&L. A.D.S.S./Forms/C. 2118.

Army Form C. 2118

WAR DIARY
or
INTELLIGENCE SUMMARY.
(Erase heading not required.)

Instructions regarding War Diaries and Intelligence Summaries are contained in F. S. Regs., Part II. and the Staff Manual respectively. Title pages will be prepared in manuscript.

Place	Date	Hour	Summary of Events and Information	Remarks and references to Appendices
	5th		The 128 Bty conducted aeroplane registration of several targets in the BEAUMONT - BEAUCOURT STN. Valley - The shower aborted subsequently but the Germans were exploding bursts on the ground about 15 secs after he sent the signal G. [meaning fire] As soon as the Bty was ranging on each target [sending a yellow smoke to changing was not much hindered]. Slight shelling of HAMEL & MESNIL.	
	6th		A very quiet day - The 86th fired a few rounds in retaliation to trench mortars near 333. - The 128 Battery set on fire a house in ST PIERRE DIVION which was being used as a sniping position. - MALLY received about 100 x 77 mm shells in three batches in the evening.	
	7th		At 5 pm an organised "hate" of the German villages in reply to the previous days shelling of MAILLY took place. There was no retaliation and apparently considerable damage was done as the Germans did not shell our villages for some days.	

WAR DIARY
or
INTELLIGENCE SUMMARY.
(Erase heading not required.)

Army Form C. 2118.

Place	Date	Hour	Summary of Events and Information	Remarks and references to Appendices
	8/12			
	9		Nothing of interest to report - Enemy's guns have carried out their usual shelling of trenches with 77 a.m & 5.9 in their	
	10			
	11		intervals with 4.5 in their	
	12/12		Heavy enemy shelling of LANCASHIRE POST & HAMEL - The 128 Bty replied greatly helped in pts 377 & ST PIERRE DIVION. For some evenings past the former has taken to shelling our transport near the SUCRERIE on the SERRE Road. They have stopped by concentrating shelling of the gun pits (suspected known) near BEAUMONT.	
	13/12		Enemy's heavy howitzers very active in the Northern zone - The 9.5" Shells were knocken in return.	
	14"		Two batteries of the 101" How Bde 22nd Div. were attached to his Bde for a few days to conduct a practice camp positions were found for them one at COLINCAMPS & one at MAILLY. They come in tonight	

WAR DIARY or INTELLIGENCE SUMMARY

Army Form C. 2118.

Place	Date	Hour	Summary of Events and Information	Remarks and references to Appendices
	16th		The Hun attacked Bks C.101 & D.101 commenced typhulate. In the afternoon they received orders to leave that night instead of tomorrow till the 18th as was originally in(tended) & funny for Jerries. A Big Jar practise. This Huns implicate the Batteries were well equipped, shot with lots seen appeared to be good.	
	17th		In the evening the Germans shelled MAMETZ & MESNIL heavily while our relief were taking place. Big Bty shelled the houses from near BEAUCOURT Sin & also ST PIERRE DIVION. German howitzers rather more active than usual shelling the REDAN & COLINCAMPS — A premature 4.2" was seen & hearing holes.	
	18th		A German Battery firmly allegued to be in an orchard near ST PIERRE proves to be mythical. Shoved from the same battery as yesterday. Another premature 4.2"	
	20th		ENGLEBELMER well shelled with about 50 77mm & 130 fm be retaliated on the Batteries end of GRANDCOURT where 3 known depots the gunner billets to be effected. Large clouds of thick dust were seen.	

Army Form C. 2118.

WAR DIARY
or
INTELLIGENCE SUMMARY.
(Erase heading not required.)

Place	Date	Hour	Summary of Events and Information	Remarks and references to Appendices
AUCHONVILLERS	21st		Received further news from naval source of german guns. 120 R# [?] left an Enemy station at THIEPVAL.	
	22nd		A carefully devised "hate" batteries on its Enemy villages of PUISIEUX + GRANDCOURT was carried out during the day. In the Enemy Retaliating fairly. In some hate was expected. with an additional 30 rounds from the French heavy Rty on MIRAUMONT where Div HQ are situated. During the day PUISIEUX, GRANDCOURT + MIRAUMONT received a total of 90 — (45 + 120 orig) — Its The Summans (archives Hr.3) Guns only produce 5"=4.2 at MAILLY	
	23rd		The 88 Rty. fast at a German Rty 4263 which could be seen firing. The effect was good and the German ceased. Early in the morning a flock of French Biplanes but one over the lines — with so many shots at The German practice was Somewhat wild	

Army Form C. 2118

WAR DIARY
or
INTELLIGENCE SUMMARY.
(Erase heading not required.)

Instructions regarding War Diaries and Intelligence Summaries are contained in F. S. Regs., Part II. and the Staff Manual respectively. Title pages will be prepared in manuscript.

Place	Date	Hour	Summary of Events and Information	Remarks and references to Appendices
	23		At 2.30 pm a combined demonstration by all available guns commenced on the trenches near BEAUMONT & those stones south of the "Ravin-en-Y" just to the South. 100 HE per Bty.	
	24	10 am	Demonstration continued two areas being shelled out the original trenches & french mortar area near the SERRE road & the other the Ravin en Y. Very little retaliation.	
	25		Demonstration continued, three bombardments being carried out on the same areas as yesterday at 10.35 am, 2.30 pm & 3 pm. The shooting on the German trenches near the ravine by all guns was most accurate. A test was carried out of Compound guns was the fuze No 100 with the old No 44. Result very much in favour of the No 44 troops were then for them perfect. A report was submitted accordingly. Heavy trains seen going S.E. from IRLES presumably conveying services to the Champagne district. Very little hostile shelling.	

2353 Wt. W2514/1454 700,000 5/15 D. D. & L. A.D.S.S./Forms/C. 2118.

Army Form C. 2118

WAR DIARY
or
INTELLIGENCE SUMMARY.
(Erase heading not required.)

Instructions regarding War Diaries and Intelligence Summaries are contained in F. S. Regs., Part II. and the Staff Manual respectively. Title pages will be prepared in manuscript.

Place	Date	Hour	Summary of Events and Information	Remarks and references to Appendices
	26		Very quiet hardly a shell being fired by either side	
	27			
	28			
	29		Enemy shelled LANCASHIRE POST with short bursts.	
	30		A German aeroplane has all day been flown over HÉBUTERNE & in various altitudes & diving by the antiaircraft guns & a Vickers biplane the first they the machine was hit by both. The machine seen to fall over MAILLY & there our Lewis crews for the troops in the village.	
Oct	1st		Very quiet day	
	2			
	3		A few shells from a 4.2" Hows which SAILLISEL being seen over the enemy before, an observing officer of the 9th French Heavy Battery observed all day at 128 Bty observing St. waiting to shoot. The Hows however did not fire.	

WAR DIARY or INTELLIGENCE SUMMARY

Army Form C. 2118

Place	Date	Hour	Summary of Events and Information	Remarks and references to Appendices
	4ᵗʰ		Trench mortars active in the Northern zone – 86 Bty retaliated.	
	5ᵗʰ 6ᵗʰ		have fired mortars in the neighbourhood of the RESAN + new SERRE Road, also a certain amount of shelling. The enemy appear to be treating considerable use of "Pouff" Batteries. Some are skillfully worked & some not.	
	8		126 Bty shelled a trench mortar near the "RAVIN EN Y" which had been located by an infantry Obs. after a reconnaissance in their daylight. Only 20 rounds could be spared & although most of these were within 10ᵡ of the entrenchment to direct hit could be obtained. The O.C. 28 Bde Beauregarde a forward position for a sector of shooting at 28 Bty about 1500ᵡ N.W of BEAUMONT, for the purpose of shooting at MIRAUMONT, BEAUREGARDE should it be necessary! these places being outside our range from present positions.	

Army Form C. 2118.

WAR DIARY
or
INTELLIGENCE SUMMARY.
(Erase heading not required.)

Place	Date	Hour	Summary of Events and Information	Remarks and references to Appendices
	9		Trench mortars active in the Northern Zone – Petitshaha	by BB Bty.
	10		A flash battery was worked in GRANDCOURT.	
	12		In consequence of the activity of enemy's trench mortars near LANCASHIRE POST, a combined trench mortar shoot was organised. The 16 Siege, 32nd Bde & 128 Bty took part owing to the line of HE the 128 Bty could only fire shrapnel.	
	13 14 15 16		Very quiet days.	
	17		Trench mortars active again in Northern Zone – BB Bty fired 40 shells, nothing very available	
	20		As a result of the heavy shelling of our trenches near SPREE yesterday afternoon a rate was organised for tonight on the enemy trenches opposite	

WAR DIARY or INTELLIGENCE SUMMARY

Army Form C. 2118.

Place	Date	Hour	Summary of Events and Information	Remarks and references to Appendices
	20 (cont)		50. 6" HE, 40. 4.5" HE, by 86 Bty + 50 18pr HE. This took place at 2.15 pm. Shooting was good but the number of partial detonations disappointing. The Germans made practically no reply, their work about it being mostly [?]/[?] apparently finished.	
	21		The 4/5 London How Bde (57B, 57C, 10 London, 11 London) arrived + went into action. Two Btys at MAILLY + two at COURCELLES. They are here for 10 days instruction + are attached to this Bde.	
	22		Enemy shelled our trenches in Northern Zone heavily from 10 am – 12. 86 Bty retaliated with Shrapnel. Fuzes not erratic.	
	23		11th London Bty. registered on edge of SERRE wood. Enemy trench mortars were active during the afternoon in front of SERRE.	

Army Form C. 2118.

WAR DIARY
or
INTELLIGENCE SUMMARY.
(Erase heading not required.)

Instructions regarding War Diaries and Intelligence Summaries are contained in F. S. Regs., Part II. and the Staff Manual respectively. Title pages will be prepared in manuscript.

Place	Date	Hour	Summary of Events and Information	Remarks and references to Appendices
	24.		86th Battery fired with shrapnel near R.36.c., in retaliation for trench mortar firing. Germans fired 16 H.E. into our trenches in front of THIEPVAL.	
	25.		Mist prevented observation all day. No firing.	
	26.		128th Battery fired a few shrapnel at communication trench in R.7.c. Hostile artillery quiet. 11th London Bty. and c/57 registered various points in R.7.a. Much traffic observed on BIHUCOURT – ACHIET railway. Hostile observation balloon came up at 1.50 P.M. observed at 2.20 P.M.	
	27.		Germans observed firing dummy batteries with puffs behind spot	

2353 Wt. W2514/1454 700,000 5/15 D. D. & L. A.D.S.S./Forms/C. 2118.

Army Form C. 2118.

WAR DIARY
or
INTELLIGENCE SUMMARY.
(Erase heading not required.)

Instructions regarding War Diaries and Intelligence Summaries are contained in F. S. Regs., Part II. and the Staff Manual respectively. Title pages will be prepared in manuscript.

Place	Date	Hour	Summary of Events and Information	Remarks and references to Appendices
	27. (cont.)		C/57 Bty. registered.	
	28.		Hostile artillery quiet. B/57 Bty. shelled BEAUCOURT station, obtaining 4 direct hits, with No. 100 fuze, none of which detonated. C/57 Bty. registered. 10th & 11th London Bty.s also registered.	
	29.		96th Battery fired at German trenches in front of REDAN with great effect; 16th Siege co-operated, their firing was very accurate, but burate of shells bad. 1/10 + 1/11 Bty.'s fired on German trenches.	
	30.		128 H. Battery fired 40 rounds H.E. with 100 fuze, at German trenches in front of THIEPVAL wood. Only one proper detonation was obtained.	

Army Form C. 2118.

WAR DIARY
or
INTELLIGENCE SUMMARY

(Erase heading not required.)

Place	Date	Hour	Summary of Events and Information	Remarks and references to Appendices
	30. (cont)		Germans retaliated with a few 3.in. shell in HAMEL. Other batteries did not fire.	
	31.		Hostile artillery quiet. Neither battery fired to the London Brigade left before daylight	

W. Felusman Lieut Col
Cmdg 1st N.M.R.F.a

2-11-15.

4th Division

127th Brigade R.F.A.

Nov. 1915

Vol II

Army Form C. 2118

WAR DIARY
or
INTELLIGENCE SUMMARY.   127th Brigade. R.F.A.   (4th Div)

(Erase heading not required.)

Instructions regarding War Diaries and Intelligence Summaries are contained in F. S. Regs., Part II. and the Staff Manual respectively. Title pages will be prepared in manuscript.

Place	Date	Hour	Summary of Events and Information	Remarks and references to Appendices
Nos. 156.	2nd		Batteries did not fire. Everything Quiet on our front.	
"	3		— do —	
"	4		86th Battery fired H.E. into trenches K.29.c.10.0 in retaliation for trench mortars during the morning. 86th fired 50 rounds H.E. into German trenches, 25 with No. 100 fuze & 25 with No. 44 fuze. 128th Battery did not fire.	
"	5		86th Battery did not fire. 128th fired a few rounds of lyddite at a point to open ground to test the Nos. 100 & 44 fuzes.	
"	6		Everything quiet on our front.	
"	7		Everything quiet on our front.	
"	8		Batteries did not fire.	
"	9		Both Batteries retaliated on BEAUCOURT, 86th on SERRE & BEAUMONT & 128 on GRANDCOURT as well, for German shelling of ENGLEBELMER.	

Army Form C. 2118

WAR DIARY
or
INTELLIGENCE SUMMARY.

(Erase heading not required.)

Instructions regarding War Diaries and Intelligence Summaries are contained in F. S. Regs., Part II. and the Staff Manual respectively. Title pages will be prepared in manuscript.

Place	Date	Hour	Summary of Events and Information	Remarks and references to Appendices
Nov.	9 (cont.)		88th also fired on trenches in front of SERRE in retaliation for trench mortars. Batteries did not fire. Everything quiet on our front.	
"	10		88th Battery fired during the morning in retaliation for trench mortar bombing. 128 Battery did not fire.	
"	11		128 Battery fired at trenches Q.17.2 & 2.3. Considerable traffic was observed on the ACHIET-LE-GRAND — BIHUCOURT road & 2 trains on the railway between the same two places. Everything quiet on our front.	
"	12		Batteries did not fire.	
"	13		88th Battery shelled trenches near K.36.c.2.4 and Q.6.a.3.4.	
"	14		128 Battery re-registered a few points.	
"	15		128. Battery retaliated on point R.19.c.3.5 for hostile shelling in front of HAMEL. 88th did not fire.	
"	16		Neither battery fired. Black powder battery near GRANDCOURT was active	

Army Form C. 2118

WAR DIARY
or
INTELLIGENCE SUMMARY.
(Erase heading not required.)

Instructions regarding War Diaries and Intelligence Summaries are contained in F. S. Regs., Part II. and the Staff Manual respectively. Title pages will be prepared in manuscript.

Place	Date	Hour	Summary of Events and Information	Remarks and references to Appendices
Nov.	17		88th did not fire	
"	18		128 Bty. shelled two houses in BEAUMONT, one which was used by snipers being completely demolished – set on fire	
			88th Bty. fired on trenches in R.29.D in retaliation for trench mortaring	
"	19		128 did not fire	
			88th Bty. fired on same place in retaliation for trench mortaring	
"	20		128 Bty. did not fire	
			88th Bty. shelled trenches near R.36.a.10.10 and R.29.b.7.5 in retaliation for trench mortars	
			128 Bty. shelled trenches in Q.24.b.7.5 Fire ft both batteries very effective	
"	21		88th Bty. bombarded trenches from R.35.c.3.4 to R.35.c.3.9	
			128 Bty. did not fire	
"	22		88th Bty. fired at trenches Q.5.a.2.9 and R.29.b.7.8 in retaliation for trench mortars	
			128 Bty. did not fire	

WAR DIARY
or
INTELLIGENCE SUMMARY.

(Erase heading not required.)

Army Form C. 2118

Place	Date	Hour	Summary of Events and Information	Remarks and references to Appendices
Nov.	23		All quiet on our front. Batteries did not fire.	
"	24		Germans bombarded our front line heavily from BEAUMONT northwards, also heavy mortar bombs being fired into trenches of left Battalion. 81st Bty. fired 76 H.E. in retaliation, with good effect. 128 Bty. fired 30 H.E. into BEAUMONT, & trenches in front. 128 also carried out bombardment in conjunction with 18-prs and 6 in with excellent results.	
"	25		86th Bty. carried out bombardment of enemy's trenches in front of SERRE. Enemy did not retaliate. 128 Bty. did not fire. 86th Bty. did not fire.	
"	26		128 Bty. shelled ST PIERRE DIVION in retaliation for German shelling of MESNIL.	
"	27		86th Bty. fired on trenches in K.29.b and K.35.e in retaliation for trench mortar bombing.	

WAR DIARY
or
INTELLIGENCE SUMMARY.
(Erase heading not required.)

Army Form C. 2118

Place	Date	Hour	Summary of Events and Information	Remarks and references to Appendices
Nov.	28		86th Bty. registered communication trenches in a.5.c	
			128 Bty. did not fire. All quiet on our front.	
"	29		86th Bty. fired on trenches opposite the REDAN and in R.29.b in retaliation for trench mortars. Infantry reported 'effect' most excellent.	
			128 Bty. did not fire.	
"	30		86th Bty. shelled trenches opposite the REDAN in retaliation for trench mortars, and also registered a trench in R.30.c	
			128 Bty. did not fire.	

ABSchreiber
Lieut Col
Cmdg 1.7.I. Bde. R.F.A

30/11/15.

127th Bde. R.F.A.
Doc.
Vol III

WAR DIARY or INTELLIGENCE SUMMARY

Army Form C. 2118.

127th Bde R.F.A.

(Erase heading not required.)

Place	Date	Hour	Summary of Events and Information	Remarks and references to Appendices
Dec.	1st		86th Bty. fired 8 rounds opposite the REDAN in anticipation of daily french mortaring, & fired on German 2nd line trenches from K.27.b.7.4 to K.27.b.9.7 in conjunction with fire demonstration. 128th Bty. retaliated on ST. PIERRE DIVION for German shelling to MESNIL. 86th Bty. shelled apparent dressing station at Q.6.c.5.1. 128th Bty. fired on trenches from Q.17.b.2.2 in retaliation for shelling of our trenches. Enemy trench mortar active from about Q.18.c.5.6 128 Bty fired twice during the day at this spot.	
	2		All quiet on our front. 86th Bty shelled communication trench in Q.6.c. & Q.6.c.2.5.1 suspected to be an observing station.	
	3		128th Bty- fired at Q.24.& 6.7 and Q.24.& 4.6, a great many blind shell. Enemy replied by shelling our trenches S.of ROVIM-EN-Y 128 th retaliated on their front trenches about Q.17.& 2.5	
	4		86th Bty. did not fire.	
	5		128th Bty retaliated on German trenches for shelling of our trenches in Q.17.a. Enemy vigorously trench-mortared our trenches in front	

WAR DIARY or INTELLIGENCE SUMMARY

Army Form C. 2118.

Place	Date	Hour	Summary of Events and Information	Remarks and references to Appendices
Dec.	5		A HAMEL battery retaliated on German front trenches in 8.18.c German observation balloon up	
	6		All quiet on our front. Batteries did not fire	
	7		86th Bty fired on trench in K.29 & 28	
			12th Bty shelled trench from R.14.c.27 to R.19.a.10. Observation difficult owing to rain & many shell	
	8		86th Bty fired opposite REDAN in retaliation to trench mortars	
			128th Bty carried out bombardment of German trenches in 8.17.& with good results. Enemy retaliated very feebly.	
			86th Bty fired on working party in 8.6.c.5.1	
	9		All quiet on our front. Batteries did not fire	
	10		— do —	
	11		— do —	
	12		RFA Bty fired on trench 8.6.c.6.1	
			Two Batteries and HQ. of 151st. Bde. RFA attached to this Bde. for training.	

151st Bde. A & D batteries registered.

WAR DIARY
or
INTELLIGENCE SUMMARY.

Army Form C. 2118.

Place	Date	Hour	Summary of Events and Information	Remarks and references to Appendices
Dec.	13		8th Bty. fired on trenches 8.6.c.4.8 & 8.6.c.6.1. 151st Bde. A&D batteries registered	
	14		All quiet on our front. 151st A & 151st D registered fire on German trenches.	
	15		8th Bty. bombarded German front line trench K.29.d 1.2 ± to K.29.d.3.5, with good effect.	
	16		All quiet on our front. Batteries did not fire.	
	17		8th Bty. shelled trench at Q.5.a.2.9 at request of infantry in retaliation for shelling & trench mortaring. Infantry reported result good. Also shelled front line trench at K.35.c.4±.2.9, and trench parapet.	
	18		10.8th Bty. shelled BEAUMONT in retaliation for shelling of MAILLONVILLERS 108 ft. Bty. retaliated on BEAUMONT for enemy shelling of MAILLONVILLERS	
	19		8th Bty. fired on trenches K.29. & 5.5 at request of infantry in retaliation for 4.2" howitzers. Many rounds fell in trench.	

Army Form C. 2118.

WAR DIARY
or
INTELLIGENCE SUMMARY.
(Erase heading not required.)

Instructions regarding War Diaries and Intelligence Summaries are contained in F.S. Regs., Part II. and the Staff Manual respectively. Title pages will be prepared in manuscript.

Place	Date	Hour	Summary of Events and Information	Remarks and references to Appendices
Dec.	19		128th Bty shelled a new trench in Q.10.d.6.6. Firing very accurate, effective and well-conducted. Enemy did not retaliate.	
	20		All quiet on our front. Batteries did not fire	
	21		86th Bty fired at junction of front trench and lodge in R.23.d.7.0 where at least two machine gun emplacements were located. Considerable damage done. Enemy retaliated with field guns sixth trench mortars about R.23.d.8.0	
	22		96th Bty fired two salvoes on German trenches in X.5.a & X.5.c 128th Bty retaliated on RAVIN-EN-Y for German trench mortars and fired at a supposed trench mortar Q.10.d.7.7	
	23		128th Bty shelled German front line trenches in Q.11.a. Germans retaliated very feebly with light field guns only.	
			"C" Bty 151st Bde registered	
	24		Several men were seen working in tent or dug-outs at Q.6.a.4.7 & in trench close by. Fire was opened by 86th Bty with excellent effect, planks & beams being seen to fly into the air	

WAR DIARY
or
INTELLIGENCE SUMMARY.

Army Form C. 2118.

Place	Date	Hour	Summary of Events and Information	Remarks and references to Appendices
Dec.	24		151st. Bde. "B" & "C" Batteries both registered. Neither battery fired. All quiet.	
	25		Considerable traffic on BIHUCOURT railway observed.	
	26		96th Bty. fired on German front line trench between K.23.l.8.1 & R.29.b.7.8 in conjunction with trench mortars.	
			128th Bty. fired at earthworks in R.7.a.6.7, and retaliated on front line trench Q.18.a.0.1	
	27		151st. Bde. "B" Bty. registered.	
			96th Bty. shelled German trench at K.29.b.8.8 in retaliation to shelling. Results reported by 125 Bty. as excellent, all rounds falling in German trench or wire, and a large breach made in German trench parapet.	
			151st. Bde. "C" Bty. registered.	
	28		128th Bty. fired at front trenches Q.17.b.10.0. Carried out pre-arranged bombardment on German trenches Q.17.d.9.1 to Q.18.a.1.0 with good results. Retaliated on Q.17.b.2.2 for shelling of REDAN	

WAR DIARY
or
INTELLIGENCE SUMMARY.

(Erase heading not required.)

Army Form C. 2118.

Place	Date	Hour	Summary of Events and Information	Remarks and references to Appendices
Dec.	29		98th Bty. shelled R.29.&7.8 in retaliation for German shelling of our front line trenches, and fired in retaliation at trenches in SERRE. 128th Bty. fired at trenches in Q.17.c in retaliation for shelling of our trenches in Q.17.a. 98th Bty. did not fire.	
"	30		128th Bty. fired at Q.17.&.6.1 and Q.18.c.&.6 in retaliation for German shelling at Q.17.c & 8.2. Fired 40 rounds into ST PIERRE DIVION in retaliation for German shelling of HAMEL.	
"	31		98th Bty. fired on trench Q.6.a.4.7 where movement was seen. 128th Bty. shelled trenches at R.19.d 3.5 in conjunction with 51st Division. Enemy artillery very active all day.	

Wesley Egan
Lieut Col
Comdg 117 Bde R.F.A.

4th Division

War Diaries

127th Bde R.F.A.

January To 21-5-16

1916

BDE Broken up

4th DIVISION.

127th BDE. R. F. A.

JANUARY 1916.

Army Form C. 2118.

WAR DIARY
or
INTELLIGENCE SUMMARY.
(Erase heading not required.)

Instructions regarding War Diaries and Intelligence Summaries are contained in F.S. Regs., Part II. and the Staff Manual respectively. Title pages will be prepared in manuscript.

Place	Date	Hour	Summary of Events and Information	Remarks and references to Appendices
January	1st.		128th Bty. fired at a machine gun emplacement in Q.24.d.4.8.	
	2		86th Bty. fired to register trenches in Q.29.b. 128th Bty. fired into German trenches at Q.18.c.3.8. and into ST. PIERRE DIVION in retaliation for the shelling of HAMEL.	
	3		86th Bty registered K.30.d.1.9. to find the error of the day.	
	4		86th Bty. carried out bombardment of K.36.c.2.4 & K.35.c.4.4. Shells burst well, & fire seemed very effective. 128th Bty. fired into ST. PIERRE DIVION several times during the day, and on trenches Q.18.c.6.5 with good effect, to stop heavy German bombardment of HAMEL and our trenches.	
	5		86th Bty. shelled BEAUCOURT, 128th Bty. shelled the MOUND S/16. and trenches in Q.16.a, Q.24.b, Q.17 & Q.22 to Q.18.c.4.6. in conjunction with fire demonstration.	
	6		Misty day. Front all quiet.	

WAR DIARY
or
INTELLIGENCE SUMMARY.
(Erase heading not required.)

Army Form C. 2118.

Place	Date	Hour	Summary of Events and Information	Remarks and references to Appendices
January	7		98th Bty. shelled the barricade on the SERRE road, obtaining many direct hits.	
	8		98th Bty. fired to cut wire left by 18-prs. in front of trench about R.35.a.30.05. 128th Bty. fired at trench mortar in R.18.c.7.5.	
	9		Front quiet.	
	10		Light trench mortar fired on R.35.c.25.40. 98th Bty. retaliated on light trench mortar in R.18.c.5.2 in retaliation for its activity. 128th Bty. fired at the trench mortar in R.18.c.5.2	
	11		98th Bty. fired on front trenches about R.29 & 7.0 and at R.23.2 at request of infantry who had been shelled by 105 m.m. howitzer. Infantry reported fire to be effective.	
	12		Our front all quiet.	
	13		" " " "	

WAR DIARY
or
INTELLIGENCE SUMMARY.
(Erase heading not required.)

Army Form C. 2118.

Place	Date	Hour	Summary of Events and Information	Remarks and references to Appendices
January	14		8th Bty. fired on front trenches from Q.5.a 27.61 to R.35.c 2.0 in conjunction with the demonstration. Fire seemed to be more effective than usual, the parapet being breached in several places. One round severed a bright flare which may have been a trench mortar bomb store. Germans retalited feebly on the REDAN and on our front trenches in Q.4.b and 2. Their fire was inaccurate, some rounds falling nearly 100 yds short. 128th Bty. fired on an aerial torpedo mortar reported to be firing from Q.11.d 2.7	
	15		8th Bty. shelled front trench at R.35.c 4.6 where there have appeared to be either a machine gun emplacement or an observation post. Several rounds fell in trench & one round on top of a dug-out, throwing up sandbags etc. fired on trench junction K.29.d 4.5 in retaliation for shelling of my trenches opposite. 127th Bty. observer reported fire very effective	
	16		128th Bty. fired into trenches in Q.18.a with good effect.	

WAR DIARY
or
INTELLIGENCE SUMMARY.

Army Form C. 2118.

Place	Date	Hour	Summary of Events and Information	Remarks and references to Appendices
January	17		Our front all quiet.	
	18		86th Bty. fired at N. & E. of Quadrilateral (R.35.a) in retaliation at respect of infantry. 128th Bty. fired at a trench mortar in the Ravin-en-y (Q.11.c) and at the Hawthorn Redoubt (Q.10.& 77) in retaliation for aerial torpedos into our trenches in Q.10.a. 88th Bty. fired on German salient Q.4.d.9.5, where infantry reported.	
	19		a machine gun fired at trench mortar reported to be firing from 128 ft Bty. fired at trenches Q.10.b & 8.7 and at Trenches Q.10.b & 8.7. A new machine gun emplacement or O.P. clearly visible in BEAUCOURT. resulted Q.12.4.9.3 also fired at. One round blew in a dug-out close to it, throwing up several boards into the air.	
	20		Front all quiet.	
	21		86th Bty. fired on trenches about R.35.a 5.2 & R.35.c & 4.6	

WAR DIARY
or
INTELLIGENCE SUMMARY.

(Erase heading not required.)

Army Form C. 2118.

Place	Date	Hour	Summary of Events and Information	Remarks and references to Appendices
January	21		Germans started with 5.9 in howitzer on our trenches in R.34.b.	
	22		88th Bty fired on German trenches according to programme of fire demonstration. Germans retaliated strongly on our trenches in R.34.	
	23		128th Bty. fired on strong German works at R.7.c.7.6. 88th Bty. fired on trench Q.6.c.4.1. believed to be used as an listening station. 128th Bty. fired at a white mound on the right of HAWTHORN redoubt at Q.10.& 65.65. Many direct hits were obtained, and the mound was greatly reduced in size. 88th Bty. fired on earthworks in Q.6. a 5.9 at request of 107th Infantry Bde.	
	24		128 R. Bty. fired a few rounds into HAWTHORN redoubt, and shelled retaliation for shelling of MESNIL.	
	25		BEAUCOURT at Q.4.& 9.9. 88th Bty fired into German trenches Enemy let off a mine at lodge & machine gun position about R.23.b. 66.00. opposite. Fired at lodge & machine gun position A flight of 7 German aeroplanes came over a dug-out blown in our lines flying due west	

WAR DIARY
or
INTELLIGENCE SUMMARY.
(Erase heading not required.)

Army Form C. 2118.

Place	Date	Hour	Summary of Events and Information	Remarks and references to Appendices
January	26		Our front all quiet.	
	27		" " "	
	28		" " "	
	29		Faint smell of gas from 7.15 a.m. to 9.30 a.m. (ALBERT had been shelled with gas shells.) THIEPVAL wood very heavily bombarded from 12.46 to 7.15 p.m. 128th Bty. fired at frontline trenches R.19.c.1.5 & R.Bty fired on trenches about R.29.b & 4.6 125th Bty. reported shooting very effective. Fired on trenches N.E. of Quadrilateral and opposite the REDAN	
	30		Flash of a 77mm Bty. was seen. Enemy again bombarded THIEPVAL wood. A possible position R.20.a.3.1. true bearing 85° from Q.22.2.8.6. 128th Bty. shelled THIEPVAL village opposite the REDAN (Q.5.a.3.9.) in	
	31		9th Bty fired on trenches for enemy shelling. Weather cold & foggy.	

V Schelwann Lt.-Col. RFA
Comdg 127th Brigade RFA

4th DIVISION.

127th BDE R. F. A.

FEBRUARY 1916.

WAR DIARY
or
INTELLIGENCE SUMMARY.
(Erase heading not required.)

Army Form C. 2118.

Place	Date	Hour	Summary of Events and Information	Remarks and references to Appendices
February	1st		Hostile Artillery was less active than usual. No trench mortars or machine guns were fired on our front. Observation was unfavorable till noon owing to mist. Weather cold, slight wind from S.S.E. No movement of enemy visible.	
	2nd		Hostile Artillery quite inactive. The trench mortar or machine gun activity. A new machine gun emplacement or O.P. is visible in 2nd line trench at A.24.F.9.c. Two men were seen close to the Labaune (R.25.b.y.b.) pointing towards GRANDCOURT. Uniforms could not be distinguished. They were dispersed by 2 round from Division on our right. Weather fine and clear. Wind S.W.	
	3rd		Hostile Artillery inactive. Hostile Artillery in the Division on our right active. Trench mortars inactive. Two machine guns at Q.14.b.5.1 and Q.18.c.1.9 fired a few rounds at us of our aeroplanes at 11-0 a.m. Weather cold. Temperature about 41°F. Gusty S.W. wind	

Army Form C. 2118.

WAR DIARY
or
INTELLIGENCE SUMMARY.
(Erase heading not required.)

Instructions regarding War Diaries and Intelligence Summaries are contained in F. S. Regs., Part II. and the Staff Manual respectively. Title pages will be prepared in manuscript.

Place	Date	Hour	Summary of Events and Information	Remarks and references to Appendices
February	4th		Hostile Artillery inactive.	
			About 6 trench mortar bombs fired into the REDAN at 12 noon in retaliation for our mine.	
			No machine guns active.	
			Usual traffic of Supply Wagons and men on ACHIET – BIHUCOURT road.	
			1.7 pm train going from left to right on ACHIET – BAPAUME railway. 6 closed and 4 open trucks.	
			Light good. Wind S.W. strong.	
	5th		Hostile Artillery normally active.	
			No trench mortar or machine gun fire.	
			Usual amount of transport on ACHIET-LE-GRAND – BIHUCOURT road.	
			Following trains observed on ACHIET – BAPAUME railway.	
			(1) 10-15 am left to right.	
			(2) 10-30 a.m. " " "	
			(3) 12 noon right to left.	
			(4) 1-5 pm " " "	
			Four German balloons visible true bearings from A.22.d.8.6. 36° 42° 45° 96°	
			11-15 a.m. 1 bomb from German aeroplane fell in MAILLY.	
			Weather fine.	
	6th		Hostile Artillery less active than usual.	
			No trench mortar or machine gun fire. Weather fine in the morning a little rain later. Wind S.W.	
			At 4-15 am 86 Bty fired 30 rds HE with good effect on the HAWTHORN REDOUBT. Enemy retaliated with a few rounds from 4.4 mm guns.	
			At 11-20 am 125 Bty fired 30rds on trenches on Q.19.a. 9.6. but result was poor owing to high wind.	

2353 Wt.W2511/1454 700,000 5/15 D. D. & L.   A.D.S.S./Form/C. 2118.

WAR DIARY
or
INTELLIGENCE SUMMARY.

(Erase heading not required.)

Army Form C. 2118.

Place	Date	Hour	Summary of Events and Information	Remarks and references to Appendices
February	7th		Hostile Artillery activity less than usual. No Trench Mortar or Machine Gun fire.	
		9-15am	Two Germans seen looking out from trench at R.19.d.2.8. 128th Battery fired at this spot. 5 Germans seen running away over the crest.	
		2-0pm	6 horses exercising in field near ACHIET – BIHUCOURT road.	
		2-30pm	Party of 20 horsemen seen entering ACHIET-LE-GRAND from BIHUCOURT.	
		2-35pm	One horseman in blue grey uniform seen riding into MIRAUMONT from BEAUCOURT. Wind strong and gusty. N.W. Light good. 128 Battery fired 3 rounds at R.19.d.2.8. at 9-0 a.m. and during the morning fired 48 rounds on Q.19.b.2.2. with fairly good effect. At 12-20pm 86 Bty fired 5 Rds on Dugout in Trench K.36.C.15".15" of which 3 appeared to fall on dug-out. Hostile Artillery inactive. No Trench Mortar or Machine Gun fire.	
	8th			
		10-58am	128 Battery shelled the trenches in Q.19 & Q.2.2. (Pts 369 and 391) with 8 rounds H.E.	
		2-30pm	86 Battery fired 30 rounds with H.E. good effect at Machine Gun Emplacement in Q.4.D.9.0.	
	9th		Hostile artillery activity greater than usual, especially from 9-45 to 10-30am this morning. No Trench Mortar or Machine Gun fire. Usual amount of traffic on ACHIET – BIHUCOURT road. Two German balloons observed up at true bearings of 75° and 55° from Q.2.d.4.8.9.5. Weather fine at little snow during night. Wind S.W. At 12-30pm 86 Bty shelled enemy's 2nd line trench at Q.5.a.9.1. and Q.5.a.5.8. with 32 rds H.E. a number of which landed in trenches south of no results.	

WAR DIARY
or
INTELLIGENCE SUMMARY.

(Erase heading not required.)

Army Form C. 2118.

Place	Date	Hour	Summary of Events and Information	Remarks and references to Appendices
February	9th	3-0 pm	128 Battery fired 10 Rounds H.E. at German Observation Post on R.3.a.2.5.	
		6-30pm	86 Bty fired 12 Rounds on hostile trenches opposite REDAN. Infantry reported fire very effective.	
	10th		Hostile Artillery activity rather greater than usual on left half of zone, inactive on right half. No Trench Mortar or Machine Gun fire.	
		11-20 am (9th)	German balloon up at true bearing 55° from Q.2.d. 48.95.	
		11-50 am (9th)	Two hostile balloons went up at true bearings 94° and 85°30' from Q.2.d 48.95.	
		1-40 pm (9th)	Balloon observed at true bearing 108° taken from Q.2.d 48.95.	
			Following trams were seen on 9th.	
			1-30 pm Left to right 30 trucks	
			1-45 pm " " " "	
			2-50 pm " " " "	
			3-20 pm Right to left. 8 passenger carriages	
			3-35 pm " " 40 trucks	
				5 trucks
	11th	12-15pm	Weather sunny and hazy.	
			86 Bty fired 13 rds H.E. into trenches opposite REDAN. At 5-15 pm 128 Bty shelled Pt 369 with 12 Rds H.E.	
			Hostile Artillery Activity normal. 2-5 pm (10-2-16) Machine Gun fired from Q.18.c.O.5 at no of our aeroplanes. The same machine gun also fired at 2-40 pm and at 3-0 pm. No Machine Gun or Trench Mortar fire.	
		11-0 am (10th)	Enemy observation balloon seen being towed Northwards about 2 miles E. of MIRAUMONT. No movement seen. Light very bad owing to rain.	
		At 11-0 am	128 Bty fired 39 rds H.E. on Q.19.b.2.2. nearly all good detonations	
		At 4-45 pm	128 Battery fired 40 Rounds into Q.18. & Y.5.	

WAR DIARY
or
INTELLIGENCE SUMMARY.
(Erase heading not required.)

Army Form C. 2118.

Place	Date	Hour	Summary of Events and Information	Remarks and references to Appendices
February	12th		Hostile Artillery very active. No French Mortar or Machine Gun fire. No movement seen. Light fair. Wind N. 128 Battery shelled BEAUCOURT (R7 D 3.9) in the afternoon but observation of effect was impossible owing to mist.	
	13th		Hostile Artillery more active than usual. No French Mortar or Machine Gun fire. Weather rainy and misty. Two men seen on BEAUCOURT road in R.7.C. Uniforms could not be distinguished.	
		8-15am	At 10-0 am and again at 10-30 am 86 Battery subjected the trenches in the vicinity of the REDAN to a very heavy shelling with appreciable results.	
	14th		Hostile Artillery activity normal. No French Mortar or Machine Gun fire.	
		3-0pm (13th)	A Heavy Battery from behind GRANDCOURT was firing in the direction of the SUCRERIE, smoke could be seen.	
		(14th)	The top of a convoy & Motor Lorries about 30 in number were seen moving in a S.E. direction. Line leading to road 64° taken from Q 22 d 8.6. Light good, strong wind.	
	15th		Hostile artillery activity less than usual. No French Mortar or Machine Gun fire. No movement seen. Light good. Wind high and gusty. Two rounds were fired by 86 Battery into Q 6 a 3.9 for the benefit of the I.O.M. The second were doubtful being the same make and old looking shell as a premature fired the day before. Both rounds reached the target before exploding	

WAR DIARY
or
INTELLIGENCE SUMMARY.
(Erase heading not required.)

Army Form C. 2118.

Instructions regarding War Diaries and Intelligence Summaries are contained in F. S. Regs., Part II. and the Staff Manual respectively. Title pages will be prepared in manuscript.

Place	Date	Hour	Summary of Events and Information	Remarks and references to Appendices
February	16th		Hostile Artillery inactive. No Trench Mortar or Machine Gun fire. All quiet on our front. No movement seen. High wind and rain.	
	17th.		Hostile Artillery inactive. No Trench Mortar or Machine Gun fire.	
		2-20pm (16th)	From seen moving from left to right on ACHIET-BIHUCOURT railway. Engine and 6 trucks.	
		2-27pm (16th)	A bright light like a halo was seen twinkling in THIEPVAL CHATEAU.	
		9-10am (17th)	Train going from right to left on ACHIET-BIHUCOURT railway. Several G.S. wagons seen going to and from the valley about 2000 yards N. of MIRAUMONT. There seems to be a good deal of work going on there. Weather fine. Strong wind. S6 Battery shelled the trenches N. of (Auchonvillers)—BEAUMONT-HAMEL road (A.4.d.9.5.6 A.5.c.1.8) Observation bad. General effect of fire good. 5% duds.	
	18th		Hostile Artillery inactive. No Trench Mortar or Machine Gun fire. A screen has been put up at R.y.a.5.0 this may be to hide the road at this point or possibly to hide gun flashes. Strong defensive works are being made at R.2.d.6.2. no work is being done by day apparently. No movement to be seen. Light rain. Wind high.	

Army Form C. 2118.

WAR DIARY
or
INTELLIGENCE SUMMARY.
(Erase heading not required.)

Instructions regarding War Diaries and Intelligence Summaries are contained in F.S. Regs., Part II. and the Staff Manual respectively. Title pages will be prepared in manuscript.

Place	Date	Hour	Summary of Events and Information	Remarks and references to Appendices
February.	19th.		Hostile Artillery inactive. No Trench Mortar or Machine Gun fire. A few parties of men seen on the BEAUCOURT – MIRAUMONT road but no movement seen near our trenches. Light fairly good, wind blowing a gale.	
		At 6-0 pm 56 Battery began shelling trenches opposite REDAN and to right and left from Q.5 a 2·7/ to K 35 c 3·4. 296 rounds were expended. Rapid rate of fire being maintained with good effect. In reply to heavy German shelling 128 Battery retaliated on Q.5 a 3·6 and road and communication trenches in Q.5 B.	
	20th.		Hostile Artillery active. No Trench Mortar or Machine Gun fire.	
		10-30am (19th)	A German was seen working a scythe at R 12 a 35·85. He was joined by another and they each carried away a large bundle of hay.	
		11-30pm (19th)	A suspected Zeppelin was heard travelling in a Westerly direction passing over MAILLY and BEAUSSART. Between 11-15 and 11-45 pm an aeroplane dropped lights at a point near AUCHONVILLERS near the 8 inch Hows and behind MAILLY.	
		6-0am (20th)	One green light was fired from trenches in front of BEAUMONT. No action on the part of hostile Artillery followed this. A very faint smell of gas was detected at O.P at Q 22 d 8·6 presumably from gas shells fired last night.	
		9-30am	German observation balloon up true bearing 92° from Q 22 d 8·6. 106° from A 2 c 9·5. 6 rds were fired by 128 Bty on Communication Trench in R 19 c 4·4. They were found to check ranges of centre section guns which were found to shoot 150° shorter than the other guns	

Army Form C. 2118.

WAR DIARY
or
INTELLIGENCE SUMMARY.
(Erase heading not required.)

Instructions regarding War Diaries and Intelligence
Summaries are contained in F. S. Regs., Part II.
and the Staff Manual respectively. Title pages
will be prepared in manuscript.

Place	Date	Hour	Summary of Events and Information	Remarks and references to Appendices
February	20th		128 Bty also fired a few rounds on Q.5.c.29. 86 Bty expended two rounds on trenches opposite REDAN for re-registration. Report on Evening of the 19th. At 6·0 p.m. the enemy opened an intense bombardment on our trenches between the Quadrilateral and BEAUMONT. A rapid rate of fire was immediately opened by 86 Battery on their right lines and by a section of 128th Battery on the communication trenches to the East and South of the REDAN. The 29th Brigade also called up the detached section of the 86th Battery which fired on the F.A.N. Redoubt. None of the enemy infantry left their trenches on our front. The hostile fire slackened and finally died away altogether about 7·0 p.m. Our Batteries ceased fire at about 7·10 p.m having kept up a slow rate of fire for some time. Hostile Artillery activity normal. French mortars were rather active on left of zone during the evening of the 20th. No Machine Gun fire.	
	21st	4·50 p.m (20th)	Train observed going from right to left on BAPAUME – ACHIET railway.	
		9·0 am (21st)	German observation balloon up true bearing 56° taken from Q.2.d.75.95. No movement seen	

2353   Wt. W2514/1454 700,000 5/15 D. D. & L.   A.D.S.S./Forms/C. 2118.

Army Form C. 2118.

WAR DIARY
or
INTELLIGENCE SUMMARY.
(Erase heading not required.)

Instructions regarding War Diaries and Intelligence Summaries are contained in F. S. Regs., Part II. and the Staff Manual respectively. Title pages will be prepared in manuscript.

Place	Date	Hour	Summary of Events and Information	Remarks and references to Appendices
February	21st	12-10pm	86 Battery Re-registered A.6.c.5.3.	
	22nd		Hostile Artillery inactive. French Mortars and Machine Guns inactive. Aeroplanes on both sides much more active than usual. Easterly wind blowing all day.	
		11-15am	(21st) and at 12-40pm trains were seen travelling from left to right on the ACHIET-BIHUCOURT railway. 4-0pm Another train from left to right. No movement seen. 86 Battery again re-registered A.6.c.5.3.	
	23rd		Hostile Artillery inactive. No French Mortar or Machine Gun fire. No movement seen. 128 Battery shelled ground and road on R.3.a.	
	24th		Hostile artillery inactive. No French Mortar or Machine Gun fire. No movement seen. 125th Battery fired a few rounds of Trenches on A.14.d. 10½ stopped firing owing to observation becoming impossible later on the day. The Battery fired 22 rounds at French Mortars in A.15.c.	
	25th		Hostile Artillery inactive. No French Mortar or Machine Gun fire. Observation impossible. Driving snow from N.E.	
	26th		Hostile Artillery inactive. No French Mortar or Machine Gun fire. No movement seen. 128th Battery fired three rounds into R.19.d 35°80. An enemy collected snowfall fight was attempted thus appears to be many dugouts here as the Huns disappeared at once.	
	27th		Hostile Artillery activity normal. No French Mortar or Machine Gun fire.	
		11-30am	(26A) German balloon up true bearing 96° from Q.22.d.8.6 at 12 noon the balloon descended.	
		12-47pm	(26A) from going from right to left on BAPAUME-ACHIET-LE-GRAND railway consisting of two engines two passenger coaches 36 closed trucks broken flats with 2 wheeled vehicles and two G.S.	

Army Form C. 2118.

WAR DIARY
or
INTELLIGENCE SUMMARY.
(Erase heading not required.)

Instructions regarding War Diaries and Intelligence Summaries are contained in F. S. Regs., Part II. and the Staff Manual respectively. Title pages will be prepared in manuscript.

Place	Date	Hour	Summary of Events and Information	Remarks and references to Appendices
February	24th.		Wagons on them	
		1.20 pm (26+)	Two Germans digging for [jup?] at R.8.6.3.8. disturbed by 18-pr Battery During the afternoon more parties of Germans than usual were seen on the BEAUCOURT-MIRAU-MONT road going in both directions. Tracks could be seen leading to a bank E. of GRANDCOURT (not on map) Telephone wires run to and from what appear to be large dug-outs. True bearing from Q.22.d.8.6. 90°. A machine gun emplacement at Q.10.6.90.44 was shelled by 128 Battery without retaliation from hostile guns	
	28th.		Hostile Artillery inactive. No trench Mortars or Machine Gun fire. No movement seen. 128 Battery fired a few rounds on Road in R.1.6. Effect of fire unobserved owing to mist. The shelling of the same place was repeated later on the day	
	29th.	7.20am	Hostile Artillery activity normal. Some french Mortar firing on left of Divisional zone. No Machine gun fire except at our aeroplanes from on ACHIET-BIHUCOURT railway. 3 Observation balloons visible true bearings from Q.22.d.8.6. 42° 45° 96° One balloon seen from Q.2.c. 45° 90 true bearing 196° Balloons observed from Q.2.d. "18".95. true bearings 52° and 104°	
		9.35am	Hostile aeroplane dropped 2 bombs N.E. of MAILLY. Two new strong emplacements a R.4.c.6.2 (just E of BEAUCOURT Redoubt were shelled by 128 Battery	

Army Form C. 2118.

WAR DIARY
or
INTELLIGENCE SUMMARY.
(Erase heading not required.)

Place	Date	Hour	Summary of Events and Information	Remarks and references to Appendices
February	29th		early in the afternoon. Later, the same Battery shelled Registered trench in R 2 d 4.5. and THIEPVAL. with good effect throwing clouds of brick dust up into the air. In retaliation for enemy shelling of our front trenches in front of BEAUMONT. 56A Battery fired on Q.6.C.8.4. and trenches opposite REDAN.	

APPilgrim
Lieut Colonel R.F.A.
Commndg 124 (How) Brigade R.F.A

4th DIVISION.

127th BDE R. F. A.

MARCH 1916.

MARCH

WAR DIARY
or
INTELLIGENCE SUMMARY.
(Erase heading not required.)

Army Form C. 2118.

Place	Date	Hour	Summary of Events and Information	Remarks and references to Appendices
1st.			Hostile Artillery inactive.	
	2nd	2.15pm	Trench Mortar Bombs fired into on trenches opposite SERRE.	
		11.am	188th Battery shelled road in R.3.a. Several good detonations	
2nd.			Hostile Artillery inactive.	
			128th Battery shelled known target in their line further S of front action out to incoming artillery fire of 154th Brigade.	
3rd.			Hostile Artillery normal.	
4th.			128th Battery fired at trenches in Q.5.c.+8. Section of 86th ? Battery returns by sections of 151st Brigade. Hostile Artillery Quiet.	
5th.			Remaining section of 128th Battery + one section of 86th Battery relieved by sections of 154th Brigade. Detached section of 86th Battery relieved by section of 485th Div Artillery. Battery spent the night at waggon lines at ORVILLE. Whole Brigade moved out to rest at MONDICOURT.	

WAR DIARY
or
INTELLIGENCE SUMMARY.

Army Form C. 2118.

Place	Date	Hour	Summary of Events and Information	Remarks and references to Appendices
6th–31st			Brigade at rest at MONDICOURT.	

W H Shipman Lt. Colonel.
Cmdg 127th Brigade. R.F.A.

4th DIVISION.

127th BDE. R. F. A.

APRIL 1916.

Army Form C. 2118

WAR DIARY
or
INTELLIGENCE SUMMARY.
(Erase heading not required.)

APRIL

MAP References
RANSART and FONQUEVILLERS

Place	Date	Hour	Summary of Events and Information	Remarks and references to Appendices
1st-3rd			Brigade at rest at MONDICOURT.	
	3rd		On the night of the 3rd one section of "B" Battery 160th Brigade RFA relieved a section of "B" Battery 128th Brigade RFA at BERLES (W.15 d.4.6) second section of 128th Battery relieved section of "C" Battery 128th Brigade RFA near BASSEUX (W.5 b.58) Section of 96th Battery relieved a section of "A" Battery 126th Brigade RFA at BIENVILLERS (E.8 a.2.4) Brigade Head Quarters came after LA CAUCHIE in the afternoon.	
	4th		Section of 128th Battery at BERLES had one man killed and his wounded. Indies Evening section 96th Battery relieved the remaining section of "A" Battery and put two guns across the road to the four guns at E 8 a.1.1 The remaining section 96th Battery relieved section of "C" Battery at BASSEUX.	

WAR DIARY or **INTELLIGENCE SUMMARY.**

(Erase heading not required.)

Army Form C. 2118.

Map Reference RANSART & FONQUEVILLERS 1/10000

Place	Date	Hour	Summary of Events and Information	Remarks and references to Appendices
	5th April		Quite Morning. Office 5th 126th Brigade Headquarters handed over to Sn Headquarters at LA CAUCHIE. Whole relief completed. Ammunition column moved up from MONDICOURT to LA CAUCHIE. Batteries registered.	
	6th		Batteries registered	
	7th		86th Battery retaliated on German front support trenches at E 5 c 85 60.	
	8th		Nothing to report.	
	9th		128th Battery registered targets	
	10th		8th Battery fired at trenches in E 5 a 45 with good results	
	11th-12th		86th Battery retaliated at Enemy Mortar area Z.5. Enemy mortars ceased fire. 126th Battery carried out harassing bombardment on hostile trenches at W 18 d 4373, on infantry entering former	

Army Form C. 2118.

WAR DIARY
or
INTELLIGENCE SUMMARY.
(Erase heading not required.)

Month: APRIL

MAP REFERENCE
RAMPART and YONGEVILLERS 1/10000

Place	Date	Hour	Summary of Events and Information	Remarks and references to Appendices
14th			Trenches and covering casualties. Enemy artillery quiet on the whole. 86th Battery retaliates, for enemy Mortar firing, onto "big Z". Section 8 regt. 18guns moved into New position at W5b 45-75.	
16th	3.30pm		86th Battery fires at trenches at E5d 4330-0586 and 2270 with good results in conjunction with demonstration.	
	3h		128th registered from new gun position	
	3.2h		16th Camera onto prearranged containment. Trenches at E5d. Hostile artillery inactive	
			86th Battery retaliates for German shelling, trenches at F11d 5793	
16a			128th Battery registered trenches W24a. b.c.	

WAR DIARY or INTELLIGENCE SUMMARY

Army Form C. 2118.

Map Reference: RANSART & MON QUEVILLERS

Month: APRIL

Place	Date	Hour	Summary of Events and Information	Remarks and references to Appendices
	17th	11.25 am	86th Battery fired after 2's in retaliation for 105 mm	
		3.35 pm	86th Battery and 18th Battery fired at Germans running at W9c. as per arranged Bombardment run to our infantry wiring a new strafe trenches after its 5 minutes Bombardment the Relieve upon its 1st second line trenches which 15 Infantry have to account. The rain was very successful the Infantry having several hostile trenches bombing numerous dug-outs formed up & new staff and machine gun emplacements. Our Casualties were very slightly wounded. Message of congratulation were received by us from the Woolwich Regt. 18th Infantry Brigade to 9th RB	

Army Form C. 2118.

WAR DIARY
or
INTELLIGENCE SUMMARY.
(Erase heading not required.)

Instructions regarding War Diaries and Intelligence Summaries are contained in F. S. Regs., Part II. and the Staff Manual respectively. Title pages will be prepared in manuscript.

Map reference RANSART & FONQUEVILLERS 10000

Place	Date	Hour	Summary of Events and Information	Remarks and references to Appendices
			4th Div and 4th Corps.	
	18.	6.45 p.m.	88th Battery retaliated for German trench Mortars on trenches at E.27.c. with good effect.	
	19th	4.30 p.m.	86th Battery fired at front line trenches at W.29.c.15/15 in retaliation for trench Mortars. Fire very effective. Hostile artillery Normal.	
	20th		86th Bdge. Batteries retaliated severely to hostile trench mortars on our trenches. Increased activity by hostile artillery.	
	21st	3.30 p.m.	Both batteries carried out a short bombardment on German trenches at W.29.c. Very effective fire.	
	22nd		Nothing to report.	

Army Form C. 2118.

WAR DIARY
or
INTELLIGENCE SUMMARY.
(Erase heading not required.)

Map references. RANSART & FONQUEVILLERS

Title pages APRIL

Place	Date	Hour	Summary of Events and Information	Remarks and references to Appendices
	23rd	11.45am to 2.45pm	128th Battery fired W29a, W29b, W30A } in retaliation for two shellings S8	
			BERLES.	
		5.15pm to 5.40pm	86th Battery fired at the "Z"s and trenches at E.11.6 in retaliation for enemy Mortars. North extreme here active two hours	
	24th	1.25pm to 5.15pm	86th Battery fired at Fort trenches at E23c + E29b. Fire was excellent results	
			128th Battery registered Enemy very active	
	25th	3.10pm	86th Battery carried out Bombardment Stevenes at E23c 3793 + E29b 8164 in conjunction with 9.2"s 18prs	

Army Form C. 2118.

WAR DIARY
or
INTELLIGENCE SUMMARY.
(Erase heading not required.)

Instructions regarding War Diaries and Intelligence Summaries are contained in F.S. Regs., Part II. and the Staff Manual respectively. Title pages will be prepared in manuscript.

Month: APRIL

Map reference
Place: RANSART & FONQUEVILLERS 10.000

Place	Date	Hour	Summary of Events and Information	Remarks and references to Appendices
	25th	10.53am	128th Battn shelled W29 6.5.5 in retaliation for shelling of BERLES. Ransart	
		3.35pm	128th Battn shelled X7C 10.3 at request of Infantry	
		5.15pm	128th Battn fired by aeroplane at X20 & 85.10. Hostile artillery very active in vicinity of BERLES.	
	26th	2 pm (4 pm)	85th Battn fired at E11 6 and two letter Z in retaliation to the shelling of Sgm Trenches.	
		2.30pm (5 pm)	128th Battn fired by aeroplane at X20 & 50 10. Two O.K's. Retaliation asked for	
	27th	9.15 am	8th Battn fired at F5 a, c & d by 10th Infantry Brigade.	
		2.20pm	128th Battn retaliation	

WAR DIARY or INTELLIGENCE SUMMARY

Army Form C. 2118.

(Erase heading not required.)

Instructions regarding War Diaries and Intelligence Summaries are contained in F. S. Regs., Part II. and the Staff Manual respectively. Title pages will be prepared in manuscript.

Month and Year: **APRIL**

Map reference: Ransart & Fonquevillers 1/10000

Place	Date	Hour	Summary of Events and Information	Remarks and references to Appendices
	27th	2.55 pm / 5 pm	18th Battery fired by aeroplane at hostile Battery at X20d 19.46. First quiet.	
	28th	6.45am / 7.15 am	128th Battery fired at trenches at X1d. in retaliation for the shelling of our trenches. 128th Battery fired at Machine Gun Emplacement X1a 6.4. Good result, also at W24c 66.13 (by aeroplane) X25 b 10.50 am a Suspected Gun Emplacement at X26 a 8.8. 88th Battery fired at a Suspected M.G. Emplacement at E28 d27, effect good. First quiet.	
	29th	12.15 pm	128th Battery fired at Machine Gun Emplacement at X7 c 11.83. 7 hits. Emplacement seemed to be very strongly built.	

Army Form C. 2118.

WAR DIARY
or
INTELLIGENCE SUMMARY.
(Erase heading not required.)

APRIL

Place	Date	Hour	Summary of Events and Information	Remarks and references to Appendices
	29th		18th Battery fired at Gun Emplacement at X 26 a 88 (Observing aeroplane) One hit caused an explosion. Hostile artillery inactive	
	30th		365 Battery obtained several hits on F 5 a of 11 b, at the request of Infantry. Hostile artillery quiet	

Wilkinson Lt Col
Commanding 157th Howitzer Brigade RFA

4th DIVISION.

127th BDE. R. F. A.

MAY 1916.

WAR DIARY
or
INTELLIGENCE SUMMARY.
(Erase heading not required.)

Army Form C. 2118.

Map reference Ransart o Tanquinlun 10000

Place	Date	Hour	Summary of Events and Information	Remarks and references to Appendices
	1st		86th Battery retaliated for the fire of trench mortis anti-aircraft F.11.b.6.3. Hostile artillery fairly quiet	
	2nd		128th Battery shelled at O.P. Crolier, Beliette N.C.T. Tütchler by our and our put out of action by penetrating thin turrent being slightly wounded.	
		5 pm	128th section fired at concealed H.S. gun in second line trench at X.26.a.3.6. The Battery at and gun did not fire the next morning as usual. Working party seen in X.7.c.7.6 was fired on when 128th Battery and dispersed.	
	3rd		128th Battery fired at gun emplacements at X.26.a.3.6 and X.20.a.20.15 with good effect at upper fire 45 shells O.P.4.45 sector at REPLER line at Monnicourt and 128th sector. Both Batteries fired in retaliation to heavy	
	4th	2.15 am -3.30 am		

127' RFA
Army Form C. 2118.

WAR DIARY
or
INTELLIGENCE SUMMARY.
(Erase heading not required.)

MAY

Place	Date	Hour	Summary of Events and Information	Remarks and references to Appendices
	4.		Bombardment 8b on trenches. Germans endeavoured	
			even on trenches but were driven out.	
	5.		Negotiating for the remaining echelons 8b Bde Batteries	
			and the B.A.C. moved out to MONDICOURT.	
	6.		Brigade Baths is moved down to AUTHEUX to	
			rest. The Brigade was relieved while 16th Brigade	
			R.F.A. that we relieved when we moved up.	
			Rest.	
			Lieut Henry Jones got Bahin from 1st Brigade.	
	6.4/5		8b 2/Lt Remier relinquishes 1st Brigade.	
	15.		lieut Walker 8bth Rg and a Sergeant Search Bahin	
			Souper Mailly to Superitina to Rueberg 8?	
			Gun positions etc. They are attached to	

WAR DIARY
or
INTELLIGENCE SUMMARY.
(Erase heading not required.)

Army Form C. 2118

Place	Date	Hour	Summary of Events and Information	Remarks and references to Appendices
	10th		15th I.B. at BERTRANCOURT	
	11th 12th 13th		Brigade at rest at AUTHEUX	
		13-20	Brigade had a rest. 3 fm Gun Batteries outspde his batteries each reaching her left section. The new Battery sprette 82nd Brigade and is called D/82. Commanded by Capt Mackie. 86th Battery spotted 125th battery 26th Brigade. 14th Brigade and 125th Brigade R.F.A. is nowhere	

Army Form C. 2118.

WAR DIARY
or
INTELLIGENCE SUMMARY.
(Erase heading not required.)

Instructions regarding War Diaries and Intelligence Summaries are contained in F.S. Regs., Part II. and the Staff Manual respectively. Title pages will be prepared in manuscript.

Place	Date	Hour	Summary of Events and Information	Remarks and references to Appendices
			FINIS	

W.S. Seligman Lt Col
Cmdg 157 Brigade RFA
20/5/16.

www.ingramcontent.com/pod-product-compliance
Lightning Source LLC
Chambersburg PA
CBHW080838010526
44114CB00017B/2329